ERRATA

Due to errors in pagination
the following pages should be read
in this order:
. . . 169, 171, 170, 172, 173 . . .
. . . 211, 213, 212, 214, 215 . . .
. . . 257, 256, 258, 260, 261 . . .
. . . 351, 353, 352, 354, 355 . . .

Confes
W
Spo

Confessions of a Washed-up Sportswriter

including various digressions about sex, crime, and other hobbies

By Gary Cartwright

Texas Monthly Press

Texas Monthly Press, Inc.
P.O. Box 1569
Austin, Texas 78767

A B C D E F G H

Library of Congress Cataloging in Publishing Data

Cartwright, Gary, 1934–
    Confessions of a washed-up sportswriter.

    1. Texas—Social life and customs—Addresses, essays, lectures. 2. Texas—
Popular culture, Addresses, essays, lectures. I. Title.
F391.2.C34 1982   306'.09764   82-10296
ISBN 0-932012-39-6

"Border Towns"
© 1976 Dallas Times Herald
Reprinted by permission

TWO MORE BOTTLES OF WINE, words and music by Delbert McClinton.
© Copyright 1975, 1978 by Duchess Music Corporation, New York, NY.
Rights Administered by MCA Music, A Division of MCA, Inc.,
    New York, NY.
Used by permission.   All rights reserved.

VICTIM OF LIFE'S CIRCUMSTANCE, words and music by Delbert
McClinton.
© Copyright 1975 by Duchess Music Corporation, New York, NY.
Rights Administered by MCA Music, A Division of MCA, Inc.,
    New York, NY.
Used by permission.   All rights reserved.

Other portions of this book previously appeared in *Harper's*, *Inside Sports*,
Rolling Stone, and *Texas Monthly*.

Book design by Larry Smitherman

To my parents,
Roy and Vera Cartwright,
with love and
remembrance

Contents

1

Confessions of a Washed-up Sportswriter

"Listen, Tojo and Hirohito and you Nomuru and you Kurusu, and all the rest of you heathen sons of heaven, you won't understand this, it'll be far over your pagan heads, but, even so, you ought to hear about it."
—C. E. McBride, Kansas City *Star*, March 27, 1944. Reprinted in *Best Sports Stories 1944* (Dutton).

Crew Slammer never made *Best Sports Stories*. He never got farther than the bulletin board at the Fort Worth *Press*. He was a victim of the industry, for he collided time and again with the mentality ceiling that bears down on every newspaper I know anything about. Nevertheless, I believe that Crew Slammer in his way was a better sportswriter than C. E. McBride, Stanley Woodward, or even Red Smith. He was inquisitive, sardonic, satirical, cynical, opinionated, hedonistic, and what intelligence he had was easily offended. He hated sport. "To watch it," he thought, "is a deadly bore." Baseball was something that the twentieth century had a right to do without. Spectator golf ranked in importance with bridge tournaments and Junior League rummage sales. Football, tennis, hockey, and boxing interested him for aesthetic reasons. Crew Slammer fancied that he wrote like Hemingway. A typical lead describing a junior swimming meet would begin, "In the late summer of that year we lived in a house in a village that . . ."

Crew Slammer was like all my friends in those days. He wanted more. He had a competitive drive to be the best. Why did he become a sportswriter? That is the question we were all trying to answer. Inevitably we turned to the *Best Sports Stories* anthology, there to prosper or rot. I am sad to say that Crew Slammer did not prosper, but pretend you don't know that for a while. For Crew Slammer was a myth, a symbol of our tragic graveyard, a commentary on conditions. He lived only in our imaginations, which of course means that he lived nonetheless.

When I started writing sports in 1958 at the *Press*, I already knew something about basic reporting. I covered the night police beat for two years at the Fort Worth *Star-Telegram*, much to the despair of a night city editor named Ed Capers, who used to tell me, "Your trouble is, your fingers are too fast for your mind." I thought he had it backwards, so I quit and joined the sports staff of the *Press*. Instinctively I realized that the only way to move forward was to change newspapers every two years—a pattern I followed to the Dallas *Times Herald*, the Dallas *Morning News*, and finally the Philadelphia *Inquirer*, where, like Crew Slammer, I became a victim of the mentality ceiling. But almost every important thing I learned, I learned at the *Press*.

The Fort Worth *Press* is one of those dilapidated brick-box institutions that Scripps-Howard used to stake between the railroad yard and the farmers' market. Its city room with the eras of dirt and the rancid smell of machine oil reminds you of a train depot in a college-size town. For years it has been vanishing in a cloud of soot, and momentarily it will reappear as a parking lot. It is maintained as you would maintain a shoe box of old letters by a few faithful servants who are nearing retirement age. Good writers have come and gone, and the others have joined the scenery. I cannot visualize the *Press* city room without calling up Delbert Willis, the one-legged city editor who periodically takes a leave of absence to hunt for the Jap who got him; Caroline Hamilton, a husky, old-maidish feature writer in cowboy boots; or Marvin Garrett, a meek silver-haired farm and county editor. Marvin is sitting at his desk, barely visible behind an enormous mound of publicity releases (which we would sometimes take, turn over, and use for copy paper in times of austerity), and all day he is shuffling papers and clucking.

The *Press* is P.M., meaning that it publishes in the afternoon, and that we had to report at 6 A.M. The morning dark does things to the creative man. My friend and fellow sportswriter Dan Jenkins used to complain that it made his hair hurt. His wife would set her alarm for 3 A.M., watch his hair from her side of the bed, and make notes, but they never isolated the problem. I never made it at 6 A.M., but I came close that first day. Twelve minutes late, in a panic, peeling off coat and sweater as I climbed the single flight of dark stairs, I smashed glue-eyed through the swinging gate that separated sports from the other departments. Suddenly I realized that the only other person in the room was Puss Ervin, a retired postman who had signed on as our bowling writer. Puss was hunched over his typewriter, drinking vodka from a paper cup and puzzling over the previous night's bowling averages. It was the dead of winter, so the heater — the coal chute, we called it — was running full blast. Puss had removed his coat, tie, and shirt, and draped them over the back of his chair. He didn't know me yet, but I guess he had heard I was coming to work at the *Press.* He wouldn't look up. Between sentences he muttered: "You'll never make it, son." I knew he was right. Half an hour before deadline, our slot man, Sick Charley Modesette, arrived. Charley had been out all night, looking for his car. There was a professional detachment about Charley, a combat residual bred in men who have learned to expect nothing. "All the bastards slept in again, huh?" Charley observed, and started plugging the first edition with old pictures and dated syndicated columns by Joe Williams and Harry Grayson. We made deadline with seconds to spare. It was always this way.

Many times I put out the paper alone. All the sportswriters did. We staggered in, tore the night's run of copy from the United Press machine, selected the stories according to the page dummies supplied by the advertising department, assigned headlines and wrote them, clipped box scores and other trivia from the morning *Star-Telegram*, selected pictures and sent them to the engravers, made up the cutlines, then hurried to the composing room, where a printer named Max would be waiting to change everything. Like Charley, Max was a professional. All he ever said was, "Who the hell do you think you are?"

We survived on the assumption that no one read our paper anyhow. It is the same feeling you get on a college newspaper or on mind-expanding drugs. There are no shackles on the imagination; there is no retreat, only attack. One of my jobs was to make up little "brights" or boxes:

> John Doughe made a hole-in-one yesterday at Glen Lakes Country Club when a snake swallowed his tee

shot, a dog swallowed the snake, and an eagle carried
off the dog, dropping him in the cup after colliding head
on with a private plane flown by Doughe's maternal
twin.

We went heavy on the irony. Under these circumstances you might think we got a lot of letters to the
editor, but I don't remember any.

II

The starting salary for a college graduate was about
$45.67 a week. It went up in pennies. For that reason
we ate our meals at the Lavender Cafeteria. Three biscuits soaked in cream gravy cost twenty-six cents.
Cowboy Hardley, a photographer, favored gravy
over cantaloupe, which cost slightly more but got
results from those of us who had to watch him eat it.
Cowboy was a chow hustler. We called him Everman
Fats for his hometown of Everman. He would bet his
breakfast against yours that you wouldn't finish.

I did not know it at the time, but the *Press* sports
staff was ten years ahead of the game. In 1955 the
Press was perfecting what most, but not yet all, sports
staffs believe they have just created: a competitive art
form. Significant television competition was years
away, but already the *Press* was rebelling against the
stiff, bleak who/what/when/where architecture of its
predecessors, exposing myths, demanding to know
why, and treating why as the only question. It was
funny about 1961 when *Newsweek* devoted its press
section to the wry progressive sports editor of *Newsday*, Jack Mann. *Newsday* hired good, creative
writers. They worked as a unit, pruning clichés from
wire copy, pepping up hard news by tracing angles all
over the country, barreling over dogma where they
confronted it. Was Yogi Berra a lovable gnome, like

it said in *Sporting News*? Did he sit around reading comic books and eating bananas? Or was he a non-communicative boor whose funniest line was, "How the hell would I know?" *Newsday*, the magazine pointed out, demanded an answer.

There was no way for *Newsweek* to know it, but sports editor Blackie Sherrod had been preaching a better anarchy at the *Press* in 1950. Sherrod surrounded himself with such men as Dan Jenkins and Bud Shrake, now well-known and excellent writers at *Sports Illustrated*, not to mention the irresponsible Crew Slammer. He let them write from the gut.

What obsessed us all was the species. We could watch for hours out the window of the *Press* composing room—which overlooked the New Gem Hotel, where God knows what the blacks were up to—speculating out loud what the species might otherwise become. Without sport, what would Mickey Mantle do? He would drive a forklift, Crew Slammer was certain. Joe Kuharich would be night watchman for a company that manufactured caskets. Joe Namath raised carrier pigeons and sold hubcaps. Roger Maris operated a liquor store on the Illinois-Missouri border. Bud Wilkinson was Norman Rockwell's chauffeur, and Vince Lombardi operated an academy for the sons of South American dictators. Rice football coach Jess Neely, a slight, shallow-faced man with a Southern drawl who has since retired, was a kindly Southern scientist who devoted his life to crossbreeding the boll weevil with the bull elephant. He always seemed to be at cross-purposes.

It was a great joke, of course, but after a while Jess Neely did suggest something unusual. I remember being assigned to do what we called a jockstrap story after an SMU-Rice game in Houston about 1960. It appeared from the press box that Rice lost the game because Neely refused to gamble on fourth down late in the fourth quarter when the alternative was certain defeat. In the twenty minutes before deadline I had to race to the Rice dressing room to gather some quotes from Neely and write six hundred words. All I could think to ask was, "Coach Neely, what were you thinking out there on fourth down?" Neely gave me a sorry scowl and said, "Why, young man, to score more points than my opponents, naturally." At the time I questioned his sincerity. Now that I am older and wiser I believe that Neely was answering as well as he knew how. Frank Howard, the former coach at Clemson, was one of the best men I ever interviewed. In a situation much like the one Neely found himself in, Frank Howard first talked about the other team ("Those big old fine-looking athletes"), then concluded, "We were gonna get our tails whipped, it was a question of by how much."

In most cases the argot of the sports industry can be traced to the sports pages. An American Football League player discussing the ability of a rival kickoff-return man observed recently, "He good! He good! He have developed the knack to alter directions on a dime." He read that somewhere. On the other hand, originality and imagination can be trouble, as Darrell Royal frequently discovers. Royal, the University of Texas football coach, thought himself amusing a few years ago when he likened the rival team from Texas Christian University to "a bunch of cockroaches." And he was. The trouble started because a few sportswriters stopped short of explaining that while TCU had not won many games, it had occasionally risen to the moment and spoiled a good thing for someone else. This slip is still a psychological spook anytime TCU plays Texas.

Press conferences such as this one are hazardous. Sportswriters are too absorbed by their own questions to understand the answers. Harold Ratliff, sports editor for the Associated Press in Texas, is the dean of the press conference because he has made himself a focal point for years. Harold likes to bait his subject. He is always asking coaches to predict how much they will win by, or better yet say something rotten about the opponent. While he is never successful, he believes that he is. A recent AP story out of Dallas begins, "Coach Tom Landry of the Dallas Cowboys professed concern over his team's future Wednesday although the Cowboys hold a three-game lead . . ." On the face of it, this is a strong story. Good Lord, the entire future of the Cowboys? Well, not quite, as the story goes on to explain. What happened, I am certain, is that Ratliff asked Landry something like "Coach, your team about has it [the championship] wrapped up, wouldn't you say?" Landry would not. Landry pointed to the difficult schedule in the final weeks of the season, and he said, "We could still lose it . . ."

III

I remember a discussion that several of us had with Landry one afternoon. The subject was "field position," a term you hear more frequently from college coaches than professional coaches. The concept of the game of football is attack and retreat, the same as war. The ultimate object is to capture the opponent's goal, but a secondary consideration is keeping the ball as far as possible from your own goal line. Professional teams, with their superior striking power, are less cautious about field position but no less concerned, as Landry was explaining. After taking some time to ferment his question, Ratliff cornered Landry and asked, "Tell us, Tom, what do you consider the best field position?" I looked at Landry. He didn't need anyone to remind him to answer with care. He said, "Harold, I am personally attracted to my opponent's one-inch line."

I respect Landry. One reason is that he defended me before a mob of super-fans who wanted to know why Landry had neglected to have me fired for writing terrible things about his team. (It somehow amazes the super-fan to learn that writers are not hired or fired by the teams they are assigned to cover.) Landry told them, "You have to remember one thing, when the game is over and we're all feeling bad about losing, he is the one with the typewriter." I have thought about what Landry said. Especially in the escaping minutes after a night game, plunging into the irretrievable deadline, I have written my story upside down and backwards and then hoped to hell I could find a first paragraph to justify it. Don Meredith, the Cowboys' quarterback, is a good friend of mine, but one afternoon when he failed to rise to the occasion, I started my game story: "Outlined against a gray November sky, the Four Horsemen rode again: Pestilence, Death, Famine, and Meredith."

Meredith read it and thought it was funny. His fans did not. Fans of Kansas City Chiefs linebacker Sherrill Headrick thought it was funny when I wrote that he had "the face of an Oklahoma chicken thief." Headrick's wife did not. Buddy Dial's wife canceled her subscription to the Dallas *Morning News* when I wrote that he had been benched because Landry felt he wasn't playing well. I didn't even write that. I was drunk. Three friends wrote it for me. I have done as much for them. Sportswriters will pull you out of a ditch.

All of our hearts went out to the old sportswriter from the Rio Grande Valley—I forget his name—who stumbled into the Cotton Bowl press box one New Year's Day. Someone on the field fired a cannon and he fell out of his chair. I asked him, "Didn't you get to bed last night?" He said, "Damn near. Only missed it about that far," holding his hands to indicate a foot or so.

IV

Professional football players are easily the best-educated, most congenial, and most sensitive group of athletes I know. They have a different kind of courage, almost masochistic.

I fell into the habit of dropping by the Cowboys' training room before a game. It was the warmest place in any stadium, but I also needed a B-12 shot or something more stimulating. No one talks about it, but training rooms are portable pharmacies. It is the trainer's job to have his forty men ready by Sunday afternoon. If a player is injured, they shoot him full of cortisone. If his pain threshold is low, they give him morphine or another opium derivative. If his metabolism is skimpy, they give him amphetamines. When Commissioner Pete Rozelle outlawed the free use of amphetamines a few years ago, several players and maybe a few sportswriters were ruined. I suspect the National Football League was on the verge of a scandal. Certainly Big Daddy Lipscomb didn't help the image by taking an overdose of horse. Rozelle got pep pills out of the aisles and under the tables. One trainer got around the rule by putting out two pots of coffee, one straight and the other laced with dope. It was explained to me recently by an NFL player, "Every man lets the trainer know his requirements. When you get to the stadium there is a paper cup of whatever you need waiting in your locker."

Almost any football player would be astonished to

have explained to him the deliberate change that football has made to his body chemistry. Ernie Stautner, a wide, strong, innocent, hard-living former defensive end who now coaches for the Cowboys, nearly died from being given the wrong drug before a game in Cleveland. Stautner should have been in the hospital that day, but he was determined to play for the Pittsburgh Steelers. After the team doctor inadvertently stoked him up with twelve hundred milligrams of Demerol instead of Novocain, he *was* in the hospital — dying, he suspected. "Nurses and doctors were running around like a British comedy," he told me later. "I kept thinking: I'm just a statistic now. I thought about this testimonial dinner they were having for me in two weeks back in Pittsburgh. Boy, that's gonna be a dead affair! Pittsburgh! Boy! That's the irony — the only team in the league I never wanted to play for, and here I was dying on their time."

Someone called a priest and Stautner made his final peace with the Maker. "Father," he said weakly, "I don't have much time, so if it's okay with you I'll just hit the highlights."

V

Just as an athlete, if he's any good, will rise to the occasion, so will a sportswriter. That is the essence of his profession, and one of the reasons there are so few good sportswriters. The other reason is editors. Unfortunately, there is not a hint of a parallel between the average coach and the average newspaper editor. There was an abundance of writing talent in Texas at the time when Crew Slammer and the rest of us still considered the impossible dream to be a dateline from College Station. Few sports editors were talented enough to recognize it. The Dallas *Morning News'* Bill

Rives had Tex Maule working the slot. His reasoning was that it took more judgment to arrange stories than it did to write them. Maule hated the job. Now he is senior editor at *Sports Illustrated* and one of the top sportswriters in the country. Roy Terrell, *Sports Illustrated*'s assistant managing editor, was stuck away somewhere in Corpus Christi.

The sportswriters everyone heard of in the 1950's were Jesse Abramson, New York *Herald Tribune;* John Carmichael, Chicago *Daily News;* Red Smith, New York *Herald Tribune;* Maxwell Stiles, Los Angeles *Mirror;* Ed Danforth, Atlanta *Journal;* Earl Ruby, Louisville *Courier-Journal;* Milton Gross, New York *Post;* Joe Williams, New York *World-Telegram & Sun;* Jimmy Cannon, New York *Post;* Prescott Sullivan, San Francisco *Examiner;* Tim Cohane, *Look;* Bob Hunter, Los Angeles *Examiner;* Si Burdick, Dayton *News;* Shirley Povich, Washington *Post.*

As E. P. Dutton & Company spread the word in its anthologies of *Best Sports Stories,* names like Furman Bisher, Atlanta *Journal;* Jack Murphy, San Diego *Union;* Murray Olderman, NEA; and Bill Rives, Dallas *Morning News,* joined the pack. Still later, Blackie Sherrod clamored over the wall of the Fort Worth *Press,* found an outlet at the Dallas *Times Herald* and became — along with two Los Angeles columnists, the *Times'* Jim Murray and the *Herald Examiner*'s Mel Durslag — one of the best day-in, day-out sportswriters in the business. These men worked for the big papers and covered the big stories, and E. P. Dutton sorted them out each year for recognition. Others, such as Dan Jenkins and Bud Shrake, would occasionally break through on pure ability. The men in *Best Sports Stories* wrote with a diversity of styles and emphasis that only helped to confuse a novice. I can't think of his name, but there was an old-timer from Philadelphia who started every game story like this: "Army's powerful Cadets defeated Navy's game but outmanned Midshipmen for the second straight year here Saturday, 14–6, before a crowd of 81,342." The second sentence was always, "Army won the toss and elected to receive." Having created that, he tacked on the play-by-play and got drunk. We could see that this style went nowhere. We were in danger of being replaced by the ape.

As far as I know, this exercise is still tacked to the bulletin board of the Fort Worth *Press*:

By CREW SLAMMER

The World's Greatest Sportswriter

*Baltimore, Nov. 27—*Late in the fourth quarter when Army's Black Knights of the Hudson had traveled on their bellies long enough to be mistook for Arlington National Cemetery, and had risen in an agonizing mass and smashed the United States Navy's football team to bobbing bits and pieces, Army coach Red Blaik craned his neck toward the score board clock, whispered to an assistant, and squirmed off in the direction of the men's room. Army had won, 23 to 7, and Blaik was ready to wash his hands of the whole affair.

Conditions conspired to prevent this from being a flawless opening paragraph. After all, it was written for the bulletin board, not the five-star final. Crew Slammer was fifteen hundred miles away, emptying the wastebasket, when Army defeated Navy. There was something else, though, which Bill Rives (by then assistant managing editor of the Dallas *Morning News*) explained to me a few years later: "You can't use *men's room* in a family newspaper!" I also learned from Rives that you can't use *Jap-a-Nazi Rat* in a family newspaper, even when you are quoting Jules Feiffer's *Great Comic Book Heroes*.

VI

Rives looked like an aging Rudolph Valentino. He was a fanatic for words. The walls of his department were posted with signs ordering KEEP IT SHORT! or WRITE LIKE YOU TALK! The trouble was, neither Rives nor any of the other name writers followed those orders. Maxwell Stiles would open a story on the United States women's golf championship: "Last Saturday at the Waverly Country Club in Portland I saw the face of America peer at me through a pair of dark eyes alight with the radiant glory of one who has brought honor and dignity to her native land." Then we would study Sherrod, painting his first impressions of a Kansas sophomore named Wilt Chamberlain: "If they're going to let him play basketball . . . they ought to let the Grand Canyon play ditch." Rives would start: "Julius Nicholas Boros, swarthy-skinned son of Hungarian immigrants, captured the National Open championship Saturday with a score of 281, one over par," and *Best Sports Stories* would leap on it.

Dan Jenkins could mock them all with his sweep and simplicity: "Tommy Bolt, with astonishing ease, won the 1958 U.S. Open golf championship today on a vicious course that broke Sam Snead in two days and wrenched Ben Hogan's wrists." And who was Jenkins? He was our first big-timer from the Fort Worth *Press*. He wrote for *Golf Digest*. He could be counted on to have a pocketful of press-box tickets or parking passes. Anytime he passed Ben Hogan on the veranda of the Colonial Country Club, Hogan was likely as not to say, "Hi, fella," the only two words Hogan used well. An ex-TCU football player named Red ("How's ya mom and them?") Marable had even confided to friends in high places that he did not want to hit Jenkins, merely "grab him and shake him around."

Bud Shrake followed hard behind Jenkins. He is a giant of a man with a poet's soul and a lumberjack's appetite. He was the accidental winner of a chili-rice-eating contest one time while serving as contest referee. Shrake is an enormously talented sports-writer and a keen observer of the species. For a while Shrake and I shared an apartment in Dallas. From time to time a well-known college football coach from a big-time school whose name I will not mention would show up with a bag of groceries, often on the night before a major game. We would eat and drink until about 3 A.M., then drive through town looking for girls. We never talked football.

Shrake had a suspicious habit of being with me each time I disgraced myself, my newspaper, and my country. I have always reacted in curious ways to the pressures and exigencies of my profession. It was not Shrake who suggested that I dress up like a waiter, crash the Fort Worth Colonial Country Club's first (and last) annual poolside luau and fashion show, and leap off the three-meter diving board, spraying dinner rolls among the floating orchids.

Yet Shrake had an invitation and I had none. He helped me find a linen closet in the basement, and he was there when club manager Virgil Bourland inter-cepted me on the way to the poolside. "What's this?" Bourland asked, lifting a roll from the wicker basket. "Them's rolls!" "What for?" Bourland challenged. "For hungry people." Bourland asked, "Is this some kind of joke?" and I assured him that hunger is never a joke, stomping away indignantly and crouching in the hedges while a search party was organized. It was not Shrake who threw up all over Michigan State football coach Duffy Daugherty when Daugherty told a nau-seous joke (punch line: "I don't know what it *is*! I found it in my nose!") in the hotel suite of "Coach of the Year" Murray Warmath. It was me. Yet Shrake was a ready accomplice, I confess, just before that, when we ripped off Warmath's bedding, contrived an effigy and hung it from his transom, much as his students at the University of Minnesota had been doing earlier in the year. Shrake was clear across the room when I took off my clothes and sang "Danny Boy" at Blackie Sherrod's Christmas party. He was there when I swung at and missed Norm Van Brocklin at a night spot in Birmingham. And he had grave reservations the time we found a dead carp on the banks of a gravel pit, and had it cooked and served to Bill Rives, a Catholic. The answers to why we do such things are buried with the minute and uncelebrated details of the events themselves, and may be too fragile for the Freudian window sash. I know this: in a time my memory cannot identify, in a place I cannot remember being welcome, there is someone's voice, full of respect and anticipation, saying, "For Chrissake, here he comes *again!*"

VII

Influenced in part by men like Blackie Sherrod, Dan Jenkins, and Bud Shrake, almost all sportswriters were experimenting with words in the name of literature by 1960. It is impossible to overestimate the damage this has done to subsequent sportswriters, as this lead, selected at random from the October 22, 1967, Dallas *Morning News*, suggests:

Houston — There was mutiny of SMU's Good Ship Destiny here Saturday night and the Rice Owls found themselves marooned all alone on the Southwest Conference's unbeaten Isle of Desire.

In the fifth paragraph the writer lets you in on the secret: Rice defeated SMU, 14–10.

Dan Jenkins is probably the best sportswriter I have ever read, but until he went to *Sports Illustrated* it was difficult to plead his case. Take the creative mind and lash it to a pillar in the city room some Saturday night. Bombard it with the rattle of Western Union printers. Give it headlines to write and other people's stories to read and paste up, and you will understand why from time to time rats have been trained to play the piano. Boredom may be the mother of genius; certainly it comes equipped with its own safety valve.

Boredom is the reason why at the Dallas *Times Herald* in 1960 we came to invent the mythical football power from Metcalf R. The name honors the late newspaper poet James J. Metcalf (the R. stands for nothing in particular, it just sounded better than Metcalf U. or Metcalf Poly). On any Sunday among the agate lines of type telling who won, a *Times Herald* reader was privileged to find the results of the Metcalf R. game. Metcalf R. scheduled such worthies as Indiana McGruder and Southeastern Oklahoma Central, and always won by three points.

Do not suppose this went unchallenged. On one occasion when the Metcalf R. score was accidentally lost on the composing room floor, a neighbor of the city editor complained. This complaint was the inspiration for our next move: the invention of the Corbet Comets, a small high school football power of unspecified location.

The Comets streaked along on the energies of their twin halfbacks, Dickie Don and Rickie Ron Yewbet—named for TCU football coach Abe Martin's speech pattern ("We gonna play some foobuhl, yewbet we are!"). Every Friday night we inserted under a 14-point headline a paragraph celebrating Corbet's newest triumph. Corbet did not lose for two seasons,

in which time Rickie Ron got mumps and died. Someone had blue and black Corbet window decals
printed, and someone else suggested a story to the
editor of the women's page when E. O. (Shug)
Kempleman, Corbet Ford dealer, donated the world's
largest tuba to the Fighting Corbet Band. Later, when
I worked for the Dallas *Morning News*, someone
slipped into print the results of the city of Corbet
municipal elections. F. D. Orr defeated E. O. (Shug)
Kempleman, 43 votes to 38. Rives, by then an assistant managing editor, blamed me. He called me "flip"
and suggested that I read *The Texas Almanac* sometime and grow up.

What is much harder to forgive is what Rives did
to my "Study in Black and White" story, the year that
the Mississippi State University basketball team conquered everyone except its state legislature. There
was a law in Mississippi prohibiting integrated sports
events. On the day before the MSU basketball team
was supposed to leave for the NCAA tournament in
Louisville, this law was stretched to include sports
events anywhere in the world so long as they involved state teams from Mississippi.

This was a banner story anywhere in the country.
No one had to tell me to place a long-distance call to
the captain of the MSU team. I don't remember the
captain's name, but I remember that he was surprisingly candid. To his way of thinking there was justice
in the fact that the Mississippi State basketball team
could not claim a national championship until it had
played and beaten teams of Negroes. In a touching
aside, he told what happened the night of his senior
dance in his hometown of Poplarville, Miss. That
night, some of the town rednecks kicked down the jail
door, hauled out a Negro named Parker, tied him
with rope, and threw him in the river. The MSU cap-

tain could not remember what the victim had done to rile the population, but the lynching dampened his heart where it would never dry. "The night of our senior dance!" he repeated. "Imagine." I wrote the story straight and Rives killed it. He gave this reason: "This puts the Dallas *News* in the position of taking sides." Well, my God, what if it does? Rives could have just dropped it there. Instead, in an amazing burst of rationale, he added, "If it were a wire-service story, maybe it would be different. But this story . . . this story is written by our own man. Our own man!"

Rives wasn't there a few years later when the *Morning News* destroyed another story, this one considerably closer to home. I learned from a friend that the Dallas Country Club was discreetly planning to drop its annual invitational tennis tournament rather than open it to black tennis star Arthur Ashe. The friend put me in touch with an influential club member who confirmed the story and added, "We can't very well have an invitational tennis tournament without inviting the best player in the country. And the mossbacks who run this place can't very well bring themselves to let Arthur Ashe in the front door."

For several years running I had been assigned to cover the tournament. I didn't like it, but there it was in my assignment folder. Dallas Country Club is where The Establishment that Dallas claims does not exist runs the city, including both of its newspapers. Hence the annual Dallas Country Club Invitational Tennis Tournament was displayed by both Dallas newspapers as you would display WORLD WAR THREE . . . right up till the moment when my story that the whole thing had been dropped was dumped in the editor's wastebasket. After a day and a half of soul-searching, I learned, the rival Dallas *Times Herald* also reached the conclusion that there was no story here.

Then an unfortunate thing happened. *Sports Illustrated* got wind of the story and printed it completely, including the part that made mention of the fact that *Times Herald* executive editor Felix McKnight was a board member at the country club. McKnight is a onetime sportswriter and wire-service reporter with a reputation as a no-holds-barred newsman. It was shortly after McKnight took over that *Times Herald* staff members adopted a motto for their paper: "We wait until the bandwagon gets rolling, then throw ourselves under it."

VIII

By this time I knew I would never be a good sportswriter. Yet to turn away from the only profession you have ever known would not be an easy thing. Especially a profession with all those beautiful conflicts of interest. Sportswriters get in free, to sports events or most anything else. They are fed and liquored and given unusual considerations. There are cocktail parties, and wealthy sportsmen with yachts and planes and private islands in the Bahamas, and moonlight jobs in communications. The pay is poor, but no one bothers to live on his salary.

There is no spectacle in sport more delightful than witnessing members of the Baseball Writers Association, who invented the box score, trampling each other at the buffet table. The first time I actually saw Dick Young, the New York *Daily News'* very good baseball writer, he was smearing deviled egg on the sleeve of Arthur Daley's sport coat and discussing Casey Stengel's grammar. Ben Hogan was rude and gruff, but he impressed me when I learned that the caviar at his annual press party cost forty-five dollars a jar. Tony Lema had a genius for public relations at least as great as his genius for golf. Champagne Tony! I covered his funeral. It was an assignment that I did not want, but I was there, thinking that it might be years before I tasted champagne again. They served some on the flight home. Bear Bryant used to insist that the way to handle a sportswriter was with a fifth of scotch. Sportswriters deplored this attitude, but no one ever thought to sue Bear Bryant.

Editors across the land dove for their memo pads a few years ago when the trade magazine, *Editor & Publisher*, exposed the practice permitting sports teams to pay traveling expenses for writers assigned to cover them. The practice still exists. Some editors see no special evil in the fact that their writers accept cash per diem from the team, usually twenty-five dollars a day for room and meals. I know a sportswriter who accepts per diem *and* signs for all expenses. The team pays double, but this is how he keeps a daughter in college.

W. O. McGeehan is credited with drafting the industry's code. "If it's a bribe," McGeehan allegedly told a public relations man, "it's not enough. If it's a gift, it's too much." Still, ethics is a nebulous question to a profession that has never really defined its purpose. To report? To expose? To speculate? To entertain? To criticize? To subsist and endure? A good sportswriter does it all. I do not know a sportswriter who would accept, say, one hundred dollars to print something he did not believe.

On the other hand, I can believe damn near anything. In 1960, after I had written that their training camp was "A Mickey Mouse Operation," an official of the Dallas Texans (now the Kansas City Chiefs) put an envelope into my shirt pocket. It contained, I learned after I had thanked him and walked off, three one-hundred-dollar bills, the only three I had ever

seen. It was an offer in the nature of a living allowance, for we were guests at the training camp. The
club was training in the spartan quarters of the New
Mexico Military Institute (NMMI) in Roswell. In
keeping with tradition, sportswriters lived there too.
Windowpanes and indoor plumbing had not yet
weakened NMMI, which I suppose was part of the
reason the Texans selected it as a training site, aside
from the fact that it was cheap. I had been sitting on
my cot, sweating and drinking gin from a chipped coffee cup, when destiny happened by the open window—
Paul Miller, a defensive end who once trained with
the uptown Los Angeles Rams. Miller was a constant
but authoritative bitcher. He became the source for
my Mickey Mouse story. The morning after it appeared in print, this club official pushed the three bills
in my pocket. All he said was, "I guess things haven't
been too easy on you guys these last few weeks."

Well, it was true: they had not. What is more, I had
seen the Texans' owner Lamar Hunt squander that
much money warming up the engines of his airplane.
The Hunts were perhaps the richest family in the
world. Lamar and all of his brothers and all of his
children and all of his brothers' children each inherited twenty million dollars at birth. Bunker, his
older brother, is fat and right-wing to a fault, but I
liked him and had traveled places with him in his airplane. I think of Bunker now, half-asleep on the team
bus waiting outside the Polo Grounds in New York
. . . bitter cold, blowing snow, Christmas music, and
the blind blue faces of the people outside in the
crowding darkness. An old woman in a stocking cap
stomped her feet to keep from freezing. A boy—he
couldn't have been ten—pressed close to a burning
trash basket. Something stirred Bunker; he started
and saw them too. He looked at them awhile, then
he told me, "Boy hidy, that's what I call 'the Great

Unwashed.' "

I carried the three hundred dollars with me all morning. I really was broke, having ripped through my expense money from the *Times Herald* in defense of sanity. But I gave back those three bills. I finally realized they were payment for all the Mickey Mouse stories I would ever write.

That is the only time anyone ever offered me money. There is a more subtle practice, however — hiring sportswriters to do program stories or other inconsequential writing jobs for the team they are assigned to cover. It pays well, up to fifty dollars for a couple of pages. I could nominally consider myself a professional writer, so I accepted this sort of arrangement. It is about the same as baseball writers' accepting twenty-five dollars a game to serve as "official scorer."

The answer to conflict of interest, Texas E. Schramm used to explain, is to write positive. Schramm is president and general manager of the Dallas Cowboys, but he learned the business as publicity man and later general manager of the Los Angeles Rams. Los Angeles was and still is a sportswriters' holy place. Athletes step softly. Management is generous. Nevertheless, a big game is a big game, and tickets can be hard to come by.

When the Rams' management prohibited passing out free tickets to the 1951 championship games in the Coliseum (in accordance with league rules), local newspapermen talked it over and decided that the event was not worth covering. They stuck by the position until the Rams reassessed their own and purchased at full price from the league office several hundred "complimentary" tickets.

As a publicity man, Schramm sometimes wrote a column under the by-line of a well-known Los

Angeles sportswriter. While Schramm slanted the columns in favor of his employers, he wrote nothing that the columnist might not have written for himself, had he been up to it. All Schramm did was accent redeeming qualities. Ex–Tulane publicity man Larry Karl provided a similar service for a New Orleans sports columnist in the 1950's. Karl would write the column, deliver it, fix it with a standard headline, and tuck it in the columnist's typewriter. On one occasion Karl appendaged the column with a personal note—"Ed," (or whatever) "the plane leaves at noon." He discovered how far things had gone when the message appeared in print as the final sentence to the column.

Let me make one thing plain: most sportswriters have no business in journalism. They are misfits looking for a soft life. The worst sportswriters are frustrated athletes, or compulsive sports fans, or both. The best are frustrated writers trapped by circumstances. Westbrook Pegler called sportswriters "historians of trivia," but Pegler learned his craft by writing sport. Scotty Reston, Heywood Broun, Damon Runyon, Ring Lardner, and Paul Gallico wrote about sport. Winston Churchill covered cricket during the Boer War. The *New York Times'* John Kieran was a sportswriter, but he was much more. When students at Yale protested that a *sportswriter* had been invited to address them, Kieran delivered his speech in Latin.

Sportswriting should be a young man's profession. No one improves after eight or ten years, but the assignments get juicier and the way out less attractive. After eight or ten years there is nothing else to say. Every word in every style has been set in print, every variation from discovery to death explored. The ritual goes on, and the mind bends under it. Ask a baseball writer what's new and he'll quote you the record book. Baseball writers are old men, regardless of age. Crew Slammer contended it was the sport that gets too heavy for the human soul. Men who have traveled the deadly dull cycle too often are forever deafened to what they started to say. One writer with the Philadelphia *Bulletin* has been with the Philadelphia Eagles Football Club so long that he refers to them as "we." Difficulty with pronouns is a terminal sign for the journalist.

A writer whose ear is gone can become an editor, which is to say he can become a censor and accountant. Newspaper editors pretend to be appointed guardians of the old mentality ceiling ("write to the sixth-grade reader": never mind why he is sixth grade), yet in reality they *are* the mentality ceiling. Crew Slammer and the rest of us formulated the theory that the higher a man climbs in the newspaper business, the less he becomes. It must be like a pencil sharpener up there.

I never did learn the name of the man in the Tower who had me fired from my last job as sports columnist of the Philadelphia *Inquirer*. I saw him once. He was pale and, as I recall, walked with a limp. I believe the last time he came down from the Tower was in '07, to overturn a *Bulletin* truck or something. His reason for letting me go was he couldn't understand what I was writing. I appreciated his position.

April 1968

Postscript

This was the first non-sports story I ever published in a national magazine. As I read it again fifteen years later, I am relieved it was the first; if it had been the tenth or seventeenth I would have been well advised to pursue my original plan to become a lawyer, or perhaps a salesman of women's footwear. In places, the writing is embarrassing. "The Freudian window sash," for example, whatever the hell that means.

Still, it's a good picture of how it was in the city rooms of the 1950's, before computers and word processors. I can still hear the rattle of Western Union printers, and smell machine oil, feel the soot. One measure of this story's immaturity is the obvious bitterness I still felt for the newspaper editors of my early experience. I suppose I have mellowed, but newspapers have come a long way, too. Maybe we had something to do with bringing about changes. (See "Stop the Press!" for another view of this subject.)

There is an inclination to make changes in all stories, but I decided against it. I leave them to history, warts and all.

I still believe that sportswriting is a good way for a young journalist to get indoctrinated into the profession, though a few years on the police beat are essential to an understanding that the games are sometimes deadly and permanent. Sportswriters *are* "historians of trivia," but they're historians nevertheless. There is a freedom in sportswriting not found anywhere else on a newspaper. But beware of the debilitating effects of the deadly cycle: when a writer realizes that he (or she) has written all this before, it's time to move on. I haven't heard of Crew Slammer in years, but I'd like to believe he's somewhere in the Himalayas, doing pieces on the snow leopard.

2

Who Was Jack Ruby?

All I know about the best man in my wedding is he didn't exist.

Five days before John F. Kennedy was assassinated in Dallas, I got married for the second time. It was a Sunday, the day after I'd covered the SMU-Arkansas game at the Cotton Bowl, and Jo and I—who had known each other a good three weeks—were convinced by this romantic con man who called himself Richard Noble that we should drive to Durant, Oklahoma, and get married. Richard Noble personally drove us in his air-conditioned convertible. He paid for the blood tests and license. We used his 1949 Stanford class ring in the ceremony, and we drank a quart of his scotch and sang "Hey, Look Me Over" ("Remember when you're down and out, the only way is up!") on the way back to Dallas.

There was no such person as Richard Noble, and the Stanford class ring was bought in a hock shop.

Whoever the man was who called himself Richard Noble had set up a bogus sales office in a North Dallas apartment complex inhabited mainly by airline stews and indomitable seekers and had managed to ingratiate himself with his personality, credit cards, liquor supply, and national WATS line. A month or so after the assassination, which I assume he had nothing to do with, Richard Noble vanished in the night. The FBI came around asking questions, and that was the last I heard.

A lot of bizarre people were doing some very strange things in Dallas in the fall of 1963, and Richard Noble was only one of them. Madame Nhu bought a dozen shower caps at Neiman-Marcus and tried to drum up support for the Diem regime in Saigon, even while her host in the U.S., the CIA, laid plans to assassinate Diem himself. Members of the American Nazi party danced around a man in an ape suit in front of the *Times Herald* building. Congressman Bruce Alger, who had once carried a sign accusing Lyndon Johnson of being a traitor, went on television to denounce the Peace Corps as "welfare socialism and godless materialism, all at the expense of capitalism and basic U.S. spiritual and moral values." Zealots from the National Indignation Committee picketed a UN Day speech by Ambassador Adlai Stevenson; they called him Addle-Eye and booed and spat on him and hit him on the head with a picket sign. When a hundred civic leaders wired strong and sincere apologies to the ambassador, General Edwin Walker, who had been cashiered by the Pentagon for force-feeding his troops right-wing propaganda, flew the American flag upside down in front of his military-gray mansion on Turtle Creek. There were pro-Castro cabals and anti-Castro cabals that overlapped and enough clandestine commerce to fill a dozen Bogart movies. Drugs, arms, muscle, propaganda: the piety of the Dallas business climate was the perfect cover. A friend of mine in banking operated a fleet of trucks in Bogotá as a sideline. Airline stewardesses brought in sugarcoated cookies of black Turkish hash without having the slightest notion of what they were carrying.

Jack Ruby was having one of his customary feuds with an employee of his Carousel Club, but this one was serious. His star attraction, Jada, claimed that she feared for her life and placed Ruby under peace bond. Newspaper ads for the Carousel Club during the week of November 22 featured Bill Demar, a comic ventriloquist — hardly Ruby's style, but the best he could do.

And someone took a potshot at General Walker in his own home. People said later it was Lee Harvey Oswald.

If there is a tear left, shed it for Jack Ruby. He didn't make history; he only stepped in front of it. When he emerged from obscurity into that inextricable freeze-frame that joins all of our minds to Dallas, Jack Ruby, a bald-headed little man who wanted above all else to make it big, had his back to the camera.

I can tell you about Jack Ruby, and about Dallas, and if necessary remind you that human life is sweetly fragile and the holy litany of ambition and success takes as many people to hell as it does to heaven. But someone else will have to tell you about Oswald, and what he was doing in Dallas that November, when Jack Ruby took the play away from Oswald, and from all of us.

Dallas, Oswald, Ruby, Watts, Whitman, Manson, Ray, Sirhan, Bremer, Vietnam, Nixon, Watergate, FBI, CIA, Squeaky Fromme, Sara Moore — the list goes on and on. Who the hell wrote this script, and where will it end? A dozen years of violence, shock, treachery, and paranoia, and I date it all back to that insane weekend in Dallas and Jack Ruby—the one essential link in the chain, the man who changed an isolated act into a trend.

Jack Ruby had come a long way from the ghettos of Chicago, or so he liked to think. He described the Carousel Club as a "fucking classy joint" and patrons who challenged his opinion sometimes got thrown down the stairs. The Carousel was a dingy, cramped walk-up in the 1300 block of Commerce, right next to Abe Weinstein's Colony Club and close to the hotels, restaurants, and night spots that made downtown Dallas lively and respectably sinister in those times of official innocence. You can see more flesh in a high school biology class now than you could at any of the joints on the Strip in 1963, but that wasn't the point. Jack Ruby ran what he considered a "decent" place, a "high-class" place, a place that Dallas could view with pride. "Punks" and "characters" who wandered in by mistake were as likely as not to leave with an impression of Jack Ruby's fist where their nose used to be.

Cops and newspapermen, that's who Ruby wanted in his place. Dallas cops drank there regularly, and none of them ever paid for a drink. Any girl caught hooking in his joint would get manhandled and fired on the spot, but Ruby leaned on his girls to provide sexual pleasures for favored clients.

Jack Ruby was a foulmouthed, mean-tempered prude who loved children and hated ethnic jokes. He didn't drink or smoke. He was violently opposed to drugs, though he maintained his own high energy level by popping Preludin—an upper—and it was rumored that he operated a personal clearinghouse for mob drug-runners. He was involved in shady financial schemes, and the IRS was on his back. A swindler who called himself Harry Sinclair, Jr., told

Secret Service agents that Ruby backed him in a bet-and-run operation. Ruby supplied cash and introduced Sinclair to likely victims. (H. L. Hunt was supposed to have been one.) If Sinclair won, he'd collect; if he lost, he'd write a hot check and split. Ruby got forty percent of the action.

Sex shocked and disturbed him, and that's how Ruby had his falling-out with Jada, who had been imported from the 500 Club in New Orleans so that the Carousel could compete with the much classier Colony Club (where Chris Colt was stripping) or Barney Weinstein's Theatre Lounge around the corner, where you could catch Nikki Joy. Ruby was childishly jealous of the Weinsteins, who drove Cadillacs and Jaguars and took frequent trips to Las Vegas; and he assuaged his envy by drafting complaints to the strippers' union, the Liquor Control Board, and the IRS, accusing the Weinsteins of whatever. Even the FBI, to its sorrow, knew of Ruby's antipathy for the Weinsteins. Of all the Ruby rumors that have flourished and died through the years—that Ruby fired at Kennedy from the railroad overpass, that Oswald visited the Carousel Club a few days before the assassination—only the most current one, that Ruby was an informant for the FBI, seems to have much truth to it. Hugh Aynesworth, a *Times Herald* reporter who knew Ruby well, verified it: "In 1959 the FBI tried eight times to recruit Jack Ruby. They wanted him as an informer on drugs, gambling, and organized crime, but every time they contacted him, Ruby tried to get his competitors in trouble. 'Ol' Abe over at the Colony Club is cheating on his income tax. . . . Ol' Barney at the Theatre Lounge is selling booze after hours.' After a while the FBI gave up on the idea." The Weinsteins, not surprisingly, considered Ruby a creep.

I first met Jada about a month before the assassination. Bud Shrake and I shared an apartment on Cole Avenue that autumn, and since we were both sportswriters, Ruby considered us favored customers. He invited us to the Carousel one night, and Shrake came home with Jada. We all became good friends, and when Jo and I got married a few weeks later, Jada gave us our first wedding gift—a two-pound Girl Scout cookie tin full of illegal weed she had smuggled across the border in her gold Cadillac with the letters JADA embossed on the door. Jada cleared customs with one hundred of the two-pound tins in the trunk of her car. She was accompanied by a state politician (who knew nothing about the load) and wore a mink coat, high-heel shoes, and nothing else. The first thing she did at customs was open the door and fall out, revealing more than the customs official expected. That was one of Jada's great pleasures, driving around Dallas in her mink coat and high heels, her orange hair piled high and the coat flaring open. It was a better act than the one Ruby paid for.

Ruby planted the story that Jada was trained in ballet, had a college degree in psychology, was a descendant of John Quincy Adams, and a granddaughter of Pavlova. Jada's name was Adams, Janet Adams Conforto, but she hadn't been inside a classroom since she ran away from a Catholic girls school in New York at age fifteen, and she couldn't dance her way out of a doughnut. Her act consisted mainly of hunching a tiger-skin rug and making wild orgasmic sounds with her throat. As a grand climax Jada would spread her legs and pop her G-string, and that's when Ruby would turn off the lights and the hell would start.

The other strippers and champagne girls hated Jada. She was a star and acted the part. The bus-station girls from Sherman and Tyler came and went—Ruby automatically fired any girl who agreed to have sex with him—but Jada treated Ruby like a dog. She called him a pansy and worse, and she spread word among the customers that the hamburgers served out of the Carousel's tiny kitchen were contaminated with dog shit.

One night while Jada was ravaging her tiger skin, a tourist stepped up and popped a flashbulb in her face. Ruby threw the startled cameraman down the stairs. Jada popped her G-string about a foot, and Ruby threw her off the stage. All this took a few seconds, but for those few seconds Ruby was an absolute madman. Then he walked over to our table and said in this very weary, clear, huckster voice, "How's it going, boys? Need anything?" I don't think he remembered what had just happened.

On the morning of the assassination, Ruby called our apartment and asked if we'd seen Jada. Shrake said we hadn't. "I'm warning you for your own good," Ruby said. "Stay away from that woman." "Is that intended as a threat?" Shrake inquired. "No, no," Ruby apologized. "No, it's just that she's an evil woman."

Unlike the other clubs on the Strip, the Carousel was strictly a clip joint where Ruby's girls hustled $1.98 bottles of champagne for whatever they could get.

"We kept the labels covered with a bar towel," a onetime Ruby champagne girl told me. The woman, who is now married to a well-known musician, went to work for Ruby when she was seventeen. "Jack would tell us to come on to the customers, promise them anything—of course he didn't mean for us to deliver, but sometimes we did on our own time. The price for a bottle of cheap champagne was anywhere from fifteen to seventy-five dollars. We'd sit with the customer as long as the bottle lasted, drinking out of what we called spit glasses—frosted glasses of ice water. We worked for tips or whatever we could steal.

"Actually, Jack had a soft heart. He was always loaning us money and knocking the snot out of anyone who gave us a bad time. He liked that image of himself—big bad protector. He'd fire you, then ten minutes later break in on you in the john and demand to know why you weren't on the floor pushing drinks. One girl there got fired about three hundred times."

The only "decent" woman in Jack Ruby's life was Alice Nichols, a shy widow who worked for an insurance company. He dated her on and off for eleven years. The reason Ruby couldn't marry Alice, he told many of his friends, was that he had made his mother a deathbed promise that he wouldn't marry a gentile. Ruby's mother had died in an insane asylum in Chicago.

Ruby had the carriage of a bantam cock and the energy of a steam engine as he churned through the streets of downtown Dallas, glad-handing, passing out cards, speaking rapidly, compulsively, about his new line of pizza ovens, about the twistboards he was promoting, about the important people he knew, cornering friends and grabbing strangers, relating amazing details of his private life and how any day now he would make it big. He once spotted actress Rhonda Fleming having a club sandwich at Love Field and joined her for lunch. You could always spot him at the boxing matches. He'd wait until just before the main event, when they turned up the lights, and he'd prance down the center aisle in a badly dated hat and double-breasted suit, shaking hands and handing out free passes to the Carousel.

He was always on his way to some very important meeting, saying he was going to see the mayor, the police chief, some judge, Stanley Marcus, Clint Murchison. And every day he'd make his rounds— the bank, the Statler Hilton, the police station, the courthouse, the bail-bond office, the Doubleday

Book Store (Ruby was a compulsive reader of new diet books), the delicatessen, the shoeshine parlor, radio station KLIF.

KLIF was owned by Gordon McLendon, whom Ruby once identified as "the world's greatest American." McLendon, who billed himself as "the Old Scotchman," made his reputation recreating baseball games on the old Liberty Broadcasting System until organized baseball conspired to shut him down. The Old Scotchman would sit in a soundproof studio a thousand miles from the action he was describing, reading the play-by-play from the ticker, his voice shrill and disbelieving, while his sound man (Dallas' current mayor Wes Wise was one of them) beat on a grapefruit with a bat and faked PA announcements requesting that the owner of a blue 1947 Buick please move his car out of the fire lane. Later McLendon pioneered the Top Forty music/news format, introduced a series of right-wing radio editorials, ran unsuccessfully for Ralph Yarborough's Senate seat, and launched a one-man campaign against dirty and suggestive songs like "Yellow Submarine" and "Puff, the Magic Dragon." The Old Scotchman, Jack Ruby liked to say, was his idea of "a intellectual."

Ruby wasn't a big man—five foot nine, 175 pounds—but he had thick shoulders and arms, and he was fast. He swam and exercised regularly at the YMCA, and was a compulsive consumer of health foods. He had an expression that dated from his street-fighting days in Chicago: "Take the play away." It meant to strike first. He usually carried a big roll of money, and when he carried money he also carried a gun.

Hugh Aynesworth saw the many personalities of Jack Ruby as clearly as anyone. Aynesworth recalled a night at Ruby's second club, the Vegas, when a drunk came in after hours with a bottle bulging from his inside coat pocket. Ruby took the man's two dollars, showed him to a table, then smashed the bottle against the man's rib cage.

Another time Aynesworth encountered a dazed, bleeding wino staggering near the Adolphus Hotel. The wino had tried to bum a quarter from Ruby, who smashed him in the head with a full whiskey bottle. Yet at times Ruby could be embarrassingly sentimental.

"Ruby was a crier," Aynesworth recalls. "I mean, he could go to a fire and break out crying."

Aynesworth has been investigating the events of that week for twelve years and has concluded that the Warren Report is mostly accurate. Two nuts, two killings. "In Ruby's case the conspiracy theory is totally ridiculous," he told me. "Ruby would have told everyone on the streets of downtown Dallas. *Ho, ho, ho, they asked me to help kill the President. Of course I'm not gonna do it.*"

Joe Cavagnaro, one of Jack Ruby's best friends, made the same observation. "Nobody would have trusted Jack with a secret," he said. "He talked too much."

Cavagnaro is the sales manager of the Statler Hilton, a neat, manicured, gregarious man who exudes the personality of downtown Dallas, but he was just a man in need of a friend when he arrived in 1955. Cavagnaro was eating at the Lucas B&B Restaurant next to the Vegas Club one night when Ruby sauntered in, said hello, and picked up the check.

"He was a fine person," Cavagnaro said. "Much different than the picture you read. He had a big heart. He was good to people. Anyone down on his luck, he'd help them to the point of excess. There was a policeman whose wife and kid were in an accident, he took over a sack of groceries. He'd read something in the paper about some poor family and he'd go to the rescue. Sure, he had a short fuse, but remember, he had to police his own business; otherwise they'd close him up. The vice squad was always hanging around his place. Some drunk would act up and Jack would remove him without the vice squad being aware it ever happened."

Cavagnaro and Ruby had coffee at the Statler a few hours after the assassination. Ruby was extremely upset, and blamed the *Morning News.*

"He said it would be a cold day in hell before he placed another ad with the *News*," Cavagnaro told me. "Jack was a true patriot. He was also a Democrat. He thought Kennedy had done a lot for the minorities. Just from a business standpoint, he said, something like that could kill a city."

Did he say anything about killing Oswald?

"I think everyone in Dallas said something to the effect that 'I'd like to kill that S.O.B.' "

But Ruby *did* it; that is the difference. What did Cavagnaro think when he heard the news?

"I thought, yes, Jack *could* do that. I'd seen him hit a guy once for insulting a girl. The guy practically left his feet and flew across the street."

In the same block as the Statler Hilton and the Dallas police station, in a spot called the Purple Orchid, Ruby's ex–champagne girl joined eighty million viewers of Ruby's astounding crime on television. The girl turned to the bartender, who had also worked for Ruby, and she said: "Well, Jack's finally gonna get recognized."

Times Herald editorial page editor A. C. Greene and his wife had just driven home from church. Betty Greene ran ahead to answer the telephone, and when A.C. walked in the kitchen door she told him that someone had just killed the man who killed the President. He was someone who owned a downtown nightclub, Betty Greene said, bewildered. *Oh, God,*

A.C. thought: *Jack Ruby!*

While Ruby was shooting Oswald, Jo and I were driving from Columbus, Ohio, where I had just met my new in-laws, to Cleveland, where the Cowboys were playing the Browns. The NFL was the only shop that stayed open that weekend. They claimed that it was a public service, and in retrospect I think they were right. Shrake met me at the press box entrance and told me what had happened.

"Jack Ruby!" I said. "Why not."

"Why not," Shrake said, shaking his head.

If you believe that Jack Ruby was part of a conspiracy, a "double cutout" as they say in the spy trade, then you must also conclude that the conspiracy involved dozens or even hundreds of plotters, including Captain Will Fritz of the Dallas police department. Time and events make Ruby's role in a conspiracy almost impossible. Oswald was to have been transferred from the city jail to the county jail at 10 A.M.—that was a solid commitment Chief Jesse Curry made to his intimates among the press corps. If Ruby had been gunning for Oswald, if he had premeditated the crime that eighty million witnesses saw him commit, he would have been at the police station at 10 A.M. But he wasn't. There were several reasons for the delay in transferring Oswald, but the main one was Will Fritz's insistence on interrogating the suspect one more time in city jail.

Ruby knew when the transfer was scheduled. He had covered the event like a reporter on a beat: Parkland Hospital, the assassination site, the press conferences. He was always at the center of the action, passing out sandwiches, giving directions to out-of-town correspondents, acting as unofficial press agent for District Attorney Henry Wade—who, like everyone else on the scene, simply regarded Jack Ruby as part of the furniture. Twice during a press conference Wade mistakenly identified Oswald as a member of the violently anti-Castro Free Cuba Committee. The second time a friendly voice at the back of the room corrected the DA. "No, sir, Mister District Attorney, Oswald was a member of the Fair Play for Cuba Committee." The voice was Jack Ruby's. How did he know that? Well, it was in all the news reports, but there is a more intriguing theory: an FBI report overlooked by the Warren Commission suggests that one of Ruby's many sidelines was the role of bagman for a nonpartisan group of profiteers who stole arms from the U.S. military and ran them for anti-Castro Cubans.

Ten o'clock came and went, and still Oswald hadn't been transferred. It was after ten when Ruby received a telephone call from one of his strippers who lived in Fort Worth. The girl needed money; she needed it right then. Ruby dressed and drove to the Western Union office in the same block as the police station. He couldn't have missed the crowd lingering outside on Commerce and on Elm. At 11:17 A.M. Ruby wired the money. He walked up an alley, passed through the crowd, and entered the ramp of the police station, a distance of about 350 feet. He was carrying better than two thousand dollars in cash (he couldn't bank the money because the IRS might grab it) and his gun was in its customary place in his right coat pocket.

Three minutes after Ruby posted the Western Union money order, he shot Oswald.

If the world at large was shocked at that precise minute, consider the bewilderment of Jack Ruby as the Dallas cops pounced on him. What was wrong? Had *he* done something he wasn't supposed to do? Didn't *everyone* want him to kill Oswald? What the hell was this?

"You all know me," he said pathetically. "I'm Jack Ruby."

Jack Ruby had to believe that he was guilty of a premeditated, calculated murder. The alternative—to admit he was crazy—was too awful to contemplate.

During the trial he told his chief attorney, Melvin Belli, "What are we doing, Mel, kidding ourselves? We know what happened. We know I did it for Jackie and the [Kennedy] kids. I just went in and shot him. They've got us anyway. Maybe I ought to forget this silly story that I'm telling and get on the stand and tell the truth."

The silly story that Belli, Joe Tonahill, and other members of the defense team were attempting to pass along to the jury was that Ruby killed Oswald during a seizure of psychomotor epilepsy. Belli and Tonahill still subscribe to this contention.

"The autopsy confirmed it. Ruby had fifteen brain tumors," Joe Tonahill told me. Tonahill, a huge, deliberate, friendly man, maintains that the Ruby trial "was the unfairest trial in the history of Texas." Judge Joe Brown, exhibiting a classic downtown Dallas mentality, appointed Dallas advertising executive Sam Bloom to handle "public relations" and overruled the defense on almost every motion. Ruby himself considered hiring a public relations man—or that's what he wrote in a letter to his intellectual hero, Gordon McLendon.

"Jack Ruby needed help long before Kennedy came to Dallas," Tonahill said. He was seated at the desk of his law office in Jasper, in front of a four-by-eight-foot blowup of Bob Jackson's Pulitzer prize–winning photograph of the Oswald murder. "He was a big baby at birth—almost fifteen pounds. That could have had something to do with it. His mother died in an insane asylum in Chicago. His father was a drunk and was treated for psychiatric disorders. A brother and a sister had psychiatric treatment. Ruby tried to commit suicide a couple of years earlier. His finger was once bitten off in a fight. He had a long history of violent, antisocial behavior, and when it was over he wouldn't remember what he had done. What provoked him? Maybe the flashbulbs — that's a common cause in cases of psychomotor epilepsy — or the TV cameras, or the smirk on Oswald's face."

I asked Tonahill what he thought of Ruby as a person.

"He was a real object of pity," Tonahill said. "Anytime you see a person overflowing with ambition to be someone, that person is admitting to you and the world that he's a nobody. Ruby was like a Damon Runyon character — a total inconsistency."

If Jack Ruby was not crazy when he gunned down Oswald, it's a safe bet the trial drove him that way. Day after day in the circus atmosphere of Judge Brown's courtroom, Ruby was forced to sit as a silent exhibit while psychiatrists called him a latent homosexual with a compulsive desire to be liked and respected, and his own attorneys described him as a village clown. He didn't even get to tell his own story, and by the time the Warren Commission found time to interview him months later, Ruby was convinced that there was a conspiracy to slaughter all the Jews of the world.

"In the beginning," Tonahill told me, "Ruby considered himself a hero. He thought he had done a great service for the community. When the mayor, Earle Cabell, testified that the act brought disgrace to Dallas, Jack started going downhill very fast. He got more nervous by the day. When they brought in the death penalty, he cracked. Ten days later he rammed his head into a cell wall. Then he tried to kill himself with an electric light socket. Then he tried to hang himself with sheets."

Ruby wrote a letter to Gordon McLendon claiming he was being poisoned by his jailers. Many Warren

Report critics take this as additional evidence of a conspiracy. If someone did poison Ruby, it was a waste of good poison. An autopsy confirmed the brain tumors, massive spread of cancer, and a blood clot in his leg, which finally killed him.

The trial of Jack Ruby may have been one of the fastest on record. The crime was committed in November and the trial began in February. "The climate never cooled off," Tonahill said. "He was tried as it was peaking. There was this massive guilt in Dallas at the time. The only thing that could save Dallas was sending Ruby to the electric chair."

Though there are unanswered questions in his mind, Tonahill supports the conclusions of the Warren Report.

"If there was a conspiracy, and it was suppressed, it had to involve maybe a million people. That's a bunch of crap.

"The worse mistake the Warren Commission made was yielding to Rose Kennedy and suppressing the autopsy report. There was something about Kennedy's physical condition the family didn't want made public. I don't know what it was. Possibly a vasectomy—there was a story he had a vasectomy after the death of his baby. Being good Catholics, the Kennedy family wouldn't have wanted that out."

One close participant in the bizarre happenings of Dallas who isn't satisfied with the Warren Commission investigation is Bill Alexander, the salty, acid-tongued prosecutor who did most of the talking for Henry Wade at the Ruby trial. Alexander and former state Attorney General Waggoner Carr both urged the commission to investigate FBI and CIA personnel for information linking the agencies to Lee Harvey Oswald. There is no indication that such an investigation took place.

"I'm in Washington telling the commission to check

out this address I found in Oswald's notebook, in his apartment, the day of the killing," Alexander recently told the Houston *Chronicle*. "None of those Yankee hot dogs are paying any attention to me.

"So I say, 'Waggoner, c'mon, let's get a cab.' We jump in and tell the driver to take us to this address. We get there and what do you think it is? The goddamn Russian Embassy. Now, what does that tell you?

"To this day, I don't think anybody from the commission followed that up."

Although Alexander, known to members of the press as "Old Snake-Eyes," was the main reason Henry Wade got the death penalties that the leaders of Dallas were convinced would deter crime, he is no longer on the DA's staff. Shortly after his infamous declaration that Chief Justice Earl Warren didn't need impeaching, he needed hanging, Alexander resigned to enter private practice.

When I telephoned Alexander for an interview, he told me he didn't want to talk about the assassination.

"I'd like to kick the dog shit out of every Yankee newspaperman, club the fuckers to the ground," he said. "You can still see them, right up to this day, hanging around the Book Depository," Alexander went on. "Fat-ass Yankees in shorts and cameras getting the roofs of their mouths sunburned. A carload of Yankees pulled up to my friend Miller Tucker and said [Alexander slipped into an Eastern accent], 'Officer, where did Kennedy get shot?' Ol' Miller taps the back of his head and says, 'Right here, friend, right here.'"

That afternoon I met Alexander in his law office and he told me about his Manchurian Candidate theory. "I worked a solid two years on this," he began. "I read the entire twenty-six volumes of the Warren Report just to protect myself, and tracked down every lead I could get my hands on, and I don't have any evidence that anyone acted with Oswald.

"Now," he said, raising a finger and slipping into third person singular so that it would be clearly understood he was speaking hypothetically, "who knows how a person has been brainwashed—motivated—hypnotized?

"A man is cashiered out of the Marine Corps—he moves to Russia—he marries the niece of the head of the OGPU spy school—he stays a certain amount of months, then turns up at the American Embassy and says, 'King's X, fellows, I want to go home. Do you think you people might could pay my way back to New York?' Wouldn't somebody debrief that man? Hell, the FBI knew he was in New Orleans. They sent his folder to Dallas before the assassination."

On the other hand, Alexander has not the slightest doubt that Ruby acted alone in a legally sane, premeditated manner. Alexander and Dr. John T. Holbrook were among the first to question Ruby after the shooting.

"I'm paraphrasing now," Alexander said, "but it was like he wanted to open the Jack Ruby Show on Broadway, get a TV show, write a book. He asked me if I thought he needed an agent."

Alexander spat tobacco juice in a can and said, "Jack Ruby was about as handicapped as you can get in Dallas. First, he was a Yankee. Second, he was a Jew. Third, he was in the nightclub business.

"That's horseshit about him being a police buff. He didn't think any more of a policeman than he did a pissant. It was just good business. The vice squad kept plus and minus charts on the joints 'cause the licenses came up for renewal each year. The vice squad can kill a joint if they get in the wrong mood. Who wants to drink beer with a harness bull looking over his shoulder?

"Quit kidding me about how much Ruby loved people. Or how much he loved the Kennedys. Hell, where was he while the motorcade was passing through downtown? In the goddamn *Dallas News*, placing an ad for his club."

The ex-prosecutor sat back and sighed.

"It's a real experience to see how real, factual history can be distorted in ten years so that people who lived it can't recognize it."

> And the end of all our exploring
> Will be to arrive where we started
> And know the place for the first time.
> —T. S. Eliot, from *Little Gidding*

On a warm day twelve years removed from that time of Ruby and Oswald, my son Mark and I walk the streets of downtown Dallas and know the place for the first time.

The Blue Front where you could eat the world's best oxtail soup and watch Willie sweat in the potato salad is gone. The Star Bar is gone. Hodges, Joe Banks, the Oyster Bar, the musty little bookstores with their dark volumes, the mom and dad shops, the smell of pizza, of chili rice, of peanut oil, of stale beer, of perfume, lost now in the tomb of our memory. What you smell twelve years later is concrete. What you see are the walls of a glass canyon.

The corner of Commerce and Akard, which used to bustle with beautiful women in short skirts and quick men with briefcases, is nearly deserted, except for a few Hare Krishnas and some delegates to the Fraternal Order of the Eagles. The Carousel, the Colony, the Theatre Lounge, the Horseshoe Bar, the whole Strip has been leveled and turned into a gigantic parking lot for the invisible occupants of the glass skyscrapers. The big department stores and the theaters and the good restaurants have gone to the suburbs.

Twelve years ago you could have dropped a net sixteen blocks square from the Republic National Bank tower and been fairly sure that you had caught a quorum of the Dallas oligarchy. There is still a feeling of affluence, but the vortex of power has moved to the suburbs, out Stemmons, out Greenville, out Northwest Highway, out to Old Town—whatever Old Town is.

There are blacks on the city council, and the mayor is a former grapefruit hitter for the Old Scotchman. The Old Scotchman long ago sold KLIF and is seldom seen anymore; he is a Howard Hughes figure, dabbling, so it is said, in multinationals and worldwide real estate. When the sun disappears behind the canyon walls, what you see in downtown Dallas is blacks with mops and brooms, waiting for an elevator. Slack-faced office workers wait for a bus in front of the old Majestic theater, and black hookers with beehives appear to show the Fraternal Order of Eagles the sights.

I wonder: could there be a Jack Ruby in 1975? Where would he go? What would he do? The Dallas Jack Ruby knew is gone.

That Dallas was a city of shame, but it wasn't a city of hate. Its vision was genuine and sincere, but it had the heart of a rodent. In the subterranean tunnels of those proud spires of capitalism and free enterprise crawled armies of con men and hustlers, cheap-shot artists and money changers, profiteers and ideologues, grubbers, grabbers, fireflies, eccentrics, and cuckoos. Dallas was just like everyplace else, except it couldn't admit it. It was not Lee Harvey Oswald and the murder of John F. Kennedy that proved what Dallas was really like, but Jack Ruby and the murder of Lee Harvey Oswald.

We drive out Turtle Creek past General Walker's prim gray fortress. On the front lawn, a crude, hand-lettered marquee says DUMP ESTES, a reference, I suppose, to the Dallas superintendent of schools who apparently isn't resisting integration fast enough. Like downtown Dallas, the general is quieter these days. Ken Latimer, a resident actor at the Dallas Theater Center (DTC), tells us, "General Walker and his people used to picket us fairly regularly, but they've been quiet for some time now." Latimer played the lead in the DTC production of *Jack Ruby*, *All-American Boy*, a drama that attempted without much success to answer the question: Was Jack Ruby a typical American?

"Ruby wanted to be liked, to be respected, to be successful according to the value system of our society," Latimer says. "He was a cheap success, but in his own mind he had class. Violence was admissible to his system — toughness — let no one push you around.

"You asked me was it the climate of the times that made Ruby do what he did? No, Jack Ruby would do the same thing today."

We talk to stripper Chastity Fox, who played the role of Jada. Chastity had never met Ruby or Jada; she was a junior in an all-girls Catholic school in Los Angeles when Kennedy was assassinated. She is fascinated that I knew them and asks me four questions for every one I ask her. Chastity looks something like Jada, except better.

She refused to do Jada's tiger-rug hunch in the play. "Her show was nasty," Chastity says. "I'm more of a dancer." Chastity's best act is belly dancing, a subject she teaches at the University of Texas at Arlington. But like Jada she's come through some tough places — she remembers stripping in the Lariat Bar in Wyoming while a three-piece Western band played "Won't You Ride in My Little Red Wagon?"

"The club action in Dallas is different now than it was in Ruby's time," Chastity says. "There are still a few clip joints like Ruby ran, and there are three, maybe four, traditional strip places where you can go watch a show and not get hustled. The big thing now is topless. The traditional strip show—we call it parading—is dying out. It's sort of sad. It is an American tradition, but it dates back to the forties and fifties when you couldn't see ass or boobs walking down the street."

Although she never knew Jack Ruby, Chastity had heard of him for years from her agent, Pappy Dolsen. Pappy was one of Ruby's contemporaries, an old-time club owner and booking agent, a gentleman tough from a truly tough time. Pappy had told the story many times how Ruby telephoned him the day before Oswald was killed and said: "I know I did you wrong, Pappy, but I'll make it up to you. I'm going places in show business, and when I do, you're going with me."

Pappy has had a heart attack and is in the intensive care ward at Baylor Medical Hospital, but Chastity shows us a letter that Ruby had written to Pappy years ago. It said:

> We regret, at this time, we are unable to book the "act" you have for us—I'm sure its as wonderful as you mention but the price is to fucking high. Hoping to confront you on a more senseable base in the future. I remain.
>
> Jack Ruby

There is one more thing to do. Mark was six years old, a Dallas first-grader when Kennedy was murdered. He doesn't remember much of it. But there was an article in *Look*, written by a Fina Oil Company executive named Jack Shea, which mentioned that at one public school in Dallas, children cheered the news of the assassination. Jack Shea was a good Catholic and a top-level businessman, but his gut feeling that Dallas was big enough to hear the truth from one of its own was a serious miscalculation. Shea was fired. He is now a partner in a Los Angeles ad agency.

Jo and I named our son Shea after the Fina executive, and I was curious to read the article one more time. Funny, I had never told Mark or his sister Lea how Shea got his name. I hadn't thought about it for a long time. Too many things had happened.

Twelve years ago, when the first announcement that the President had been shot was broadcast over the PA system at Richardson Junior High School, Gertrude Hutter, an eighth-grade teacher, began crying. Bob Dudney, who is now a reporter for the *Times Herald*, recalled the moment. She turned her back long enough to compose herself, then addressed her class with these prophetic words:

"Children, we are entering into an age of violence. There is nothing we can do about it, but all of us must stay calm, and above all, civilized."

November 1975

Postscript

Every writer should have a Jack Ruby and a Dallas. Sometime in everyone's experience, something happens that changes things, even if you have to chase it halfway around the world, which I didn't.

In the story, I wondered if there could be another Jack Ruby in 1975. Now I know there could, and was. The nuts and counternuts are always with us. Wherever there is an Oswald, there is a Ruby. History just forgot to record the names.

Ted Turner delivered an editorial on Cable News Network recently, advocating the censorship of movies like *Taxi Driver*, which Turner and a lot of others seemed to believe motivated John W. Hinckley to attempt to assassinate President Reagan. If *Taxi Driver* hadn't been available, Turner argued, Hinckley would have done something *else* that day. That's nonsense. Priscilla Johnson McMillan, in her book *Marina and Lee,* reveals that Oswald identified with the hero of *High Noon.* Writers, directors, and artists reflect the world; they don't create it.

Not long after this story was published, I got a letter from "Richard Noble," the con man who was best man at my wedding. It was written from Texas state prison and wanted to know how much I would pay to write his life story. I get letters like that all the time, but I never answer them.

I saw Jada a few years ago. I found her in San Francisco by looking up the phone number for A. Lincoln, an alias she used when I knew her. She was hiding from a gang of bank robbers who believed that she had run off with their swag, which was mainly true. Jada looked faded and washed out, but after a couple of hours with her makeup kit she seemed to be a new woman. Every writer has a Jada in his life, or should.

3

Leroy's Revenge

Otis Crater was late for the fanciers' organizational meeting at the Cherokee Lounge for good reason. He had just stabbed a U-TOTE-M attendant following a discussion of the economic impact of a five-cent price increase on a six-pack of beer.

Crater kicked open the lounge door and bounced off the wall, scattering a table of Arabs who had made the mistake of thinking the Cherokee was a hangout for University of Texas exchange students. Crater carried the remnants of a six-pack under one arm and cradled his baby pit bulldog, Princess, under the other. He looked like a crazed, bloody scarecrow.

"That sorry bastard started it," Crater told those already gathered for the meeting. "I had turned my back to leave when he came at me with a butcher knife. He tore open my right side. Daddy was out in the truck with Princess and a load of cedar. I said, 'Don't ask me why right now, just give me your knife.' "

"Did you kill the sorry bastard?" Stout asked.

"I don't know," Crater said, as though he hadn't considered the question until now. "I 'spect I made him a Christian. Daddy told me, 'You're a goddamn fool springing a knife on a man when you can't even see straight. You're liable to cut yourself as him.' I think I got myself in the thigh."

Crater and his family are cedar choppers, a profession they have followed for a hundred years or longer. *Cedar chopper* has become a generic term, like *redneck*, almost without precise meaning. But there are still real people out among the evergreen hills, spring-fed creeks, and wild backroads west of Austin who earn their keep by clearing stands of scrub cedar for land developers. Their wages are the wood they cut in a day. They drive broken-down pickup trucks, deal in cash, preach self-reliance, and maintain a fundamental faith in the use of physical force.

Thus, an increase in the price of a six-pack is of genuine concern. One could well imagine Crater's old daddy embellishing the story for the domino players, who would nod approval and observe that Otis was a good boy, if inclined to be a little hotheaded on occasion. "Heh, heh," his daddy would say, "I taught him better. First slash, he missed by eight inches and cut his ownself in the leg."

Stout, a telephone company lineman, had summoned the fanciers to call to their attention an ad in *Pit Dog Report*, an earthy, nearly illiterate "Mag. of reading and not to many picturs" published in Mesquite and circulated nationally.

The ad read:
OPEN TO MATCH
any time . . . any where
BULLY, male, 54 lb.
A DEAD GAME DOG!

Parties interested could contact Mr. Maynard at a post office box in Phoenix, Arizona. It wasn't necessary to mention that challengers lacking the proper securities need not respond. They had all heard of Mr. Maynard and his legendary beast, Bully. Mr. Maynard was the Max Hirsch of pit bulldog breeding, and Bully was Man O' War. Bully had every quality a fighting dog can have — gameness, biting power, talent, stamina, bloodline. As the saying goes, a dead game dog.

"We're gonna get it *on!*" Stout declared, cackling and slamming the magazine on the table.

"He's crazy as a mudsucking hen," Crater said, addressing the table. J.K., a professional breeder who works with his daddy, ran the tip of a frog sticker under his walnut-colored fingernails and said nothing. Annabelle, a girl with an Oklahoma Dust Bowl face who lives with J.K., was practically sitting in J.K.'s lap, which was as far away as she could get from Stout.

"I got fifteen hundred bucks," Stout said. "That leaves fifteen hundred for the rest of you."

Crater looked down at Princess, who was chewing on his foot. "What are we gonna use for a dog?" he inquired. "I'm afraid Princess here is a shade might young. Boudreaux's dead . . . Tombstone's dead . . . and that dark brindle of J.K.'s wouldn't make a good lunch for a beast like Bully."

"Tell him," Stout said. Then J.K. related what fate had brought their way.

It seemed that J.K.'s daddy knew a driver who knew a dispatcher who had a brother in El Paso who had a dog named Leroy. Leroy was so god-awful bad nobody in El Paso would speak his name, but for a price his owner was willing to loan him out. J.K. and his daddy had taken a pretty game dog named Romeo out to El Paso where Leroy had had him for high tea.

But that wasn't all. J.K.'s daddy noticed that one of Leroy's toes had been cut off—cut clean, not like in a fight, but like a man had taken a chisel and cleaved the toe with a blow from a mallet.

Crater looked around the Cherokee and whistled. Stout yelled for some beer. They had all heard the story, how you never saw a genuine *Maynard* dog with a full set of toes. This was the result of a legendary training technique peculiar to the Maynard kennel. On a pup's first birthday, Mr. Maynard drops him in the pit with an older, experienced dog. As soon as the animals hit in the center of the pit and get a good hold, Mr. Maynard cleaves off one of the pup's toes. If the pup lets go his hold, if he loses heart and whines and slobbers, Maynard cleaves open his head and goes about his business. But if the pup holds on, if he keeps on fighting, Maynard has found a new beast to ward off the wolves of his trade. Anytime you see a three-toed dog, move over.

"You trying to tell us Leroy is one of old man Maynard's stock?" Crater asked.

"I'm trying to tell you Leroy is the son of Bully!" Stout cackled, banging his giant fist on the table. "Only the sainted Doctor Maynard don't know it. He thinks Leroy is dead somewhere out in California."

"He won't for long," Crater said. "Don't you think old man Maynard won't recognize his own work?"

"Me and daddy cut off a toe on his other foot," J.K. admitted. "Then I dyed him brindle."

"Hell," Stout said. "You seen a thousand pit bulls. After a few fights, who knows the difference?"

Crater had to laugh. Leroy, son of Bully. Even his own daddy wouldn't know him.

"That's still a lot of money," he said, tumbling Princess with his other boot. "How do we know he can take him?"

"That's just a chance we have to take," Annabelle

said, flinching as Stout grabbed her knee. Stout was leaning forward, grinning like a berserk grizzly bear. His shirttail was out, and you could see the bulge of a .38 Super pushed down into his jeans.

Pit bulldogs. Killers, yes. For two thousand years or longer, pit bulldogs have been bred for a single purpose — to fight. To fight to the death, if necessary. To attack anything with four legs. They do not defend, understand. They are worthless as watchdogs unless the intruder happens to be another dog, or a lion or an elephant. No, they attack. That's their only number. They were bred that way — short neck, tremendously powerful body and legs, an undershot jaw capable of applying 740 pounds of pressure per square inch (compared to a German shepherd's 45 or 50), a nose set back so they can hang on and breathe at the same time. The symbol of Winston Churchill and the English-speaking race.

The American Kennel Club refuses to register the breed. In its well-stocked library in New York, which includes such titles as *The Dog in Action*, *Spine of the Dog*, and *Canine Madness*, there are few references to the pit bulldog, or *American* pit bull terrier as they call it, careful to distinguish this nondog from such registered breeds as the ordinary bull terrier or the Staffordshire bull terrier.

Pure pit bulldogs are descendants of the old English mastiff, which Caesar greatly admired and brought back to Rome after his invasion of England in 55 B.C. Years before the Roman invasion, peasants kept mastiffs, or *tiedogs* as they were called — after the Anglo-Saxon practice of keeping mastiffs tied by day and letting them run loose at night. It was a practical method of regulating populations of wolves and other predators. Nobility, clergy, and other public-spirited citizens enjoyed dog fights and bequeathed legacies so that the common folk might be entertained on holidays.

Common folk are still entertained by the sport, especially throughout the South, the Southwest, and Southern and Central California, but also in Rhode Island, Massachusetts, Ohio, Illinois, Wisconsin, and most likely everywhere else. *Fanciers*, as they call themselves after the old English tradition, gather on Sunday mornings, in the thickets or bayous, along river bottoms or arroyos, in grape arbors, in junk yards, under railroad trestles. They bring their dogs and their wages and plenty of wine and beer and knives and guns, and they have one hell of a time.

Until recently, the fanciers bothered no one except each other, which was by free choice. Then, in the post-Watergate doldrums, newspapers in Dallas, Fort Worth, San Diego, and Chicago joined forces with the *New York Times* in exposing and deploring the sport, which they customarily refer to as a "practice." Boxing and auto racing are sport.

"This metropolitan area has more active dog fighting than any other region nationally," an investigative reporter wrote in the Dallas *Morning News*. Not only that, the story continued, but prostitutes and gamblers are rumored to congregate around the pits.

Almost every state has a law against dog fighting, but the sport is so clandestine that enforcement is nearly impossible. A vice squad detective for the Los Angeles sheriff's department told the *New York Times* that his department knew when and where the fights were held, but they couldn't get on the property to obtain evidence. Dog fighting is a Class A misdemeanor in Texas and can cost you two thousand dollars and a year in jail; the catch is you can't prosecute without a witness. There's not a pit bulldog breeder alive willing to testify against a fellow fancier.

But now that pit bulldog fighting has become an *issue*, all that may change. The Dallas *Morning News* (which supports the death penalty and Manifest Destiny and longs to invade Indochina) published an editorial titled "Despicable 'Game,' " the final paragraph of which I quote: "Every effort should be made to stop these fights. Quite simply, they are inhumane and appalling to any thinking citizen. Such senseless mayhem should not be tolerated in our midst."

Noble sentiments, but if history has taught us anything, it's that one man's mayhem, senseless or otherwise, is certain to be another's calling. Fanciers — like other individualists or subcultures — consider themselves to be a special breed, a class apart from what, to their point of view, are the drones of mainstream society. Fanciers care for their animals fanatically, certainly as conscientiously as most football coaches or generals treat their charges. Preservation of the bloodline is every fancier's solemn duty and privilege. When an insurance man advertised "White Cavalier (Pit) Bull Terriers" in the Austin *American-Statesman*, Crater and Stout called on the gentleman, pointing out that he was attempting to pass off lemons as oranges and promising to break his spinal column if the ad ever reappeared, which it did not. The American Kennel Club should take note, if not of the method, at least of the diligence.

Otis Crater's jaded old daddy had reached an age where he'd lost interest in most dog fights, but he couldn't resist this one; there he was in Stout's house trailer, spitting Garrett's snuff juice into a paper cup and recalling the morning in Dripping Springs when the legendary Black Jack Jr. went nearly two hours before turning Marvin Tilford's Big Red.

The match ended when Marvin Tilford's dog

turned, or gave up. Big Red knew when he'd had enough, but Marvin was so humiliated (and broke) that he didn't show up for a year. Big Red was later drowned by a boar coon who got him by the back of the neck in the South San Gabriel River.

"He should of never gone in water," Crater's old daddy pontificated as he rocked slowly and watched Princess chew on his boot. "Men and dogs belong on ground. Birds belong in air. Fish belong in water. When a creation starts believing they invented how things are, they forgot how things are."

"Hey, daddy," Crater interrupted, "tell 'em about the deputy sheriff."

"That's another story," the old man snorted, dabbing his gums with a frayed matchstick. "We was going pretty good when the deputy called and asked me how things was going. 'Pretty good,' I said. 'The dogs been fighting twenty minutes and the people seventeen.' "

Watching Princess tumble around the floor of Stout's trailer, you wouldn't take her for a killer. She's no larger than a football, this furry little alligator with sad eyes and a wrinkled face, chewing mindlessly, somehow reminiscent of J. Edgar Hoover. According to procedure, Crater had already clipped her ears, which now looked like two raw navels. They were adequate for hearing but impossible to bite down on.

Princess was fun to play with—the trouble was she didn't like to stop. She was playing with a big black poodle one afternoon when someone noticed that the poodle was no longer playing, or moving: the illusion of movement was caused by the steady jerking motion of Princess' head. Shortly following life's final measure of response, Princess dropped the black curly mess on the lawn and trotted over to examine a rosebush.

Before he got Princess, Crater traveled with a big brindle pit bulldog named Boudreaux. Crater was managing an Austin tavern when Boudreaux tore into a German shepherd three times his size. In the ten seconds or so it took Crater to separate them with his hickory wedge, Boudreaux ripped out the shepherd's chest.

You could already hear the yelps and groans of men and animals down at the creek bottom when Stout arrived, carrying a package wrapped in brown paper.

"I guess you heard Claxon got stabbed," Stout said.

"I heard he got some new marks," Crater said. "What happened?"

"In the bathroom at the Cherokee. Claxon called this dude a Meskin. The dude was a Indian. Hell, I could tell right away he wasn't no Meskin."

"How's he doing?"

"He's about half dead and half proud," Stout said, and his laugh sounded over-oiled, hollow, and obligatory. He tore away the brown paper and held up a framed, hand-lettered scroll. There were tears in his eyes. The scroll was a poem, written by his mama, Toots; her first poem since Stout's daddy was shot to death by three blacks who hijacked his tiny grocery and market. Toots watched her husband die as she fired off several rounds at the fleeing killers. Austin police captured two of the hijackers, and the third, so it's said, was captured by Stout's vigilantes and is now fertilizing a worthy crop in a cedar chopper's garden. Who knows?

Stout turned his head so that the others wouldn't see the tears, and he looked for a place to hang the scroll. He selected a spot on the wall next to a poster of Pancho Villa enjoying a smoke under a mesquite tree.

Toots' poem went like this:

The clock of life is
*   wound but once*
And no man has the power
*   to tell just when the hands will stop.*
At late or early hour.
Now is the only time we own,
*   live, love, toil with a mill;*
Place no faith
*   in tomorrow for*
The clock may then
*   be still.*

There was silence throughout the trailer as Otis Crater read the words of Toots' poem aloud, but Stout excused himself and slipped outside. He kept his back to the trailer and his head down, following the fossilized debris of an ancient riverbed. He stopped in front of an oak almost as wide as himself and took something from a homemade cabinet nailed to the tree trunk. It was a package of sunflower seeds. His short, knotted arms stretched for a low-hanging branch, and he filled a bird feeder with sunflower seeds.

Judging from the license plates of the campers and trucks scattered throughout the woods, the fanciers had come from as far away as California, Mexico, Florida, and even Canada. It was a young crowd, mostly in their twenties and thirties, a mixed bag of longhairs, cedar choppers, and high-risk investors, with a few blacks and Chicanos and some transients from a Houston motorcycle gang thrown in.

There were some women and enough children to make it look like a club picnic. A skinny kid named Tarlton, who stole ten-speed bikes for a living, passed out beer in paper cups. Tarlton wore a homemade T-shirt with a picture of Snoopy dragging a dead cat by the tail. There was no mistaking Mr. Maynard. He was the tall, lean, silver-haired man in a blue jump-suit and wraparound shades standing by his Winnebago talking to J.K.'s daddy. You'd figure him for a bomber pilot in World War II, but he was just another dog soldier a long way from home. The cold scars in Maynard's eyes reached back to quarrels too horrible to translate: it had been a long time since he found it necessary to look tough or talk big.

There were a dozen bulldogs chained to heavy iron stakes around the perimeter of the clearing, but there was also no mistaking which one was Bully. While the other beasts were whimpering and sniffing blood and straining at their chains for some action, Bully relaxed on his haunches, observing the scene with sad, patient eyes.

Mr. Maynard and J.K.'s daddy talked and shared a drink, not at all interested in the fight in progress or the other fanciers clumped around the hay bales that formed the pit walls. A spotted cur owned by two black kids was trying to survive the jaws of one of Marvin Tilford's pups. The match was hopelessly one-sided, which meant there was hardly any betting, and the crowd was restless.

"Why don't you do the fair thing and give that leopard of yours a rest," Marvin told the black kids. They conferred in whispers, then picked up their pet and paid off. The bet was fifty dollars.

That's how most dog fights end, with a humiliated owner "doing the fair thing," picking up and paying off. Dogs are frequently wounded and occasionally killed, but only in serious challenges where the stakes are high and the owners' reputations well traveled. Even then an owner will usually do the fair thing when his beast is clearly outclassed, greatly preferring a healthy animal to an over-exercised ego.

"Dogs that are the best performers aren't necessarily the best dogs," Mr. Maynard told me as we drank scotch in his Winnebago. He knew that I was a writer. He even helped me with my notes, spelling out names, and carefully considering dates. He was only anxious that the sport not get a bad name.

"People talk about pure Maynards as they do about Picassos," I observed.

"It's an art," he said.

"How do you do it? What's your secret?"

"No secret," he smiled. "I just breed best to best. Now, knowing what *is* best, that's a gift. I can't tell you about that any more than Sugar Ray could tell you how he boxed. The best performers aren't necessarily the best dogs, that's just one quality. You look for everything from performance to pedigree to conformation to the way a dog holds his head when he pees. 'Course, gameness is everything in a fighting dog, and you're not gonna know that until you see him scratch for the first time. I've heard it said that if fanciers had millions of dollars like horse people we could come up with the perfect fighting dog, but I haven't heard anyone claim they've come up with the perfect racehorse yet."

I asked him about the familiar story, how he tested a pup by cleaving off one of its toes, then cleaved its head if the dog wasn't game enough to suit Maynard standards.

"Naw," he said, pouring two more drinks. "That's an old story. I did it once or twice when I was getting started. I'm a businessman. A man growing corn doesn't burn his fields because a few ears aren't sweet. I raise dogs, I don't kill them. *Best to best*, that's the secret of a Maynard dog."

"Some people think this is a cruel sport," I said, understating the position as much as I dared.

"I guess it's cruel as anything else in life," he said, after considering the question from all sides. "These dogs only have one purpose in life, that's to fight."

Fanciers are not long on philosophy. They accept what they do with the same lack of introspection that they accept war and General Motors. Their sport is part of their life.

The October sun came through the Winnebago window, overexposing the pastiche of fanciers around the hay bales. From the swell of the crowd it sounded like a hell of a fight. Then I realized it was Crater and Stout doing the cat number.

The cat number is traditional at dog fights, much like clowns at a circus or halftime bands at football games. What they do is throw live cats—which they buy for fifty cents a head from the city pound—to assorted dogs who aren't fighting that day but who need exercise, self-confidence, and a show of affection. J.K. and his daddy use cats for training. Some handlers claim you shouldn't run a dog, but J.K.'s daddy runs all of his beasts, using a homemade device consisting of an axle and a crosspole on which he can leash one dog and one cat. The leashes are measured so the dog can chase the cat till doomsday and never catch up, which he usually will attempt to do. If a dog has worked well, J.K.'s daddy will toss him a reward—the cat of his recent ordeal. A cat who has had a run-in with a pit bulldog is something out of a wax museum—a statue frozen in terror, eyes wide with disbelief, front claws arched, fangs bared in a silly, final grin.

Several wax museum cats lay in the grass around the hay bales. Marvin Tilford's little boy walked by, swinging a dead cat by the tail.

It was a few minutes after 2 P.M. when Stout and Annabelle brought Leroy down from the trailer. They had changed his name to Tag. If he made it through the day, he would be Leroy again. He would return triumphantly to El Paso, but for now he was Tag, a

71

dog with no past and an unenviable future. Tag looked more like a walking anthill of petrified Jell-O than any animal that might come to mind. He had so much scar tissue that you couldn't tell what part was the original dog. J.K.'s dye job was blatantly atrocious; it looked as if Leroy had been tie-dyed.

"He wants Cajun rules," J.K.'s daddy told Marvin Tilford, who by previous agreement would referee the match.

"Yessir," Marvin said.

"He says, if you see a turn, call it. But let them maneuver. Don't let the handlers push their dogs out of corner. Check the handlers . . . make 'em roll up both sleeves, and make sure they taste their dogs' drinks. No sponges . . . no towels . . . all the handler can take in the pit is his dog's drink and a fan to fan him."

"Yessir," Marvin said.

When the handlers had carried the dogs to the pit, Mr. Maynard walked over and examined Leroy's teeth.

"Nice animal," he said. "Good head." If he thought the markings curious, or observed the stubs of two toes, one so recently cleaved that the skin hadn't grown back, he didn't let on.

"Let's roll," he told Marvin.

Both dogs scratched hard out of their corners, and Bully took the lead, going low, forcing Leroy to bite around the nubs of gristle that had once been ears. Christ, he *was* strong. But there was no doubt Leroy was his daddy's boy; he just kept coming. "It's gonna be a long afternoon," Crater said. Unless you have more money than you can possibly afford riding on the outcome, a dog fight is about as interesting as a college wrestling match: the beasts hit, lock on, and hold fast, in endless repetition. The fight quickly settles into a test of strength, endurance, and gameness. Even the blood takes on a surrealistic quality after a while, like ghost shadows in a hall of mirrors.

After forty-five minutes—when Marvin Tilford called the first pick-up and broke the dogs apart by forcing his hickory wedge between their jaws and twisting counterclockwise—it was still impossible to say who was top dog.

While the handlers were cooling off their animals, Crater and I walked down by the old Indian mound. You could feel the excitement bouncing off the limestone walls of the creekbed: it wasn't watching the dogs that did it, it was *being there*, experiencing an almost-vanished culture of blood rites and a close familiarity with death.

Then we caught sight of Annabelle, coming out from behind some bushes, buttoning her pants.

"Damn," she said, "I'm so nervous I almost wet my britches."

"You think Mr. Maynard knows something?"

She shook her head. "I'd hate to find out. Old men like him can be real bad customers."

"He didn't say nothing when he looked at Leroy's teeth."

"That's not what worries me," Annabelle said. "Wait till his beast gets off on the acid."

"What's that suppose to mean?" Crater asked, squinting into the sun.

"Ask Stout."

"I'm asking you."

"We rubbed Leroy's chest with acid," Annabelle said. "Very shortly now Leroy's daddy's gonna take his first trip on LSD."

Crater watched the light hit and fracture off the creek walls.

"Oh, me," he sighed. "I get this awful feeling the center's not holding." Crater walked to his truck and got his gun. One of the fascinating things about

Crater and his friends is the way they use the language. They are not educated, but they are amazingly literate.

At the second pick-up an hour later, both dogs were bloody but strong. Bully's handler whispered something to Mr. Maynard, but Mr. Maynard shook his head and the handler told Marvin: "Let 'em roll." Leroy was bleeding from the chest and from the stifle of his left rear leg.

The battle was into its third hour when J.K. told his daddy: "His leg is starting to pump blood."

"I can't help that," his daddy said.

"He's making you like it, Leroy. You better eat!" Annabelle hollered out suddenly. At the name *Leroy*, both Stout and Crater felt for their guns, but Mr. Maynard didn't blink.

"Work him, *Tag!*" J.K. yelled.

Bully was clearly the top dog now. Leroy was losing blood and weakening noticeably, but Bully was zonked far past the fatigue and mere dogdom. The ploy of the LSD was backfiring. The hair and blood in Bully's mouth told him that he was a sixty-ton gorilla at the Captain's Table reciting compound fractions in a tongue not previously heard on this planet. "Stand back," he said in his strange tongue. "This one will be for keeps." He took Leroy down by the front leg and chewed on the stifle, shaking hard, lifting Leroy off the ground and working him against the pit wall.

"Goddamn it, Marvin," Stout hollered, "keep 'em off the wall!" Marvin moved in with his hickory wedge, but before he could break the beasts Bully shook Leroy so hard he snapped off his hold and flew halfway across the pit. Then, by God, Leroy was on him, tearing at the soft part of his throat. This time Marvin called a pick-up, which was the proper thing to do. Marvin had to help the handler restrain Bully and drag him back to his corner.

"Jesus, he's pumping," said Tarlton, the bicycle thief. "Don't let 'em roll again."

Marvin looked at Mr. Maynard, then at J.K. "You want to roll again?" he asked. J.K. answered by releasing his beast, who lunged straight at Bully and got him by the eye.

"No more pick-ups," Mr. Maynard said quietly. "Let 'em roll."

"Let 'em roll," J.K. agreed.

So that would be it—one of the dogs would have to die or quit, and it wasn't difficult to project which alternative would prevail.

Three hours and fifty-eight minutes into the match, it happened. Bully was going for the chest, boring in like a jackhammer, when suddenly Leroy got a leg and flipped him easy as you turn a pancake. There was a wailing sound like echoes colliding, then Bully's eyes froze over. He lay still as Leroy tore out his throat. Leroy relaxed his hold, sniffed his dead opponent, then limped over and licked J.K.'s hand.

"If that don't beat all!" Otis Crater's old daddy said as they stood over the corpse of the late, great Bully. "It's like his old heart just give out on him."

J.K.'s daddy nodded. "Looks like he busted apart inside."

"If that don't beat all!" Otis Crater's old daddy said again.

Mr. Maynard walked over to his Winnebago and returned with a .44 Magnum and a sheaf of hundred-dollar bills. "Here's what I owe you," he told J.K.'s daddy.

Mr. Maynard turned the cold scars of his eyes on Stout, then on the others, taking his time.

"I don't know what you little bastards did to my dog," he said, "but you're the ones that have to live with it."

He walked over to Leroy, patted Leroy's head, then raised his .44 Magnum to Leroy's head and blew it off. No one moved or spoke a word.

"If you boys ever get to Phoenix," he said, looking each of them over one more time, "look me up."

August 1975

Postscript

This is my all-time favorite story, maybe because it was turned down by nearly every magazine in the country. *Rolling Stone, Esquire, Playboy, Sports Illustrated*, they all had a shot at the story and rejected it. It wasn't just a judgment call; they truly *hated* the story. "Good Lord, dogs killing *dogs*," *Sports Illustrated* editor Ray Cave (now editor of *Time*) told me. "My wife would never speak to me again if I printed that." The story touched some primordial sense of revulsion in all these editors; *people* were killing *people* daily, by the hundreds of thousands, but there was something about dogs that was too much for their sensibilities. I had to beg *Texas Monthly* editor Bill Broyles to accept the story, though he loved it once he saw it in print. Everyone did. Not long after publication I received a call from *Esquire* editor Geoffrey Norman, who had rejected the piece when he was still articles editor at *Playboy*, but apparently didn't remember. Norman wanted to know why I never sent any really good pieces like this to him.

People still ask me if this really happened. It did, though I changed the names and combined several dog fights into a single big event. It's interesting to note the blow-by-blow account of the fight, a holdover from my sportswriting days, no doubt: a fascination with the ritual itself. But more than that, it shares a fascination with the almost-vanished "sub-culture of blood rites and a close familiarity with death." I remember Broyles asking if Crater really said "the center's not holding"; that seemed a little eso-teric for a mere cedar chopper, but then that's what I was trying to show. These guys read books, too.

Incidentally, Patrick Henry Polk (see "The Endless Odyssey of Patrick Henry Polk") and his clan were fringe members of this subculture.

As Margaret Mead so eloquently phrased it: "I don't judge 'em, I just write down what happened."

4

Candy
Taking the Wrapper off a Texas Legend

On the road home to Brownwood in her green '74 Cadillac with the custom upholstery and the CB radio, clutching a pawn ticket for her three-thousand-dollar mink, Candy Barr thought about biscuits. Biscuits made her think of fried chicken, which in turn suggested potato salad and corn. For as long as she could remember, in times of crisis and stress, Candy Barr always thought of groceries. It was a miracle she didn't look like a platinum pumpkin, but she didn't: even at forty-one, she still looked like a movie star.

For once, the crisis was not her own. It was something she had read a few days earlier about how the omnipotent, totalitarian *they* were about to jackboot the remnants of the once happy and prosperous life of a seventy-six-year-old Dallas electrician named O. E. Cole. Candy had never heard of O. E. Cole until she spotted his pitiful tale in the Brownwood newspaper.

She didn't know if Cole was black or white, mean or generous, judgmental or forgiving. She only knew he was in trouble. For nearly fifty years Cole had been an upright, hardworking citizen of a city Candy Barr had every reason to hate; then his wife Nettie suffered a stroke and lingered in a coma for eighteen months while their savings were sucked away. According to the newspaper account, Cole spent $500 for Nettie's headstone, which left him a balance of $157. Before he could use that money to cover mortgage payments on his home and the electrician's shop at the back, a gunman shot and robbed him. Now, when he was too old to apply for additional credit, *they* were prepared to foreclose.

"This is a goddamn crime!" Candy raged, throwing her suitcase on the bed and barking a string of orders to her houseguests: Scott, her twenty-two-year-old boyfriend of the moment, and Susan Slusher, her seventeen-year-old niece who had recently come to stay with "Aunt Nita" from a broken home in Philadelphia.

Scott and Susan had been around just long enough to know when Candy blew — as she often did without warning — to look not for explanations but for something sturdy to hang on to. Try to imagine a hurricane in a Dixie cup. The laughing tropical green eyes boiled, and the innocence that had made that perfect teardrop face a landmark in the sexual liberation of an entire generation of Milquetoasts became the wrath of Zeus. They say she once sat waiting in a rocking chair talking to sweet Jesus and when her ex-husband kicked down the door she threw down on him with a pistol that was resting conveniently in her lap. She shot him in the stomach, but she was aiming for the groin. When she caught mobster Mickey Cohen talking to another woman, she slugged him in the teeth. She carved her mark on a dyke in the prison workshop; this was not a lovers' quarrel, as an assistant warden indicated on her record, but a disagreement stemming from Candy's hard-line belief that a worker should take pride in her job.

Candy had a cosmic way of connecting things, which to the more prosaic mind might appear coincidental. So it was that the ill-fated placement of a Citizens National Bank of Brownwood ad next to the article outlining the plight of O. E. Cole ignited her fuse. The bank ad suggested that had it not been for a Revolutionary War banker named Robert Morris, we might all be sipping tea with crumpets and begging God to save our Queen. What the average eye might take as harmless Bicentennial puffery hit Candy's heart dead center.

"I watched the bastards do the same thing to my daddy," Candy fumed, removing her mink from the cedar chest and raking bottles and jars of cosmetics into her overnight bag. "I sold my hunting rifle three times to help my daddy. It's a crime what they can do to people, a goddamn crime. Don't call *me* a criminal if *you're* gonna be one."

With the skillful employment of her CB radio, "the Godmother" and her two young companions made the 160 miles to Dallas in less than two hours. Candy hocked her mink for $250, then called on dancer Chastity Fox and other friends to help raise another $150. Then Candy painted her face with soft missionary shades of tan and gold and called on O. E. Cole, introducing herself as Juanita Dale Phillips of Brownwood and presenting the goggle-eyed electrician with $400 and a copy of her book of prison poems, *A Gentle Mind . . . Confused.* Cole couldn't have been more confused if he had found Fidel Castro in his refrigerator. When I spoke with Cole two weeks later, there were still some blank spaces behind his eyes, but the crisis had passed.

"I didn't know who she was till I saw her name on that little book," he told me. "Oh, yes, I knew the name Candy Barr. You couldn't live in Dallas long as I had and not know that name. But it wasn't for me to judge her. What is past is past. It's what a person is now I go on, and she was awful nice. We sat around and talked for hours. In fact, we talked *all* night long."

Cole hadn't stayed up all night in years. He had never seen Candy Barr's famous blue movie, or watched her strip at Abe Weinstein's Colony Club, or read about her romance with Mickey Cohen, or paid much attention when his fellow citizens gave her fifteen years for possessing less than one ounce of marijuana. In fact, he couldn't remember *what* he had heard about her, only that it seemed unsavory. "That was a long time ago," Cole seemed to recall. Roughly twenty years.

To place her properly in time you had to go back to Sugar Ray Robinson, James Dean, Marilyn Monroe, Bridey Murphy, Joe McCarthy, John Foster Dulles, the Kefauver Committee, RAF Group Captain Peter Townsend, Mort Sahl, and Sputnik. Texas was still the largest state in the union, and Elvis Presley's "Don't Be Cruel" was the number one song. *Playboy* magazine was an under-the-counter novelty, less than three years old and tame as a pet goose. Brigitte Bardot was being banned in Philadelphia, Fort Worth, and Abilene. The Dodgers were in Brooklyn, Russian tanks in the streets of Budapest, Fidel Castro in the jungles of Cuba. It was a time when the National Organization for Decent Literature was putting pressure on bookstores and enlisting local police to threaten booksellers who were too slow to "cooperate" in removing from their shelves such filthspreaders as Hemingway, Faulkner, Dos Passos, Zola, and Orwell. Thirteen million Americans spent

Tuesday nights watching a TV charade called *The $64,000 Question.* Someone with a dark sense of humor labeled it "the Age of Innocence."

Candy Barr was a household word then, an authentic Texas folk hero. To the absolute surprise of hardly anyone, Candy Barr would still be a name twenty years later. What precipitated a revival in her long-dormant career was a photo layout and interview in the June 1976 issue of *Oui:* how many forty-one-year-old grandmothers ever posed for split beaver shots? Now Candy was talking of college fan clubs, of posters and T-shirts. "If I don't get into it, somebody else will," she said. "I'm tired being ripped off. I'm not even aware of how to be a star, I just am one." It was time to move ahead with her autobiography. "All the lies and tackiness that have been written about me . . . now I'm going to set the record straight." She calls her as yet unwritten memoirs *Bits and Pieces* and speaks of "leaving my legacy for my daughter and granddaughter."

In the three months since the *Oui* photographs, Candy has received maybe five hundred fan letters from all across the United Sates, from Mexico, from Canada, from Puerto Rico, from the National Organization for the Reform of Marijuana Laws, from members of the U.S. Navy stationed on Diego Garcia somewhere in the Indian Ocean. There was the usual sprinkling of nut mail—a man in Syracuse sent a tracing of his private parts—but the vast majority of the letters were from true fans, properly reverent and begging only to speak, just once, of loneliness and isolation, of dark fantasies and repressed urges and wives that would never understand, of their recurring feeling that life had them by the nose and would never let go. An Indian from a place called Bull Mountain sent her a flower. A Los Angeles Dodger invited her to a doubleheader. A retired fire fighter from California wrote that he had pasted her picture to his locker years ago and there it remained "until my last days of fighting fires." A man from New Jersey accompanied a gentle note of adoration with three pair of sheer panty hose. The president of the Chamber of Commerce of a small Southern town wrote: "It seems rather bizarre to me that a thirty-six-year-old man with a responsible job, family, and being reasonably well adjusted would sit down and write a fan letter to someone he has not met, and never will meet. Yet, that is exactly what I find myself doing."

Maybe half the letters came from men, and a few women, in prison. One convict wrote that Candy's picture had once sustained his father during a long prison stretch and "now I can understand why." It was these letters from men inside the walls that moved her most. She intended to answer every one of them, although she was uncertain how she could afford to mail pictures to all those who requested them. She would have to find a way. "Nobody is ever going to make me feel dirty and cheap and ugly again," she swore.

To Scott and to Susan, neither of whom was born when Juanita Dale Slusher was transforming herself into Candy Barr, this whole episode must have seemed like a pilgrimage to a mystical shrine. Scott had forsaken his first passion, mountain climbing, to sit at the feet of Candy Barr and follow orders explicitly. Susan walked around with a glazed expression, saying "far out" and rubbing her fingers over the fading newspaper clippings as though to verify they were real. "I never really knew who Aunt Nita was, just that she was someone famous," Susan Slusher said. "When I was about nine or ten she visited us in Philadelphia. She was so beautiful in her mink coat and high heels and all. She wasn't like an aunt, she was someone I could talk to." Susan had been in

Brownwood less than one week when the O. E. Cole mission cleaved the pattern. Now she was wondering if maybe she ought to move to Dallas and look for a job. When you got past the talking, there wasn't a helluva lot to do in Brownwood.

Scott did the driving back to Brownwood, mountain climbing never far from his mind. Candy thought of biscuits and talked on the CB. The only thing those good buddies out there knew about "the Godmother" was that she had a husky, rapid-fire Loretta Lynn voice and a way with the double entendre. Could anyone look as good as that voice sounded? Candy Barr could. She still had it. What to do with it, that was the problem. That had always been the problem.

Juanita Dale Slusher encountered the joy of sex at age five with the aid and comfort of an eighteen-year-old neighbor named Ernest. She remembers that he was gentle, and not at all unpleasant. It wasn't until she encountered the Dallas police force some years later that Juanita Dale associated sex with guilt.

When she was nine her mother died and her father remarried: Doc Slusher, brick mason and handyman, a whiskey-drinking harmonica player and all-around rowdy, already had five kids, and right away there were four more, then two more after that. With all those Slushers around, you'd think the work would get done, but it never seemed to.

"I know in the fourth grade I was a real good student," Candy recalled. "I got to hand out the spelling and Spanish exams." After school it was three or four hours washing bedsheets over a rub board next to a boiling iron kettle under a chinaberry tree. "When girls ask me about tit development, I say, 'Honey, get yourself a rub board.' "

At age thirteen and painfully confused, Juanita Dale took her baby-sitting money and grabbed a bus out of Edna, an independent decision that would become socially acceptable, even laudable, to future generations, but an act worse than rebellion in those days: it was the act of a *bad girl*. For a while she lived with an older sister in Oklahoma City, then a year or so later moved to live with another sister in Dallas. The Dallas sister soon hooked up with a man, and Juanita Dale was on her own.

Many talent scouts have taken credit for discovering Candy Barr: Barney Weinstein, who paid her fifteen dollars to act as a shill for his Amateur Night at the Theater Lounge; his brother Abe who hired her away to become his headliner at the Colony; Joe DeCarlo, a Los Angeles entrepreneur and pal of Hefner and Sinatra, who got her away from Abe; and Gary Crosby, who once advised Mickey Cohen: "Goddamn, one thing about that broad, she can make ya feel like a *real* man."

To be technically correct, it was the old Liquor Control Board (LCB) that first discovered the girl who would become Candy Barr. They discovered her posing as an eighteen-year-old cocktail waitress—the minimum legal age. She wouldn't be eighteen for another four years, but girls from tough backgrounds develop early or they don't develop at all. She kept changing jobs, and the LCB kept discovering her. Once they sent her home to Edna, but she caught the next bus back to Dallas.

The only place a teenage runaway could count on steady work in Dallas was at the Trolley Courts, or the other hot-pillow motels located out Harry Hines Boulevard, or along the old Fort Worth Highway. Pimps, thugs, and night clerks traded around young girls as they pleased. Candy's arrangement with the motel consisted of making beds by day and turning tricks by night. There were buses out of town, but they went nowhere. There were other jobs, but she had already put in her time on the rub board. An old crook named Shorty Anderson decided she had too much class for the Trolley Courts, so he claimed her as his own and took her to live in his trailer under a bridge where he ran a school for young burglars. Candy's first husband, Billy Debbs, was a graduate of Shorty's academy. Billy was a good lover but a poor student. He went to the pen, got out, then got shot to death.

Somewhere in there — she can't fix the exact time — a pimp spotted her jitterbugging in a joint called the Round-Up Club and launched Candy's movie career. She must have been about fifteen when *Smart Aleck* was filmed. The thousands (perhaps millions) who have seen this American classic will recall that she was a brunette then. *Smart Aleck* was America's first blue movie, the *Deep Throat* of its era, only infinitely more erotic and less pretentious. It was just straight old motel room sex; the audience supplied its own sounds. I remember seeing *Smart Aleck* at the Wolters Air Force Base NCO Club in Mineral Wells about 1955. There had never been anything like it, and for my generation there never will again. All of us had seen stag movies before, threadbare hookers sweathogging with some jerk hung like Groggin's mule, but this was different: this was a beautiful fifteen-year-old sweetheart type and you could just tell she was enjoying it.

Candy claims that she had never seen her movie until she went to Chicago to pose for *Oui*. When I asked how it felt watching herself perform, she said it felt like nothing. "It didn't turn me on," she told me. She could barely remember having performed.

"They may have drugged me, or maybe I blocked it out of my mind," she said. "I suppose they took me to a motel, I don't know where. In Dallas, I guess. I had been forced into screwing so many times I wasn't really aware that this was different. I don't think they even paid me. I've read that that movie made me Candy Barr. That movie made it because I *became* Candy Barr."

One of the fringe benefits of being in films was that Candy got invited to all the best stag parties. Several prominent and wealthy Dallas business and professional men, on my oath that their names would not be revealed, recalled a Junior Chamber of Commerce stag where Candy was the star attraction. One auto dealer told me, "She went for two hundred, three hundred, even five hundred bucks. There was a banker who paid five hundred every time he put a hand on Candy." Bill Gilliland, the manager of the Doubleday Book Store in downtown Dallas, recalled that when he was a student at SMU in the mid-fifties Candy was the sensation of the Phi Delta Theta stag held at the Alford refrigerated warehouse.

"What I remember most about Candy was her enthusiasm," Gilliland said. "Later, when she was stripping at the Colony, I saw her many times. Sometimes my wife went with me. A lot of women were turned on by Candy. Here was one woman willing to flaunt it."

"She made me a lot of money," Abe Weinstein freely admitted. "The biggest draw I ever had at the Colony was Rusty Warren. What a sweetheart. But Candy ran her a close second."

Abe, who lives alone now in a North Dallas town house, enjoying the fruits of retirement, actually "discovered" Candy Barr, as opposed to Juanita Dale Slusher. The first time he watched Candy upstage the amateurs at his brother Barney's Theater Lounge, he said to himself, "That's raw talent." The name Candy Barr was Barney's inspiration (she really did eat a lot of candy), but it took Abe's sound business philosophy and promotional acumen to bring Candy uptown where she belonged. The Colony was the Stork Club of Dallas, the Cocoanut Grove, the butterfly of the Commerce Street neon patch where Jack Ruby ran the sleazy Carousel and conventioneers intermingled with cops and hustlers and drug merchants.

"I didn't make Candy a headliner," Abe told me as we drank coffee in the living room of his town house. "She made herself a headliner. Of course those stag parties and that famous movie — it made a flat million over the years — that didn't hurt her image, but Candy was a real pro from the start, one of the best strippers to ever hit the stage. I don't want to say anything about how she was offstage — she'd probably come up here and kill me — but onstage she was number one, the best. She drove 'em crazy, women too. No, I didn't make her a headliner, but I can say this without bragging: I knew how to make the most of what she had to offer."

Abe cited several examples of his promotional genius, including daily newspaper ads ("I called her my Sugar and Spice Girl"), the life-size cardboard cutout of Candy with her cowboy hat and cap pistols outside the Colony, and a deal Abe negotiated whereby Candy got a percentage of the door for playing the Jayne Mansfield role in a local production of *Will Success Spoil Rock Hunter?* She memorized the script in three days and opened after one rehearsal.

Another example, which Abe failed to mention, was how he seized the moment when Candy shot her ex-husband, Troy Phillips. State Senator Oscar Mauzy, the attorney who represented Candy in that case, filled in the details: "They set the normal bond in the case, about five thousand, as I recall. There wasn't much chance the grand jury would indict: Troy had a bad habit of getting drunk and kicking down her door, and he wasn't hurt very bad anyway. When Abe heard the bond was only five grand, he hit the ceiling. He called his friend [Sheriff] Bill Decker and got it raised to a hundred thousand dollars. Then he paid it and called a press conference. I heard about it and got the hell over to the Colony Club. There was Candy in her costume with the toy pistols and every TV and radio newsman in town. They were just about to start when I grabbed her and got her out of there."

Abe recalled that the Colony did near-record business in the days just after the shooting. When she got popped for marijuana twenty months later (in October 1957), the place was packed every night. And when Candy was released after serving three years and four months of her fifteen-year sentence, it was standing room only. By then Candy was making $750 a week. "I don't know how much money you make," Abe told me, "but I only wish you had half the money she brought in those three weeks." Abe showed me a copy of Candy's poetry, which, I gathered, had been placed on the coffee table for my benefit. It was inscribed: "Nov. 27, 1972. To Abe, dear Abe."

Abe shook his head sadly and said, "I read an article where she said nobody ever visited her in prison and it really irritated me. My late wife, Ginny, God bless her, and I visited her twice a month, which was all that was allowed. Never once missed a visit. Not in the whole time she was down there."

He refilled my coffee cup and asked a question he had been leading up to. He asked me what Candy had to say about Abe Weinstein.

"Nothing very unkind," I said. "I don't think she's bitter. At least she says she isn't."

"Then you've seen her."

"Yes," I said. "It took me twenty years, but I finally saw her." I told Abe that I remembered the first time exactly: it was February 1, 1956, the night after I got out of the Army. Jim Frye and I were walking down

Commerce Street toward the Colony Club, toward the life-size cardboard cutout, which was so close to the real thing I could smell it. I had dwelled on it many times: a fat cook in our barracks who later got sent up for armed robbery had a smaller version pasted to his locker. In the age of innocence *that* was the face and the body and the telltale blonde hair that seemed to focus all the guilts and fantasies of the fifties. She epitomized the conflict between sex as joy and sex as danger. The body was perfect, but it was the innocence of the face that lured you on. *I know a secret*, it said. *I can enjoy sex without guilt.* But the cap pistols in her hand were a clear warning of danger. Three days earlier Candy had thrown down on poor Troy. It was front-page stuff. Now those cap pistols had a frame of reference: they were directed at me.

"How did you like the act?" Abe asked.

I told him I never saw the act. One block before Jim Frye and I reached the Colony Club two Dallas cops jumped out of their car, wrestled us to the sidewalk, clapped us in handcuffs, and took us to jail. They said we were drunk. We weren't drunk, though that was certainly our intention. Those were the days of the old How Dare You Squad in Dallas: intent was sufficient cause for arrest and confinement. Candy knew that a lot better than I did, but I by God knew it, too. All those women's clubs and all those wives of all those fine men who paid five hundred dollars to get their hands on Candy Barr were actively applying pressure to the powers that were, most particularly to the Dallas Police Department's special service bureau and its hard-line director, Captain Pat Gannaway, scourge of the drug peddler and sex merchant and guardian of community sensibility. I wanted to ask Abe Weinstein, master of media manipulation, if he had ever considered that maybe he did his job of promoting Candy Barr too well. Had he ever considered that at least ten percent of that fifteen-year prison sentence rightly belonged to Abe Weinstein?

Old memories are masters of deceit. It wasn't *that* hard growing up on a farm, and John D. Rockefeller didn't ride around Central Park on the backs of orphans. Japs weren't all that evil, Harding wasn't that dumb, and Lindy wasn't that lucky. If we cared about the truth, Alan Ladd had to stand on a soapbox to kiss Maria Montez, and Mickey Rooney couldn't walk under a billy goat's belly. I mention this because now, twenty years later, when they should feel remorse and more than a little guilt, the nabobs and psalm singers of Dallas still remember Candy Barr as an epic force of evil.

As far as I am able to determine, Candy made only one blue movie, *Smart Aleck.* Yet many of the men I spoke with put the number at eight or ten or even fifteen. The prominent auto dealer seemed to recall that her co-star in one flick was an Army mule. District Attorney Henry Wade had a recollection that she once went before a camera with a black man, which didn't help her image, especially with the police. An old-time police reporter recalled that "everyone knew she was chipping around with the stuff," meaning drugs. One of her defense attorneys in the marijuana case, Bill Braecklein, now a state senator from Dallas, didn't remember the quantity of grass she was charged with possessing, "but it looked like one hell of a lot in that courtroom."

In fact, the Alka-Seltzer bottle of grass that Candy surrendered to Captain Pat Gannaway and his armada of undercover agents weighed 375 *grains*, or 24.3 grams. Less than one ounce—a small-time misdemeanor today. We would call it a short lid. If, as Lieutenant Red Souter testified, this was an amount sufficient to roll 125 joints, I would like to invite Red to my next birthday party.

Nobody in the Dallas police department wanted to talk about a marijuana case from twenty years ago, and Pat Gannaway, who retired a few years ago to join the Texas Criminal Justice Division, wasn't available for an interview. But I know this: Pat Gannaway spent a lot of man-hours bringing one stripper to justice. The confluence of these two forces—Candy Barr, desecrater of all that is decent, and Pat Gannaway, the terrible swift sword—is surely the quintessence of a morality frozen in time. Captain Pat Gannaway was referred to in newspaper accounts of the time as "Mr. Narcotics." As a lad he had been so eager to join the Dallas police department that he lied about his age. For twelve years, until he was kicked upstairs (he was put in charge of rearranging the Property Room in the 1968 department shakeup), he ran the special services bureau as his private fiefdom. He reported only to the chief. "His passion," reporter James Ewell wrote in the Dallas *Morning News* on the occasion of Gannaway's retirement, "was police work, down on the streets with his men." He loved the Army too. He served in Army intelligence and was an expert wiretapper. When he wasn't swooping down on the vermin that afflicted his city, Gannaway and his entire force were making speeches to civic clubs, warning of the peril. Those recent one-thousand-year sentences that made Dallas juries such a novelty may have been the direct result of Pat Gannaway's tireless crusade. Gannaway told James Ewell: "It was always a good feeling to see someone on those juries you recalled being at one of those talks. We always told our audiences if you got rid of an addict or pusher, you were also getting rid of a burglar, a thief, or a robber."

In the autumn of 1957 Gannaway assigned Red

Souter (now an assistant chief) and another of his agents, Harvey Totten (now retired), to rent an apartment near Candy Barr's apartment and establish surveillance. A telephone repairman would testify later that he discovered a "jumper tie-up" connecting Candy's telephone to the telephone in the apartment occupied by Souter and Totten, but the jury either ignored this or didn't believe it. A few days after the surveillance began, Candy received a visit from a friend, a stripper named Helen Kay Smith, who laid out a story about her mother coming to visit and asked Candy to hide her stash—the Alka-Seltzer bottle of marijuana. Candy agreed and slipped the bottle inside her bra, next to her big heart. Two hours later, as Candy was talking on the telephone to a gentleman friend (and therefore obviously at home, in case anyone with a search warrant wanted to drop in), there was a knock at the door. Candy's defense attorneys claimed the search warrant was a blank that Gannaway filled in after the arrest, but the court didn't buy that either.

Candy's gentleman friend, who asked not to be identified, told me what happened next:

"Candy said hold on, someone is knocking at the door. I heard some noises and someone hung up the phone. All I could think of was she's in some kind of trouble. I got over to her place. When I walked in I saw Gannaway, Totten, Red Souter, Jack Revill, and I think one other narcotics officer. Gannaway picked up a chair and said something like, 'Well, well, that looks like a joint on the floor.' I swear to you, it was the first marijuana cigarette I ever saw. That's when Candy, God bless her, said to Gannaway, 'He's just a square john kid. If you let him go, I'll give you what you came for.' She reached in and pulled out the bottle. Gannaway decided he would take me in anyway, and that's when Jack Revill said, 'Captain, if you do that, I'm turning in my badge.' So they took her away."

Candy's four-day trial the following February was a farce, which didn't prevent it from also being a sensation. In its year-end review the Dallas *Morning News* headline read: CANDY'S TRIAL LED '58 SCENE. Judge Joe B. Brown, who would later make his mark as the buffoon judge in the Jack Ruby trial, borrowed a camera and during one of the recesses snapped pictures of "the shapely defendant." Defense attorneys Bill Braecklein and Lester May realized from the beginning that their problem was much larger than a bottle of marijuana, although, as May explained, "In those days marijuana was worse than cancer."

"It was a time when the pendulum had swung far to the right," May told me. "If the police decided you were guilty of something, they made a case and you were found guilty. It was just that simple. Candy's real crime was she wouldn't cooperate with the vice squad."

No, the real problem wasn't the marijuana, it was Candy Barr herself. It wasn't merely her reputation, though God knows that was strong enough to kill a rogue elephant. It was that combative stubbornness, that unwillingness to throw herself at the feet of the jury and beg forgiveness. Chief prosecutor James Allen offered her two years for a guilty plea, and if Les May hadn't got her out of the room she would have spit in his eye, or worse.

They decided not to put her on the stand; without her testimony, of course, it would be almost impossible to challenge state witnesses: she *was* in possession of marijuana, regardless of Helen Kay Smith's testimony. That mysterious cigarette on the floor, though, was something else entirely. The attorneys worked out a way to let Candy make a statement to the jury without actually testifying, which meant that she could not be cross-examined. No one remembers Candy's exact words, but it must have been a stirring oration. When she had finished, the jury just retired and voted her fifteen years in the Big Rodeo. It was Valentine's Day, 1958.

"She was a very naive young lady," Braecklein recalled. "While we were waiting to come to trial, she was out in Las Vegas, doing her act. Just one week before we came to trial, I got word that she was going to be a bridesmaid in Sammy Davis, Jr.'s wedding [to a white actress]. Anyone who grew up in Texas knew you couldn't do that right before a trial."

In retrospect, observers on both sides acknowledged that the strategy to pick an all-male jury backfired. In his book *The Super Americans*, John Bainbridge quotes "a native of Dallas who is possessed of a philosophical cast of mind and a family pedigree going back to Sam Houston" with a theory that, in one form or another, I heard many times: ". . . those eleven men [there was one woman], they got a chance to go home that night and say to their wives: 'Well, Maude, you can brag on me for what I did today. We put that shameless creature away for a good long spell.' "

Although they didn't anticipate anything approaching fifteen years, the defense team had braced itself for a verdict of guilty. They had already drafted a list of reversible errors that would have choked the Star Chamber. The real shock came when they lost a 2–1 decision in the State Court of Criminal Appeals. In the eleven months that separated the trial from the appeals verdict, Candy had reinforced her public image by moving in with hoodlum Mickey Cohen: one assumes justice is blind, but just how blind is an open question.

In a hotly worded fourteen-page dissent, Judge Lloyd Davidson wrote, "If that is equal justice under law, I want no part of it. If a conviction obtained under such circumstances is due process of law, then there is no due process of law."

District Attorney Henry Wade, who took no part in the most sensational trial of 1958, beamed serenely when I asked him twenty years later if it was possible Candy Barr had been railroaded into prison. "Far as I know," he said, "that wasn't the case." One of the jurors told Wade some time later that the reason Candy's fellow citizens slapped her with so much time was something she said. She called chief prosecutor James Allen a liar. "That's when her true colors came out," the juror told the district attorney.

"At that period in time," Wade told me, "it wasn't unusual to get life for one cigarette. I recall we had a letter from the governor's office, inquiring into the severity of her sentence. The governor asked us to check our records and find out what was the average sentence for a marijuana conviction. So we did. It turned out the average sentence at that time was eighteen years. So she received *less* than the average sentence."

Referring to my notes, I told the district attorney that in 1960, shortly after the final appeal had been exhausted and Candy had gone inside, a survey conducted by the Dallas *Times Herald* revealed that nine defendants recently convicted of the same crime had received much shorter sentences for substantially larger quantities of killer weed.

"I think that if you'll check that again," Henry Wade smiled benignly, "you'll find that all nine of those defendants were women."

I checked again. Damned if Henry wasn't right.

I spent three weeks trying to arrange an interview with Candy Barr, and although I was now calling from a telephone booth beside a Brownwood liquor store less than seven miles from her lake cottage, I had the recurring feeling I wasn't even close. She told me that her mind was too scattered to talk right now, the house was a mess, she hadn't been able to locate the scrapbooks she had promised to show me, she was still worried about O. E. Cole, she hadn't even had time to shower and wash her hair.

"Why don't you look over the town," she said, not very convincingly. "Call me back after a while."

I had already experienced the pleasure of touring Brownwood. It's a pleasant, folksy little town where men wear business suits and women dress up to shop at the Safeway and motorists park in the middle of an intersection to exchange gossip with pedestrians. Big church town. Trees. Home of Howard Payne College, the Douglas MacArthur Academy, and the onetime golden boy of Texas politics, Ben Barnes, as well as small industries untroubled by labor problems, some ranches, a pecan research station, a model reform school, and a farm where little pigs — potty trained and dressed in plastic boots — never touch the ground from conception to skillet. In the summer, people play softball all night long. The remainder of the year they talk about their high school football team, which is usually one of the best in the state. Hardly a coffee break passes that someone doesn't remember 1940 when a wee halfback named Chili Rice personally defeated arch-rival Breckenridge for only the second time in thirty-six years. Every Friday during football season the town shuts down.

The people were friendly and proud to be right there. They all knew Candy Barr, of course; but, of course, they didn't *know* her. There is a custom among the businessmen of Brownwood that the first thing you say on meeting a stranger inquiring about Candy Barr is: "For Godsake, don't use *my* name." "My wife would leave me if she knew I'd even spoken to her," one businessman told me. "Not that I've ever fooled around. But just try telling that to my wife." Another man told me, "If you want to know about Candy, ask my son." It was the young men who knew her best, and if they refused to talk about her it was not peer presure but respect for her privacy. "She's been through enough," a college-aged man said. "She just wants to be left alone."

"People here know how to forgive and forget," Sheriff Danny Neal said. "Not just Candy . . . anyone who paid a price and is back on the street. Nobody here gives her a hard time."

"She comes in here and shops just like anybody else," a druggist said. "No, I can't think of anything special about her. She buys a lot of cosmetics that I wouldn't ordinarily stock, that's about all."

Though Candy lives her private life in her lake cottage with no visible means of support, she arouses little curiosity. The menfolk assume she is supported, at least partially, by a certain Brownwood banker, or by a former member of the Texas Board of Pardons and Paroles who at one time "kept her." The women just naturally assume she is a hundred-dollar-a-night hooker. Candy has learned to live with the whispers. "That's a hundred dollars an *hour*, man," she jokes among friends. Recently, Candy made an unexpected appearance at a fundamentalist church, where she gave a brief testimonial to Jesus as a "superstar." Nobody was shocked.

But why Brownwood? She had tried Dallas, L.A., Vegas, New Orleans, Mexico City, Huntsville. She had seen their bedrooms, their bars, their jails. When Candy returned to Edna after her parole in April 1963, overweight and overwrought and badly jolted by the experience, she met a woman named Gloria Carver and they became fast friends. When Gloria moved to Brownwood a few years later, Candy followed. "I felt safe here," she had told me in one of our telephone conversations.

That feeling of security didn't last too long. In 1969 she made headlines again when a Brownwood cop acting without a search warrant found a handful of seeds and stems in a shoe box in her apartment. Candy was out of town at the time. The case was dismissed, to the great relief, I gathered, of almost everyone. Brownwood wasn't *that* kind of town.

Certainly those were difficult times: sewing men's trousers in a prison workshop and appearing once a year at the rodeo hadn't exactly prepared her for a new career. Old friends like Mickey Cohen and Sammy Davis, Jr., had their own problems now. Under the conditions of her parole she couldn't even set foot in a place that sold alcoholic beverages. "What was I supposed to do, work in a root beer stand?" she had said. "They were pushing me into a corner all over again. It was either get on my back or do something silly." The one old friend who did help was Jack Ruby. Jack gave her fifty dollars, an air conditioner, and two breed dogs, "so you won't have to go out and sell yourself."

After Abe Weinstein pulled a few strings in Austin, Candy made a brief comeback at the Colony, then she just sort of wandered off. There had been a lot of talk about movie and recording offers in the weeks following her parole, but all of it came to nothing. Abe, who was still technically her manager and agent, tried to hustle her prison poetry—scrawled, overlabored cries on sheets of paper decorated like some fifth-grade art project with photographs clipped from *Vogue* and *Ladies Home Journal*. Abe even spread the word that the poetry was "in the hands of Doubleday right this minute." To Abe's way of thinking, this was true. He had stashed the pages with his friend Bill Gilliland at the Doubleday Book Store in downtown Dallas.

After Candy had saved and borrowed enough to publish her poems, she would make brief, unannounced appearances at events such as the chili cookoff in Terlingua, trying her best to promote the book. She would wait for a crowd to gather, then she would pop from a trailer, looking sexy and posing for pictures with the book in her hand. Some people bought out of curiosity, but most of them just gawked and waited for something else to happen. Nothing did.

She made many tentative agreements with writers and editors to do her life story. "She must have sold ten percent of herself about two hundred times," writer Larry King says. Then, unexpectedly, in October 1975 *Oui* offered her five thousand dollars to pose and be interviewed. The idea originated with writer Gay Talese, who suggested to a friend at the magazine, "Instead of those teenybopper dipsos, how about some pictures of a mature woman?"

Talese's motive was not altruistic. A year earlier he had visited Candy in Brownwood, hoping to do research on his own long-awaited book on sex, society, and the law. The interview had been a disaster. Candy refused to talk into a tape recorder, and when Talese asked specific questions about Jack Ruby, Mickey Cohen, Joe DeCarlo, prison, and Dallas in the fifties, she wouldn't talk at all. Instead, she wanted to talk about her memoirs, which she assumed Talese wanted to write. Talese tried to explain that he had enough problems with his own book, which he had been working on for several years. After a day and a half of wrangling and getting nowhere, Candy did one of her dramatic flip-flops. She stripped naked and positioned herself on the floor, as she had so many times when there didn't seem to be another choice. What happened next depends on which party you care to believe, but shortly afterwards Talese grabbed the first plane out of town.

The purpose of the *Oui* offer then was a second chance for Talese. Unfortunately, it developed pretty much as it had a year earlier. Candy still refused to answer questions. The interview, such as it was, was finally accomplished by flying Candy and her companion, Gloria Carver, to the Chicago offices of the magazine. Talese told me that he accepted no fee, other than expenses, for his troubles. He wished Candy well and hoped that the five thousand dollars and publicity helped.

"Good luck with your own story," he said.

When I telephoned for what I already knew was going to be the final time, Candy invited me to come for supper and spend the night.

I thought of Commerce Street and my old Army buddy Jim Frye as I stood in front of her small white clapboard cottage, shielded from prying eyes by an unpainted plywood fence and a yard of junk. She called her cottage Fort Dulce, *dulce* meaning sweet. Like candy. The license plate on the Cadillac was Dulce 1. Dulce Press, Inc., was the publisher of her poetry. On the shelves that separated the living room from the kitchen there were many jars of candy — candy kisses, lemon drops, jelly beans, peppermint, candy corn. Twenty years of waiting and I felt like a character out of a fairy tale.

Susan, three dogs, and four cats met me at the front door. She said Candy was still dressing. Two hours later, Candy was still dressing. When she finally made her appearance, shortly before 10 P.M., she hit the room like one of Sergeant Snorkel's ping-pong smashes. Her blonde hair was in curlers. She had scrubbed her face until it was blank and bleached as driftwood. Her green eyes collapsed like seedless

grapes too long on the shelf. She wore a poor white
trash housedress that ended just below the crotch,
and no panties.

"Don't think I dressed up just for you," she told me.

The next twelve hours were like being trapped on
the set of a Fellini movie, without Fellini. On one level
Candy was doing her best to cook supper, and on
another I was trying to interview her: the stereo
blasted top volume with rock and Jerry Jeff and the
kind of blues you heard in the black hovels of Dallas
in the fifties; dogs and cats prowled underfoot; a pet
spider named Brutus spun a web above a portrait of
Jesus saving New York City. I was confused because
I couldn't hear what she was saying, and she was
angry because I wasn't listening. I asked questions
about her life as a teenager on the streets of Dallas,
and she rambled about Jesus, Daddy, and Lord
Buckley, three of the men she found worth remembering. She accused me of having a secret tape recorder,
and when I told her I hated tape recorders, she
scolded me for using the word *hate* in her presence.

She smoked Virginia Slims and made bad puns
about "coming a long way," and sometimes she broke
out with a few lines from a song that happened to
cross her mind. Susan watched the TV set with the
sound turned off, and every ten or fifteen seconds
walked to the front door to let the dogs and cats in
or out. Scott attempted to make himself obscure.

"My God, what have you done!" she shrieked, lifting a dripping black iron skillet from the sink where
Susan had put it to soak. "Don't ever, *ever* put that
skillet in dishwater. And I told you to sharpen this
knife. Look at it!" Candy whacked the knife blade
into a tomato, disfiguring the inoffensive fruit. Susan
said she would try to do better.

"Before my mother died," Candy said as she dipped
pieces of chicken in flour, "she instilled in me a lot

of wonderful things like tolerance and patience. After she died, I talked to Jesus a lot. I wanted to be a missionary."

"Then tell me about that," I said.

"I walk around talking to the Chief a lot," she went on. "I tell Him: you're a groovy cat. He was far ahead of his time. I argue with Him. I ask a lot of damn questions and get some answers. Sometimes I don't agree. Sometimes He seems too severe. Hey! Give me some slack! Daddy never gave me pain seven days and seven nights. But nobody is gonna make me change what I feel about Him. Not even Him."

She started to tell me about "an incident that scared me for years, something that happened a year or two after Mama died," then she got interested in mashing potatoes and refused to think about it. Instead, she talked about what a luxury it was to visit her grandmother, the big feather bed, the indoor plumbing, the jars of candy, being able to go to church, and the unexcelled biscuits her grandmother made. Those biscuits will never be duplicated, Candy said, taking a can of store-bought biscuits from the refrigerator and cracking it against the corner of the table.

She looked straight at me and her green eyes swam. "This is very, very hard for me . . . talking to you," she said in a little girl's voice. I could see that it was. Candy's necessary illusion was control: no matter how chaotic or predoomed the situation, Candy required the illusion that she was in control. No matter how counterproductive it appeared, when Candy detected the irresistible forces of logic and authority, she became the immovable object. When Pat Gannaway put the heat on, *she* threatened to sue *him*. She remembered that when she was a child, "I kept my eyes closed so nobody could see me."

"Let's go in here for a while," she said, leading me to the bedroom with the pink wallpaper and the elaborate dressing table. It was the bedroom of a star, though one fallen on hard times. The floor was carpeted and old publicity photographs collected dust on the wall by the screened porch. The bed was extra large, and so was the bathtub. Carefully crossing her legs, Candy seated herself in front of the dresser mirror, so that the face I saw was her reflection. She raked the clutter of tubes and jars and cosmetic brushes aside.

I offered her one of my cigarettes and asked about Mickey Cohen. Cohen had personally guaranteed her fifteen-thousand-dollar bond while the marijuana appeal ran its course. In a cruel way, those were the peak years for Candy Barr. She lived in a villa in the notorious Garden of Allah on Sunset Boulevard in L.A. and earned up to two thousand dollars a week stripping there and in Vegas. Simultaneously, a pack of lawmen and profiteers howled like hungry dogs in her shadow—FBI agents, CIA agents, Treasury agents, IRS agents, L.A. cops, Vegas cops, Dallas cops. The pressure was so enormous that the El Rancho Vegas had her replaced with Nelson Eddy. She was also in and out of the hospital with hepatitis. Candy recalled that the first time she ever *heard* of Mickey Cohen was when he sent an orchid in a champagne glass to her hospital room in L.A., along with this note: "Don't worry, little girl, you got a friend."

I had heard from good sources that the reason that Cohen got rid of Candy was she was giving him a bad press. The vast majority of those agents were interested in Mickey Cohen, not his girl friend. Word came down from "the Eastern organization" that if Cohen didn't drop Candy, they would. Somewhere between Catalina Island and Hawaii.

"When I finally went to prison," she said, and I realized now, watching her face in the mirror, this was the only way she could answer the question, "it was with a great sense of relief. Otherwise, I would have been dead or laying on some gangster's couch. Of course I didn't know what prison was. I guess I thought it was a private club. I ordered all these new clothes from a place in Florida—ten dresses, twenty bras, cosmetics—hell, I was gonna be there a long time. The only thing I didn't think to take with me was the only thing I needed—money. Everything else they took away."

She reached for another cigarette and said, "I started to tell you a story earlier. About something that scared me for years. It was one night when I was baby-sitting. I was dead tired from washing bedsheets all afternoon and trying to study and the baby was crying. I walked over and put my hand on the baby's nose. That's all there was to it, a moment of darkness, but just for a moment I knew I was capable of killing. I thought about that many times in prison. Women who had killed or harmed children were horribly ostracized in prison. I could understand why they struck out at me, but those poor women—didn't they understand how those women hurt inside? Couldn't they tell by the depth of their tears? Didn't they understand that brief moment of darkness?"

Scott attempted to slip through the bedroom carrying an armload of clothes from the dryer, but Candy froze him with her eyes. She stood him in the corner by the blasting stereo and barked five or six terse, no-nonsense commands: bring in some fresh drinking water, go into town and pick up the mail, check the tires on the car. "Now repeat all that back to me," she demanded, holding him with her eyes. Scott repeated it all, a trait, I gathered, that was recently acquired.

"Goddamn," Candy snapped at me, "I'm supposed to be in there cooking supper. See what you're doing to me!"

I mixed a drink from a bottle of scotch I had

brought for just such emergencies (Candy doesn't drink) and studied the modest collection of books on her living room shelf. There were *The Complete Works of Emily Dickinson, Dream Dictionary*, a book of *Living Magic*, a book called *Oddities: A Book of Unexplained Facts*, and another called *Enigmas: Another Book of Unexplained Facts*. There were random copies of *Reader's Digest* and *Ladies Home Journal*.

A collection of men's hats hung like trophies from antlers. A rack containing seven or eight briar pipes sat solemnly beside a large can of Prince Albert.

It was after 4 A.M. when we sat down to a meal of fried chicken, potato salad, corn, red beans, sliced tomatoes, canned biscuits, and iced tea. Candy's spirits improved with each mouthful. She winked and asked was everything okay. Clyde McCoy blew his bluesy harmonica on the stereo and Candy began a monologue recalling her daddy, old Doc Slusher — how the deputy back in Edna used to ride into the yard on a white horse to question Doc about some groceries that had disappeared from the local market; how when they came to repossess his car, Doc sloshed a ring of gasoline around it, struck a kitchen match on the seat of his pants, and invited them to come ahead.

"Ride the rhyme, that's what Lord Buckley taught me," she said. "I learned to dance when I was two . . . on my daddy's knee. Daddy played the French harp. He was a blues man. Saturday was his blues day. He'd set a bottle of whiskey on the table for anybody that came around and he'd play the blues on that harp."

She went on about how she picked cotton and made soap and bacon for the family, the big black wash pots in the yard, hunting with the hounds, the taste of possum, which she couldn't stand, and fried armadillo, which was still a favorite.

Candy showed me her fan mail and some old publicity pictures. Maybe it wasn't much of a legacy, but it was a start. There were those who remembered her well, many more than you would ever think. "I know my kids have been hurt by what's been written about me," she said. "I'm not saying it's totally incorrect, it's the way they say it." Sure she'd done a little dope, and turned some tricks. She'd never stolen or hurt anyone, except when it was necessary. "I've rebelled," she said, "and I've learned that in rebellion you can become what you're rebelling against." Even now there were moments when she wasn't all that certain she had it together. Not too long ago a sheriff from Bell County had called and said he'd heard Candy was working his area. "I just cried," she told me. "Then I got it together and told him, 'If and when I do, you'll know it all right. I'll be there in my Cadillac blowing your doors off.'

"I almost let them make me feel ugly," Candy said, studying the twenty-year-old photo of the young girl with the toy pistols. "I look at these old pictures, and what I see is people grabbing my ass. From five years old on. I had my heart broke many times. I didn't even know why people were snotty to me. I was making a living. But it was like they had a bleeper on my ass. I was making eighty-five dollars a week as a cigarette girl at the Theater Lounge, and all I could think of was, I had a car, a place of my own, and now nobody could throw me back in a motel with a night porter.

"But they wouldn't let up. Do you know what it's like working onstage with a couple of harness bulls sitting two feet away? Why did *I* have to take them to the backseat? Why did I have to call them *sir* when they were watching me take my clothes off? They were on my level then."

It was nearly dawn when Candy made a bed for me on the living room sofa. She covered me with an imitation bearskin rug and tucked it in. An early autumn cold front had passed through West Texas: the thin walls of Fort Dulce rattled, and I lay there in the changing shafts of light thinking not of the woman whose essence filled the room but of a life-size cardboard cutout of Candy Barr. I knew what Jim Frye would ask. He would ask: *did you nail her?*

It was all a fantasy. Twenty years ago Candy Barr was forbidden fruit, a symbol for the agony of our tightly corked libidos, a martyr to repressed yearnings for violence and identity, a solitary being bending into the prevailing winds of injustice and insensitivity. When you got right down to it, Candy Barr did not apply to be our symbol. Like Patty Hearst, she just got carried away.

After a few hours' sleep we all felt better. The sudden cold snap had turned the lake bronze as the warmer bottom water floated to the surface. I walked down by the lake and watched Scott dig the cottage intake pipe from the mud and blow it clean so there would be clear water for Candy's morning shower. After her shower, Candy seated herself at the dressing table and, like one of those time-lapse Disney films where a desert flower appears to blossom before your eyes, performed the ancient miracle of her sex. The blonde hair brushed out soft and glossy. Mascara arches defined the eyes, which sparkled now like polished turquoise. That cave dweller's pallor that had appeared so unflattering in the harsh light of the kitchen took on tones of finely dusted nutmeg. In her tight hiphugger jeans and red halter she looked like a young girl ready for a hayride.

Momentarily, she reappeared as Candy Barr, a lost vision of great beauty, warmth, and charm.

She popped open a can of biscuits and asked me to sit beside her.

"Now we can talk," she said. "What do you want to know?"

"I want to know how you feel," I said.

"I feel like . . . like I'm not vulnerable anymore," she told me.

A Gentle Mind . . . Confused

Hate the world that strikes you down,
A warped lesson quickly learned.
Rebellion, a universal sound,
Nobody cares . . . No one's concerned.

Fatigued by unyielding strife,
Self-pity consoles the abused,
And the bludgeoning of daily life
Leaves a gentle mind . . . confused.

—Candy Barr

December 1976

Postscript

As far as I know, no writer had ever got this close to Candy before. She only agreed to see me because of the Jack Ruby story and my friendship with Chastity Fox. I heard later that Candy called Chastity and asked if I was okay. Chastity assured her I was.

I don't think Candy ever got her poster business or fan clubs organized, and I'm sure they didn't get around to making a movie about her life. Maybe they will. She's still a star in my eyes. My kids still talk about "the sexy lady in mink" who stopped in Austin to visit us a few years ago. Great survivor, great lady.

5

The Death of the Marlboro Man

A world big enough to hold a rattlesnake and a purty woman is big enough for all kinds of people.
—Oldtime cowboy saying

I never realized that the Marlboro cowboy was real until I read last May that he had drowned on a bucking bronco. *Drowned* . . . incredible . . . drowned on a nervous young colt in a newly dug stock tank on the Bill Flowers Ranch near Old Glory, in the starkly beautiful Marlboro country north of Sweetwater. No one knows exactly how it happened; as usual, Carl (Bigun) Bradley was alone at the time.

Bigun and his daddy, Carl (Banty) Bradley, had just sold the colt to Bill Flowers, but Flowers' foreman couldn't handle him. Bigun saddled the horse late that afternoon, cinching the flank rope tight as he could so the horse would feel pain every time he bucked, then he rode off toward what they call Cemetery Pasture.

Bigun was thirty-six and for as long as anyone could remember his workday started before sunup and ended after sundown, never varying except for the two days he took off to get married and the few times he was off in South Dakota doing a Marlboro commercial. It was seven days a week, week after week; it was the repetition as well as the work that kept him at it. But this particular day, for no particular reason, Glenda Bradley was worried. She telephoned Susann Flowers at ranch headquarters just after dark.

"You know how cowboys are," Susann Flowers told Glenda. "You gotta hit them in the head to get them off their horse. He'll be in in a while." Nevertheless, Bill Flowers and his foreman would take a pickup out to Cemetery Pasture and see about Bigun. "I'll call you back," Susann told Glenda.

The Flowerses were not only Bigun's employers, they were his friends, and Glenda's too, a couple about their own age. Bill Flowers was a famous rodeo roper and heir to old Pee Wee Flowers' four-ranch spread of eighty thousand acres. Bill was a real cowboy, too, but not in the way Bigun was—Bigun was a working cowboy, the son of a working cowboy, the grandson of a working cowboy, all of them born and raised on the same tenant ranch outside of Knox City, simple men working for wages and living their unrelenting existence in a world that could go mad without them knowing or even caring. Bill Flowers and Bigun Bradley had ridden together when Bigun was wagon boss of the Four Sixes (6666) Ranch near Guthrie—"neighboring," they call it, helping out when there is branding or gathering to be done—there was one stretch, Bill recalled, when they were out forty-one days, miles from the nearest asphalt or bathtub or woman or child or roof or television set. But there was always this difference — Bill Flowers was rich. He could quit anytime and go back to running his own ranch and rodeoing. Bigun Bradley never had time for the rodeo. And he didn't live long enough to own his own spread.

Bill Flowers and his foreman found nothing in Cemetery Pasture, but returning to the ranch house late that night they saw something in the headlights that sent cold chills up their boots — a horse's leg and part of a saddle blanket protruding from the muddy water near the edge of the new stock tank.

"Get the rope," Bill yelled, jumping from the pickup before it had even stopped rolling. But they had made a mistake that Bigun Bradley would never have made: they had forgotten their rope.

About midnight, Bill and Susann Flowers drove over to Glenda's house and told her they had found the horse. There was no trace of Bigun, except his lip ice, gloves, and a package of Kools. Sheriff Marvin Crawford and other volunteers had come over from Aspermont, and the dragging operation had begun. The Flowerses drove Glenda and her eighteen-month-old son, Carl Kent Bradley, back to the ranch house, where they could wait out the night.

"It was the longest night ever," Susann Flowers would say later. "We kept hoping that maybe he had been bucked and was unconscious somewhere out there. Almost the same thing had happened to my daddy's foreman in Pecos — they found his body in the Pecos River. We never knew what happened."

Working in the lights of a circle of pickup trucks and a fire truck beacon, the cowboys told stories and speculated. There were three possibilities: Bigun could have been bucked off; the horse could have spooked and charged into the water, taking Bigun with him; or Bigun could have deliberately ridden the bronco into the tank. "Some people think every horse will swim, but every horse won't swim," Sheriff Crawford said. "I've rode horses up to drink tubs . . . you get a bronco around water, the cinches tight up, they're liable as not to turn and pitch. You get a horse in water, most of them will swim right across, but they's a few'll just turn on their sides and go straight to the bottom."

"Bigun has been known to ride 'em into water," another cowboy recollected. "I seen him one time after a big rain take his chestnut right into the Little Wichita, trying to get the cattle to follow him."

Back at the ranch house, George Humphrey, an old-time cowboy who managed the Four Sixes for forty years (Bigun left the Sixes when George retired four years ago), told stories to the gathering of women and children. How in the old days when cattle were cheap the best way to subdue an old mossy horn was to shoot it through the thick part of the horns, aiming for dead center so that the pain would calm the steer and make it manageable. "What if you misshot?" Glenda Bradley asked, laughing the nervous schoolgirl laugh that was maintaining her. "You'd kill the animal," George Humphrey said. "Cattle was cheap and it was an advantage to get rid of these outlaws at any price. They spoiled the other cattle. They had to be either shot or driven off."

They dragged Bigun Bradley's body from the tank around 2 A.M. There were signs of a blow over one eye and behind his ear. "Either one was hard enough to kill him," Sheriff Crawford told Glenda Bradley.

Glenda went outside and cried, then she came back and helped fix breakfast.

"He preferred to work alone," Glenda Bradley is telling me. Her voice has started to quiver, and she clasps her hands tightly in her lap. "That's very dangerous, but he was so good . . . I think anyone will tell you this . . . he *was* good with horses. He just wasn't afraid. He didn't think anything could happen."

We are sitting in the kitchen of her parents' home in Westbrook, a tiny farming town near Colorado City. This is where Glenda grew up, and this is where she returned after Bigun's death. It has been two months since the funeral: only yesterday Glenda finally forced herself back to Old Glory, and having made the trip she feels better. Old friends and memories are too dear to ignore.

"I interviewed for a job teaching homemaking at Jayton High School—that's east of Knox City. When we were first married and Bigun was wagon boss of the Four Sixes, I taught homemaking in Guthrie. It's a comfort to at least know what I'm going to do. People in that part of the country, especially around Guthrie, they're not very progressive. They want things the way they were in the old times and do a pretty good job keeping it that way. Oh, they use pickups and butane branding irons, but that's about it. At first I thought I could never go back, but . . ."

Carl Kent Bradley, called Kent, now twenty months old, rides a stick horse around the table where we talk.

"I guess he'll be a cowboy, too," Glenda says. "I hate for him to do it, but that's what Bigun would want, and I know Banty (Bigun's daddy) is going to have it that way. Bigun was never allowed to be a little boy. Banty had him out breaking horses when he was old enough to ride. I mean breaking *horses . . . colts . . .* not riding old nags." Glenda says this without rancor. She is more composed now, and there is that nervous, laughing edge to her voice. "Bigun and Banty and all their people, cowboying is all they've ever known or wanted. To be on a horse chasing a cow was what Bigun enjoyed. Kent has already turned that way. Unless I ever remarry and my husband is so different . . . but I don't think I'd like any other life except cowboying."

Glenda Bradley is pretty, the way a high school majorette is pretty, a way that is difficult to describe. She is what you would call "a sweet girl," but tough and proud. As she talks about her five-and-one-half-year marriage to Bigun Bradley, she admits that she never knew him very well. No one did. "The truth is," she says, "we never had much time together, and when we did he didn't say much. He'd leave the house at three or four in the morning and come home after dark. He'd eat and go to bed. Every day, no days off. About the only socializing we did, every July Fourth the cowboys would take off and go to the Stamford Cowboy Reunion Rodeo."

Bigun was a thirty-year-old bachelor when Glenda met him at a rodeo dance. She was twenty-two and had just graduated from Texas Tech. He was the Marlboro man and wagon boss of the 6666. She had never met Bigun Bradley, but she knew him, knew him in a way that always embarrassed Bigun when she told the story.

"Bigun would kill me for telling you, but . . . well, it was a big joke at school [Texas Tech] that I liked *cowboys.* A friend of mine cut out Bigun's picture from a Marlboro ad in *Life* magazine . . . here's your cowboy, Sis, she said. . . . I said, fine, I'll just *marry* him, and put the picture on my dorm wall . . . you know, a silly girl thing. That summer another friend sent an article out of *Western Horseman* that gave his name—Carl B. Bradley, Jr. He got the name Bigun from his Uncle Guy who use to call him Bigun and his little brother (Doug Bradley) Littleun. Actually, Bigun wasn't all that tall, only about five eleven, but very strong. Anyway, on July Fourth that summer I went to the Stamford Cowboy Reunion Rodeo Dance with a girl friend and there he was. He took my girl friend home that night. Two nights later, I went back to the dance and he pretty well ignored me, but he did ask me for a date."

Six months later, after a courtship that consisted of going to an occasional cowboy movie in Bigun's pickup, they were married. As wagon boss at the Four Sixes, Bigun was making $310 a month, but Glenda started teaching and there was extra money from the Marlboro commercials, not all that much, but enough to get by. The Marlboro people had "discovered" Bigun Bradley while shooting some background film at the Four Sixes. He was one of several real cowboys who posed for commercials.

"One of the first things he told me," Glenda says, "is about the Marlboro deal — he'd been offered a full-time contract that included a part in a movie. He'd turned it down, but now, with us getting married, he didn't know if he'd done the right thing. But he decided he wouldn't be happy not cowboying . . . and he wouldn't, 'cause he was good and he liked it."

Bigun did not speak of the future, but it was his dream to someday own a small ranch. They put a little money in the bank . . . $120 every time Marlboro used him on TV, $1,500 for a few cover ads in *Life* or *Look* . . . and Bigun bought a few horses and cattle and went in partnership with Banty, who was now leasing the land where they had always worked for wages. Then the government banned cigarette commercials on TV. Glenda had to quit her job when Kent was born, and the savings account quickly evaporated. Bigun hadn't posed for a commercial in the two years before his death. "We were barely getting by," Glenda says. "And I mean barely."

It cost money to cowboy. Four hundred dollars for a saddle . . . forty dollars for a pair of chaps . . . one hundred dollars for shopmade boots. Except on the rare occasion when he accompanied Glenda to the First Methodist Church ("He never felt comfortable in a crowd"), Bigun wore Levis, white shirt, boots, hat, and, in the winter, a neck scarf. He never walked outside without his hat and boots.

"He was always giving things away," Glenda recalls. "Bridles . . . spurs . . . if he thought someone wanted his boots he'd sit down and take them off right there. That's just how he was. He was the most patient, most courteous man I ever knew. Even after we were married and had the baby, he would still open doors for me . . . yes, ma'am and no, ma'am . . . he wouldn't even take a serving of food off the table until I'd served myself first. That's the way May (Bigun's mother) raised her two boys. Even after we were married, whatever Mama and Daddy said do, he'd do, regardless of my opinion."

J. Frank Dobie once described the cowboy as "a proud rider, skilled, observant, alert, resourceful, unyielding, daring, punctilious in a code peculiar to his occupation, and faithful to his trust."

That's a pretty good description of Bigun Bradley.

Joe Thigpen, the young county attorney of Stonewall County, tosses a pack of Kools on his desk and tilts his straw hat on the back of his head. In his wilder days, before he finished law school, Thigpen worked for Bigun Bradley at the Four Sixes.

"I knew about the Marlboro cowboy—everybody around here did," he tells me. "It was a thrill meeting him." The first thing Bigun Bradley did was send Joe home for his saddle and bedroll; it hadn't occurred to Joe that he would need a bedroll. This was 1968, and the Four Sixes still had a chuck wagon drawn by four mules, a kind of traveling headquarters; they slept under the stars, bathing maybe twice a month. The wagon was already out when Joe Thigpen hired on, and they stayed out another two and a half months.

Joe Thigpen tells me: "I never met a man as patient and completely dedicated as Bigun. I never knew a man who worked harder. I don't think he ever asked for a day off. He'd wake me up every morning and tell what we had to do that day. Then we'd do it.

"Now I'm not saying he couldn't be tough on you. There was one day we were flanking cattle and I was always in the wrong place, spooking the yearlings. Bigun roped this calf . . . must of weighed four hundred fifty pounds . . . and said, 'You been messing up all day so you just flank [i.e., throw] this one by yourself.' Now there's no way one man can throw a four-hundred-fifty-pound yearling. The calf stepped on my toes and like to of broke them . . . I was sweating and puffing, all the way given out . . . never did get that yearling down. Another fellow finally had to help me. But Bigun wasn't doing it for meanness — he was teaching me a lesson."

I asked Joe Thigpen what it is that makes a man cowboy. He thought for a while, then said, "I can't tell you exactly, but I loved it better than anything I've ever done. You're outdoors, doing what you like to do. I probably never would of gone back to school, except Bigun told me that's what I ought to do. It was the best advice I ever got — a cowboy can't afford a family."

Thigpen took a check stub from his wallet and showed me his final month's pay at the Sixes — $162.50. Then he offered me a Kool and told me a story: "We had about a hundred twenty-five horses in the remuda. We were moving them one day . . . I guess we must of rode twenty-two miles . . . me being the low man on the totem pole, I had to ride drag . . . you know, back at the end, hollering and yelling and pushing horses. It was just dusty as the dickens. I was trying to smoke those Marlboros . . . I thought

that's what I oughta smoke . . . but they were burning me up . . . I'd take one puff and throw it away.
That's when Bigun came riding back. He didn't say a
word. He just took a pack of Kools out and offered
me one."

Joe Thigpen takes another cigarette and shakes his
head. Hard to believe. Hard to believe that a man
who knew so much about horses could be killed by
one. "It's something I'll never be able to get out of my
mind," he says.

It doesn't take long to tour the Old Glory community, but the tour is fascinating. Seated in a flat,
green valley of windmills and skeleton mesquites that
have been poisoned because they take too much
water from the land, Old Glory is an abandoned
cotton gin, a general store and post office, and a scattering of quaint old homes. One of the homes is the
old Raynor Court House, which sits now like a feudal
castle on a high mound. It looks like the house in the
movie *Giant*, I think as I drift below on the farm road
from Aspermont, and it turns out they modeled the
movie set after the Raynor Court House. An old couple whose name I didn't catch live there now. No one
ever goes up there, they told me at the general store.

The Germans who settled here called the spot New
Brandenburg until World War I when, in a fit of
patriotism, they decided the name sounded too un-
American and asked the oldest woman in town, Mrs.
Weinke, what they should do about it. She told them
to change it to Old Glory, and that's what it's been
ever since.

I'm in the passenger side of a station wagon with
Susann Flowers and her two young boys. Bill Flowers
has been off since before daylight, buying cattle in a
market that is on the verge of Nixonian panic, and

Susann is showing me the ranch. We drive through Cemetery Pasture, where the old German cemetery is preserved by a fence — judging from the gravestones, an unusual number of children died here in the late 1800's, a time of epidemic, perhaps — and now we slow down near the stock tank where Bigun Bradley died.

"You know what I always think when I drive by here?" Susann Flowers says. "I think about Bigun's hat. We never found it. It's down there somewhere.

"Bigun couldn't swim, you know. Neither can Bill. It scares the hell out of me to see them swimming their horses, but they do it all the time. There's no reason for it, it's just something they do. We're not supposed to question what happens on this earth, but I can't help wonder what happened that night. He could have been bucked, or the horse could have gone into the tank, but I can't help feel that Bigun rode in on purpose."

We stop in a warm summer rain while Susann fills the tank of her station wagon from a gasoline drum near the foreman's house. In an adjoining pasture there is a modern house trailer where old Pee Wee Flowers still comes occasionally to play dominoes with the hands. Susann wants to change the name of the Bill Flowers Ranch to "something Spanish," but Bill and Pee Wee won't hear of it. Susann Flowers doesn't want her two children to cowboy, but that's what they will do — cowboy like their daddy, not like Bigun Bradley. Meanwhile, Susann is organizing a college scholarship fund for little Carl Kent Bradley.

"Bigun wasn't afraid of anything," she says as we drive back to the ranch headquarters. "I heard him say one time . . . he was talking about this cowboy we all knew . . . Bigun said, 'Charley's afraid of dying.' It was something Bigun couldn't understand. He was tough as hell — that's what he was. Yet he was

121

the most considerate, most dependable man I ever knew. I'd known him for years before he stopped calling me Mrs. Flowers—and I was younger than he was."

Jeff Flowers, age five, tells me what he remembers about Bigun—Jeff remembers Bigun brought him a tiny rabbit they caught in a post hole. Jeff wears spurs on his little boots and has two horses. They're not very good horses, he tells me.

In a driving rainstorm, I turn toward Knox City, thinking about women and glasses of beer.

I stop to consult my crude map. The rain has stopped and the sun is slipping behind Buzzard Peak when I find the muddy, rutty, unmarked road that leads to the tenant house where Bigun and all his people grew up—the ranch that Banty Bradley now leases. A sign at the main-gate cattleguard identifies this as the "General American Oil Co.," and it is still another ten miles to the house, which sits on a crest overlooking miles of green hills and naked brown peaks. Fat quail and jackrabbits big as dwarf deer bounce in front of my car, and horses and cattle look me over without judging my intentions.

Banty and May Bradley are out by the stable, hoeing weeds. There are miles of weeds, weeds far as you can see, but the apron of ground around the stable is clean as a dinner plate. They hoe patiently, like people listening to the radio, like they don't care if there is an end to their struggle.

Banty is a short, husky, red-faced cowboy with wide spaces between his teeth to spit tobacco through. They say Bigun was a younger exact replica of his daddy. May, though, is pure Texas mule-iron, a lean, severe, outspoken woman who hasn't smiled since Christmas. There is no telephone here; I couldn't call in advance, and now they decline to be interviewed. I stand by my open car door, asking questions, while they go on hoeing. Then I get an idea. I tell them that I saw "Sis" (Glenda's nickname) yesterday, she says hidy and she's feeling much better. She's got a new teaching job at Jayton. Banty and May brighten as I play them a part of the tape I did with Glenda.

"Did you see Bigun's boy?" Banty asks, eagerly breaking the silence.

I describe meeting Carl Kent Bradley.

"That baby of Carl B.'s is a natural-born cowboy," May says. May is the only person I met who doesn't call her son Bigun. She calls him Carl B. "Look at him ride his rocky horse . . . natural saddle gait."

"It's getting harder," May says, "harder to go on. There is very little neighboring anymore. It's every man for himself. You used to be able to tell a cowman by his boots," she tells me. "If he was worth a speck, he had hundred-dollar shopmade boots. Nowdays, you tell a cowboy by his woreout brogans. Real cowboys can't hardly afford boots. One thing about Carl B., he couldn't care less about money. There was a pattern in his life. Things came his way. He didn't ever ask for things, we taught him that, but things came his way. He didn't ask for all that publicity. He got plenty of it, but he wasn't a *seeker*."

May does most of the talking, deferring occasionally to Banty, reminding him of a particular story. They tell me about Banty buying Bigun's first saddle when Bigun was three. May talks about their other son, Doug, how Doug never wanted to be a cowboy. Doug drives a bulldozer. Doug was always building things, while Bigun played cowboy. Blocks and stick horses. "Bigun wore out many a stick horse before he could ride," May says. "He'd play cowboy and Doug was always his calf. Doug had all the hide wore off his neck by the rope."

At May's urging, Banty tells me about Bigun snitch-
ing the latch pin off the barn door, and how Bigun
was afraid of the dark but Banty made him go back
alone in the dark and replace the latch pin. Bigun
never again messed with the barn latch. They tell me
about the agonizing weeks it took before Bigun would
mount his first wild bronco. And how, once he had
done it, he never stopped. Why does a man cowboy?
I ask. Banty grins and points to his head, as though
to say that's where his heart is. If Bigun was as good
as they say, and I believe he was, why didn't he join
the rodeo circuit? "Too many people," Banty grins.

Later, May takes me up to the house and shows me
her clippings, the clippings describing the deeds of the
Marlboro cowboy. Best all-around boy at Knox City
High, senior class favorite, FFA president, co-captain
of his football team, honorable mention all-district.
Carl B. (Bigun) Bradley, Jr.'s plain moon face, his
eyes tinted Paul Newman blue, barely seen in the
shadow of his hat, smoking what is alleged to be a
Marlboro cigarette. Why? Why would Marlboro pick
Bigun Bradley? I guess because they saw he was a real
cowboy.

There is a Marlboro sunset as I slide back along the
mud road and turn toward Guthrie. Two horses in
the road ahead turn flank and trot off into the brush.
There is a silence that lasts forever — if there were such
a word, *forever*. A windmill is silhouetted against the
dark fire of the horizon, and I can't help thinking it's
a long way home.

December 1973

Postscript

I once read that Truman Capote got the idea for *In*

124

Cold Blood from a two-paragraph story in the *Times*.
A lot of the best stories start that way. This one was
inspired by a single paragraph in the *Daily Texan*. All
I knew was, the Marlboro cowboy drowned on his
horse. The mystique was finding out who he was and
how it happened. The old *chase*. You've got to have
a taste for it.

6

Orange Peril

When Darrell K. Royal's season on earth has ended and he ascends to the Big Bowl to sit at the right hand of God Almighty, some asshole in orange slacks and white shoes will be waiting to market DKR dolls with orange halos.

The orange halos are what is known among speculators as the *edge*. If the University of Texas football team is ranked in the top ten, Orange Mullets can be counted on to swarm the marketplace in search of identity. If not, they can remove the halos and melt the dolls down for ashtrays. It would be very difficult to sell DKR dolls after an 8–3 season: after 7–4, it would be very difficult for DKR even to get into heaven. God don't sit around in his orange underwear jawing with losers.

The taste of the consumer must never be over-estimated. It is impossible to catalog the number and variety of orange trash or to comprehend the appetites of the Orange Mullets who faithfully purchase the beer mugs, drinking glasses, caps, blazers, Cadillacs, toilet seats, and key chains bearing the colors and logo of the Longhorns, but someone is getting fat and it's not Darrell. No royalties are paid, not to DKR, not to the athletic department, not even to the university.

"All we get out of it is mad," says Jones Ramsey, the UT sports information director. "After our 1963 national championship, this insurance salesman in an orange coat came by and asked me for a team picture, which I gave him. Later, I heard he had it copied and sold them for three bucks a print."

The largest selections of orange flotsam can be found in Austin, at the University Co-Op and at Rooster Andrews Sporting Goods. Under the catchline ORANGE FEVER, Rooster Andrews, who in the days of Bobby Layne was known as "the All-American water boy," stocks such items as Longhorn coaching caps, helmets, jogging shoes, stocking caps, and carry bags. As the official outfitter of the Longhorns, Rooster can be forgiven his zeal, but it's still tough on the rest of us. For example, the Hill Country Middle School requires its students to wear blue or red (the school colors) gym shorts in physical education classes, but you can't buy blue or red gym shorts in Austin. Even the street signs were orange before an Aggie bureaucrat decided to switch to more readable green and white. I fully expect to walk into Rylander's someday during football season and see orange lettuce.

For the intellectually inclined there are at least three record albums and half a dozen books extolling DKR and his young students. At least Aggie joke books are funny.

The manager of Rooster Andrews, Ron Habitzreiter, detects a cooling down of orange fever, especially in Austin. "Most of our orders come from Houston and Dallas," he says. "There is an indication that the consumers in Austin are being oranged to death." Six years ago a San Antonio record company consigned to the sporting goods firm an album called *Legend of the Longhorns.* All but a dozen copies are still in stock. I listened to the album and I promise it will make you cry.

By far the best of the DKR books is one that Royal and Dallas *Times Herald* sports editor Blackie Sherrod collaborated on in 1963. It's called *Darrell Royal Talks Football,* but the only thing dreary about the book is its title. What DKR really talks about is red beans and how ol' ugly is better than ol' nothing and why the sun don't shine on the same ol' dog's ass every day and how when that big scorekeeper finally comes to write against your name all he really wants to know is who won. DKR has a marvelous gift for the shit-kicker metaphor, but no small amount of credit for the book belongs to Sherrod, who made up some of the best quotes, such as: "Our faces were so long we could have eaten oats out of a churn." Vintage Sherrod.

"When Darrell first read the galleys of our book he called and said it was amazing how much it sounded like him," Blackie recalled recently. "I pointed out that he didn't invent all those Will Rogers quotes."

Another thing DKR never said, though it has been attributed to him dozens of times, is, "Every coach likes those old trained pigs who'll grin and jump right in the slop for him." Dan Jenkins retouched this one for *Sports Illustrated*, or so it is claimed. DKR still bristles when he reads it, and his wife, Edith, to this day groups Jenkins with Lee Harvey Oswald and Charles Manson. According to DKR's version, he said *slot*, not *slop. Slot* refers to that narrow chute steers tread en route to auction or slaughter; it is also a football expression used to indicate that fleshy caldron at the heart of a scrimmage line so in favor with blood-crazed linebackers. "*Slop* doesn't make any sense," he claims. But it obviously made sense to Jenkins and to many others who have repeated it over the years.

Understandably, DKR is thin-skinned about his slick image. It is his white plume and his meal ticket as well. A lot of mamas in Jasper and Dime Box didn't appreciate it at all when he described the game of football as "meat on meat, flesh on flesh, and stink on stink." The TCU football team was less than flattered when he compared them to a cockroach—"It isn't what he eats or totes off but what he falls into and messes up."

The latest contribution to orange literature, if the term can be used, is a book of quips and quotes from Darrell Royal compiled by Associated Press reporter Robert Heard and published by Jenkins Publishing Company last summer. Heard prefaces the 374 quotations by pointing out that 12 of them have some form of "what some people might call profanity" and then goes on to *list* them—"damned, crap, butt (two quotes), ass (three), son of a bitch, peter, piss (two quotes), and farted." DKR perused the body of the book without flinching, but the preface sent him up the wall. "He didn't object to the pisses and asses," says Jones Ramsey. "They were scattered through the book. What really got him was piling them up like that in the preface."

At Royal's request, Heard agreed to delete two fairly innocuous quotations. In return, DKR supplied a quote that Heard's research hadn't uncovered. It's one of the best in the book, and it goes like this:

"I was reading a story that a young man was interviewing Oliver Wendell Holmes, and Oliver Wendell Holmes told this young man that if he had a method, a surefire method, by which he could cause the world to bypass all troubles, that he wouldn't pass this formula on to the public or even to his friends because he felt that everyone needed some trouble in their life. And, you know, this story causes you to do some serious thinking, and I have, and my thought is: piss on Oliver Wendell Holmes."

Robert Heard freely admits that he will profit from the book in ratio to UT's winning record this season. DKR no doubt views this prospect with mixed emotions, because Robert Heard is not one of his favorite reporters. It was Heard and another AP writer, Jack Keever, who wrote the "controversial" five-part series in 1972 on black football players, or the lack of them, at the University of Texas. I place the word *controversial* in quotation marks because the series was noticeably mild, coming as it did some seven years after Heard started writing about UT football. There is an interesting footnote to the book in which Heard tells of watching DKR and one of his giant linemen hugging and dancing with each other following a miraculous last-minute game-winning touchdown against UCLA. Heard at the time mistakenly identified the lineman as Bill Atessis, when in fact it was Julius Whittier, the first black to start for the Longhorns. Contrary to what you might suppose, this accidental witness was not Heard's inspiration for the series on black players. No, Heard says he had been thinking of doing the series for some time, and when UT failed to recruit any blacks after the 1972 season, the decision was made to move ahead in the best traditions of gut-check journalism. Besides, Heard told me, he was sick of watching Texas lose all that fine black talent to Oklahoma.

If Heard's motives were less than altruistic, his methods went straight for the jugular. Heard and Keever didn't intentionally paint DKR as a racist, but that was the unavoidable impression. I've known

DKR for better than fifteen years, and I'll promise you he's no more of a racist than any other white who grew up in Hollis, Oklahoma, forty-something years ago, and less than most. His boyhood was right out of *The Grapes of Wrath:* he can still remember the stigma of being called an Okie and what it meant to wear government-issued commodity overalls. Whatever DKR was and is, he is a man with the ability to grow. In 1970, after Julius Whittier became the first black letterman at UT (a year earlier, UT had the dubious distinction of being the last all-white team to win a national championship), Royal said: "The black kids are the ones who are becoming the great athletes because they work harder than white kids. The white kids are out on their boats, and the black kids are out there using the fields, getting their recreation in sports." Ten years ago a wealthy UT alumnus in an orange coat offered me another explanation: "The reason the niggers are faster than our boys is the lions and tigers got all the slow ones."

If Heard and Keever's series was "controversial," it wasn't because of what they wrote, but what they didn't. They didn't write about the Orange Coats, that splendid assortment of dentists and bankers and contractors and regents who hired Royal in the first place, then attached themselves to the UT football program like ticks on a bird dog. Those were and still are your racists, your true orange-blood bigots. It seems almost unbelievable, but until 1963 the UT Regents explicitly *forbade* black athletes at "The University." Even after the Regents rescinded this rule (without a murmur that it was now time to break with tradition), the Orange Coats made it clear that the first black Longhorn had better be two steps faster than Jesus and able to run through a brick wall. It took a Roosevelt Leaks to integrate the Orange Coats with the twentieth century.

Since I was a sportswriter in Fort Worth and Dallas for almost eight years, I don't feel very comfortable in criticizing Heard or anyone else for neglecting the neglect of the black athlete at UT. After the Southwest Conference writers visited Austin in September, Jones Ramsey told me, "This was the first time since the five-part series that nobody asked how many blacks we had on the team." I asked Jones how many there were, and he didn't know. Later, his assistant Bill Little counted them for me. Approximately one fifth of the squad was black, including thirteen out of the top forty-four.

That's a respectable average, far more respectable than the school as a whole. UT has forty-two thousand students, and only a tiny fraction are scholarship athletes, roughly one in two hundred. But one in every twenty blacks on the Austin campus is an athlete. This suggests that UT is not exactly teeming with black students, and it isn't: eliminate the athletes and that leaves fewer than seven hundred blacks for the remainder of the campus. That, I submit, is *controversial.*

If one wants to examine Royal's attitude on the subject of race today, he would be well advised to check the Longhorn football roster. You will search in vain for any blacks from Houston or Dallas. Fort Worth is represented, as is San Antonio, but most of UT's blacks come from small towns: Galveston, Tyler, Conroe, Hamlin, Caldwell, Lampasas. Royal's brand of football is highly disciplined, and he doesn't believe that the street life of the urban ghetto is the best training ground for discipline. Whatever their color, Darrell wants boys who take off their hats indoors and say, "Yes, ma'am" and "No, ma'am."

Robert Heard calls his book of quips and quotes *Dance With Who Brung Us,* which is DKR's explanation of why he approaches the Big One with the same fundamental strategy that got him there in the first place. It has been suggested that a better title would be *Quotations From Chairman Darrell* or perhaps *The Confessions of Saint Darrell*. You're going to hear a lot of Orange Coats walking around this fall saying things like "They aren't very big, but they'll screw their navels to the ground and scratch and bite and spit at you."

DKR's best lines are not the warmed-over Will Rogers or the precooked Willie Nelson but his own vivid and sharply accurate descriptions of his own players. For example:

- On Walt Fondren — "He's quick as a hiccup."
- On James Saxton — "He could run like small-town gossip, although his compass sometimes went batty."
- On Chris Gilbert — "Did you ever try to drop a cat on its back? If you have, you know it can't be done. Chris is the same way. I bet if you'd hold his arms and legs and let go from about three feet off the ground, he'd light running."
- On Glen Halsell — "Halsell is a rolling ball of butcher knives."
- On Cotton Speyrer, the skinny pass-catcher — "He looks like he needs worming."
- On a freshman halfback who ran the wrong way — "We dialed his number, but he didn't answer."
- On Earl Campbell, upon watching Campbell trample one of his own blockers who had fallen in front of him — "Ol' Earl doesn't believe in taking any prisoners."

Royal once described defensive back Raymond Clayborn as a man who "burns a different fuel." That's a good description of DKR himself. He has run on fear for so many years that the only thing he's really afraid of is losing it. He is one of the most successful college coaches in history. He occasionally speaks of "the day I'm gonna set my bucket down," meaning retire from coaching, but he also says, "I just hope that we never reach the point where a defeat is not big news."

There is not much he can do about the DKR dolls with the orange halos. Royal is singularly responsible for the orange plague, but that doesn't mean he can stop it, except of course by losing, which he doesn't do very often. DKR seriously considered retiring after he won his first national championship, but then he thought, *What the hell.* At fifty-two, he is still a relatively young man and he'll likely be presiding over the glory of the Longhorns for another ten or fifteen years. Once when the two of us were alone and DKR was mellowed out on his favorite beverage, I asked him how long he was prepared to endure the Orange Coats and the Mullets and the stupid adoration of the charlatans and poll watchers. Royal will deny it, but this is what he told me: "Long as I got the jelly rolling and the barracudas don't smell it, I'm gonna fill my platter with white meat. The day it gets down to necks and gizzards, that's the day you can kiss ol' Darrell's ass good-bye."

November 1976

Postscript

I was dead wrong to predict that Darrell Royal would be "presiding over the glory of the Longhorns for another ten or fifteen years." He quit after the 1976 season, disgusted by pressures and sordid methods used to recruit college athletes. It just got down to the necks and gizzards, I guess. In my mind, Longhorn football has never been the same. (See "The Crude Feud.")

7

Is Jay J. Armes for Real?

Jay J. Armes was running short on patience and long on doubt. He was slipping out of character. It was possible he had made a mistake. The self-proclaimed world's greatest private detective, an internationally famous investigator who liked to brag that he'd never accepted a case he didn't solve, fast on his way to becoming a legend, was stumbling through a television interview with a crew of Canadians who never seemed to be in the right place at the right time, or to have the right equipment, or to ask the right questions.

Jay Armes calculated that his time was worth ten thousand dollars a day, which meant that the three-man crew from Toronto had gone through fifteen thousand dollars, on the house. Pretty much ignoring his suggestions, the Canadians had concentrated on what Armes called "Mickey Mouse shots" of the "Nairobi Village" menagerie in the backyard of

his high-security El Paso home, and on his bullet-
proof, super-customed, chauffeur-driven 1975 Cadillac limousine.

Worse still, the Canadians were not from the Canadian Broadcasting Corporation, as Armes had led
himself to believe, but from CTV, a smaller independent network. He had badly overestimated the value
of this publicity.

The seeds of discord had been scattered unexpectedly the previous day, at a corner table of El
Paso's Miguel Steak and Spirits, where Jay Armes sat
with his back to the wall regaling the Canadians and
two American magazine writers with tales of his
escapades, or "capers," as he called them.

He talked of the long helicopter search and
dramatic rescue of Marlon Brando's son Christian
from a remote Mexican seaside cave where the lad
was being held by eight dangerous hippies; of the time
he piloted his glider into Cuba and recovered two
million dollars of his client's "assets"; of the famous
Mexican prison break, another helicopter caper,
which, he said, inspired the Charles Bronson movie
Breakout; of the "Onion King Caper," in which a
beautiful model shot her octogenarian husband, then
turned a shotgun on herself because Armes wouldn't
spend the night with her — all incredible adventures of
a supersleuth, adventures made more incredible by
the fact that both of Jay Armes' hands had been
blown off in a childhood dynamite accident.

He raised one of his gleaming steel hooks, signaling
the waitress, still watching the faces around the table.
Too much, they said in admiration. How did he do
it? "I read the book," Armes replied enigmatically,
"and I saw the play." That was one of his best lines.

At another table strategically positioned between
his boss and the front door sat Jay Armes' chauffeur-
bodyguard, Fred Marshall, a large, taciturn man who

used to sell potato chips. You could not detect the .38 under the coat of his navy-blue uniform. When they traveled in the limousine, which was a sort of floating office, laboratory, and fortress, Fred kept what appeared to be a submachine gun near his right leg. Armes claimed there had been thirteen or fourteen — the number varied from interview to interview — attempts on his life, a figure that did not include the six or seven times he had been wounded in the line of duty. He lifted his pants leg and exhibited what appeared to be a small-caliber bullet wound through his calf.

Concealed on his left hip, under his immaculate, custom-tailored suit with epaulets and belted back, was a .38 Special; implanted in the base of the hook on his right arm was a .22 Magnum. What's more, he told CTV producer Heinz Avigdor, he held a third-degree black belt in karate — and that was the point of the ensuing argument.

"I want to show you what a black belt does, besides hold your *gi* [karate regalia] up," he smiled at the producer. "Look, I've been in a lot of films, I know what I'm talking about. Do it my way. I'll show you what it's all about."

Armes had called ahead and cleared the plan with the Miguel manager. It would be a scene right out of *The Investigator*, a proposed television series that, according to Armes, CBS would begin filming right here in El Paso, right here at the Miguel, in fact, on January 20. CBS planned a pilot film and twenty-three episodes, all of the stories adapted from Armes' personal files. Jay J. Armes, of course, would play the title role of Jay J. Armes.

This was the scenario Armes outlined for the CTV producer:

As soon as the Canadians had positioned their lights and camera, a telephone would ring. Armes would be paged. Fred would presumably go on eating his steak and chili. As Armes approached the lobby he would be confronted by a large Oriental who would grab him by the collar and say, "You've been pushing around the wrong people, Armes." Jay would project his thin smile, inform the Oriental that he was a man of peace, then flip the startled giant over his shoulder with a lightning-quick maneuver of his hooks. A second man would charge him with a pepper mill. Armes would deflect the blow with one of his steel hands, jump into the air, and paralyze the second assailant with a judo chop.

"Uh, Jay," producer Heinz Avigdor said feebly, "I think that is a bit dramatic for the purposes of our show. We're doing a documentary. I think perhaps a workout in your private exercise room, wearing your karate outfit, then some footage in your shooting range downstairs, and maybe a shot in your library. Something from real life, you see."

Jay Armes saw, all right: he saw that the producer was a fool.

"I'm offering you something from real life," he said, that edge of impatience returning to his voice.

"But, Jay, it's so . . . so staged," Avigdor argued. "*W-5* isn't that sort of show."

"It's real," Armes snapped, and the pitch of his voice was much higher. "What you're talking about isn't real. There's nothing real about working out in a gym, with a body bag, wearing a stupid *gi*. This way, I'll be in a suit and tie in a public place doing my work, exactly like real life."

Avigdor protested that his crew didn't have the manpower or equipment for the scene Jay was suggesting. Jay sighed, adjusted his hooks to the fork and knife. He changed the subject abruptly: he began telling the two magazine writers about his secret code, and about his dissolvable stationery that you could stir in a glass of water and drink.

But the affront hung in his mind, and he began to speak of the amateurish approach of the Canadians, about how when *60 Minutes* comes to El Paso in a few weeks to do the Jay Armes story the CTV crew would be eating tin cans. He estimated that the *60 Minutes* segment would be worth two million dollars in publicity and would probably get him elected sheriff in El Paso County, a post he covets not for personal gain but in the interest of justice. "When I decided to run for sheriff," he said, "I telephoned my producer at CBS and he said, 'Great, what can I do to help?'" The producer's name was Leonard Freeman, and what he agreed to do, Armes continued, was send the *60 Minutes* people to El Paso. The show would appear in January, a week before the election.

"Look," Armes told Avigdor, "I've tried to be patient with you guys. I wore the same suit two days in a row—I won't even look at this suit for at least a year now. I invited you into my home. I took time out from my work. I showed you around. I called my producer at CBS a little while ago, and frankly, he advised me to blow you off."

Armes was smiling, but it wasn't his dark, boyish face and licorice-drop eyes that captured attention. It was those powerful, gleaming steel hooks. Each hook could apply thirty-eight pounds of pressure per square inch, three times that of a normal hand. They were sensitive and deadly, these hooks, and he used them the way a surgeon uses his hands, picking rather than hacking, demonstrating, extracting, mesmerizing, proving precisely what it means for a man to turn a liability into an asset. Somewhere in those gestures was the message: I'll bet you couldn't do this. And yet what you saw was not an amazingly skilled man who could shoot and play tennis and paint and do pushups; what you saw was the dark bore of a .22 Magnum inches from your forehead. It was rimmed with black powder and projected an even more deadly threat than the threat of the hooks — the threat of sub-conscious impulse, unchecked by distance or time — for the trigger mechanism of this weapon was connected by tiny wires to Armes' right biceps. The operation cost fifty thousand dollars, Armes added, and was performed by a New York surgeon named Bechtol. Don't worry, he said, it has a fail-safe: it can't go off by accident.

"It can only be fired by my brain," Armes had told us. "It's like . . . let me put this right . . . like opening your mouth. Your brain can tell you to open your mouth, but it doesn't just fly open by itself."

That was the same day that Armes asked Avigdor and his two technicians why it was that "Canadians condone concubines." Armes said he had known many cases, especially among French Canadians, in which prominent men "kept concubines [*sic*] of fifteen and even twenty women."

I don't know if Armes noticed, but Heinz Avigdor's mouth dropped wide enough to accommodate a jackrabbit.

The first thing you see when you enter Jay Armes' office at 1717 Montana in El Paso is a mural on the wall at the end of the hallway. The mural depicts a man in a trench coat and hat, cradling the world in one arm. Painted on the face of the globe are all the cities where Jay Armes operates branch offices. On closer inspection, the man in the trench coat turns out to be Jay Armes. It is a self-portrait.

There are other Jay Armes paintings throughout the office, and throughout his home, mostly of long, graceful tigers springing at some prey off canvas.

The office has a jungle motif. The rooms are dimly lit in eerie reds and greens. "Psychological lighting,"

Armes says. Armes says he employs more than two thousand full-time agents—six hundred right here in El Paso—but the only employees visible are a secretary who sits in the front office and the faithful bodyguard Fred, who lurks nearby.

Armes escorts the visitors to his crime lab. On a long table under the weird green light, laid out like organs in an autopsy, is a curious assortment of detective gimmicks—the latest Touch-Tone portable telephone, its range worldwide; a debugger that Armes values at ten thousand dollars; a Dick Tracy–like wristwatch recorder; a tranquilizer gun that shoots sleeping gas; many small bugging devices; and two microscopes. Armes says he can do a complete laboratory breakdown here. In addition to his mastery of chemistry, Armes says he has degrees in psychology and criminology from New York University, as well as the ability to speak seven languages, including thirty-three dialects of Chinese.

Photographs on the wall and in the fat scrapbook show Armes in diving equipment, or playing with his lions and tigers, or firing on his pistol range. There is a photograph of his son, Jay Armes III, riding a pet lion. Jay III used to have a pet elephant, but a neighbor shot it with a crossbow. In a rear room with a coffee pot and copying machine, Armes points out several bullet holes in the window and door, the marks of that night when an assassin sprayed the building with a .45-caliber grease-gun.

Armes leads the visitors to his private office and sits at his desk, his back to seventy-one volumes of *Corpus Juris*. On the wall are the framed diplomas testifying that Jay J. Armes is a graduate of a number of detective academies and a member of a number of detective associations. One of the academies is the Central Bureau of Investigation in Hollywood. Curiously, there is no diploma from NYU. But Armes tells a story about how his old mentor, Professor Max Falen, discovered Armes was working his way through NYU as a dishwasher. "He blew his stack," Jay says. "He said I was shortchanging criminology." Falen arranged for his prize student to receive a paid student assistantship and moved him into his own home. As the years passed, poor Max Falen began hitting the bottle. NYU finally had to let him go. When Jay learned what fate had befallen his onetime friend and benefactor, he hired the professor and moved him to the Los Angeles bureau of the Investigators.

Although he graduated with honors at age nineteen, Jay Armes soon learned there were few openings for criminologists. That's when he decided to open his own detective agency.

"I wanted to clean up the image of the profession," he says. "In TV and the movies, private detectives are usually pictured as crooked ex-cops who keep a filing cabinet of booze and work both sides of the street." Jay pointed out that he did not smoke or drink (not even coffee), and was "deeply religious." Ten percent of everything he makes goes to the Immanuel Baptist Church in El Paso. A secretary at the church later confirmed that Armes "attends regularly and gives generously."

Although Armes is seen regularly at church, at the El Paso Club and the Empire Club, at the police station and the courthouse, and cruising the streets in his black limo, he remains a mystery man to most citizens of El Paso. Most of what they know about him comes from recent articles in magazines like *People*, *Newsweek*, and *Atlantic*, or from national TV talk shows.

According to *Newsweek*, Armes "keeps a loaded submachine gun in his $37,000 Rolls-Royce as protection against the next — and fourteenth — attempt on his life. He lives behind an electrified fence in a million-dollar mansion with a shooting range, a ninety-thousand-dollar gymnasium and a private menagerie, complete with leopards that prowl the grounds unchained at night. He is an expert on bugging, a skilled pilot, a deadly marksman and karate fighter and, perhaps, the best private eye in the country."

The article in *People* was similar, except for a couple of discrepancies. According to *People*, Armes earned his degrees in criminology and psychology from UCLA, not NYU. And it referred to him as "recently divorced."

"My wife went through the ceiling when she read that," Armes said. His wife, Linda Chew, is the daughter of a respected Chinese grocer. She is a handsome, soft-spoken woman who seems to accept her husband's chosen role with traditional stoicism. "When I leave home in the morning," Armes says, "she never knows if she will see me again."

Armes doesn't especially enjoy discussing his childhood in Ysleta. The Lower Valley, as it is called, was a mostly lower-class, predominantly Mexican American area of small farms and run-down businesses and ancient Indian teachings. It's now part of El Paso, but it was another town when Armes grew up. As Armes tells it, he was born August 12, 1939, to Jay, Sr., and Beatrice Armes. His parents were Italian and French. His father ran a grocery.

"I was a tough kid, like the sidewalk types of Chicago," he recalls. "I had to fight for what I thought was right. I was always at the head of the class, captain of the football team, a boxer, a basketball player, a star in track. Even after I lost my hands I still played all sports."

Armes remembers that he was about eleven when the accident happened. An older boy of about eighteen found some railroad torpedoes beside the track and brought them to Jay's house. The older boy stood back and told Jay to beat the torpedoes together. He did, and they blew his hands off just above the wrists. The accident hardly seemed to slow him down. He recalled holding down four jobs and running a loan-shark operation across the street from the school. "I'd loan a quarter and get back fifty cents," he said, and the memory seemed to please him. "If someone was slow in paying, I'd kick ass."

What he says happened next is straight out of the Lana Turner saga. Jay was drinking a milk shake in the Hilton Plaza drugstore when a Hollywood casting director named Frank Windsor strolled over and said: "Hey, kid, you're pretty good with those mitts." The casting director offered Jay a part in a movie called *Am I Handicapped?*, starring Dana Andrews.

Jay was barely fifteen — he recalled that he had just started taking flying lessons — when he quit school and moved to Hollywood. The next few years are vague in his recollection, but they apparently weren't dull. He graduated from Hollywood High, landed roles in thirteen feature-length movies, studied one year (1959) at UCLA, moved to New York, did three years (or, as he sometimes remembers, six) at NYU, and returned to El Paso, a triumphant nineteen-year-old determined to change the image of his new profession. Somewhere in there he also graduated from the Central Bureau of Investigation in Hollywood.

Why El Paso, the visitor wonders? With that background, why go home again?

Jay says, "I am deeply religious. It says in the Bible that you will not prosper in your hometown. How could a carpenter's son become king of the Jews? Jesus had to go to Nazareth to be recognized."

Was he then trying to outdo Jesus?

"I was trying to see if this was a fact," he says. "And it is. I am recognized now all over the world more than I am in my hometown."

While the crew from CTV is setting up outside on Montana Street, I take another look around. There is something too deliberate about the way those crime-fighting gimmicks are laid out on that table under the green light in the lab, like toys under a Christmas tree. The holes from the .45-caliber grease-gun would be more impressive if they had smashed the glass or shattered the thin layer of wood instead of leaving clean, neat punctures. I glance through the Jay J. Armes Training Academy correspondence course, which can be had for three hundred dollars. Sample question:

> Eighty per cent of people do not see accurately because:
>   (a) they have a stigmatism
>   (b) there is to much smog in the air
>   (c) because they do not pay attention
>   (d) because they usually just watch the ground.

I wonder if the Central Bureau of Investigation was like this. Then something else catches my eye — the mural at the end of the hallway, the self-portrait. I didn't notice before, but Jay Armes has given himself blue eyes. And that's not a hook holding the world, it's a hand.

Fred, the former potato-chip salesman, stands at attention, holding the rear door of the limo open for Jay Armes and his guests. There are a few rules you learn in Jay Armes' company: you do not smoke, you do not swear, and you do not open your own limousine door. A New York book editor who was in El Paso a few weeks earlier recalled the door ritual as his most vivid impression. Jay Armes always got out first, explaining, "I'm armed. I can protect my friends."

As the black limousine pulls silently into the traffic and winds past the refinery adjacent to IH 10, Armes reaches out with his hooks and activates the videotape camera buried in the trunk lid of the car. On the black-and-white screen we can see the CTV station wagon trailing us. Sometimes, Armes tell us, he uses the videotape gear to follow other people. "While they're looking in their rearview mirror," he says, "I'm right in front of them watching their every move."

The limo is also equipped with a police siren, a yelper, and a public address system, each of which he demonstrates. There is a frontseat telephone and a backseat telephone with a different number, revolving license plates, and Jay Armes' crest on each door. You might suppose all these trappings would make it difficult to remain inconspicuous, but Jay has his methods. "I read the book," he says, "and I saw the play." Sometimes he uses a panel truck with ACME PLUMBING on the side. Or the bronze Corvette with the INTERPOL sticker on the back. He even has a stand-in. Somewhere in El Paso there is another Jay J. Armes.

The limousine pulls off IH 10 and follows a narrow blacktop along rows of cheap houses, hot dog stands, and weed fields. This is not exactly your silk-stocking neighborhood.

Armes has been talking about his fifty-thousand-dollar fee for cracking a recent jewel robbery at the UN Plaza apartments in New York, and about a potential half-million-dollar fee that he turned down on the advice of his attorney. Working through his producer, Leonard Freeman, a national magazine that he is not at liberty to identify offered Armes that sum to locate Patty Hearst, which he boasted he could do in three weeks or less. "The FBI called and said, 'Hey, Jay, how can you find her in three weeks?' I said, 'cause I know my business." In return for its money, the magazine wanted Armes to guarantee an exclusive thirty-thousand-word interview with the mysterious heiress, and that's when Armes pulled out. "Even admitting to you now that I had her located," he said, "could subject me to criminal prosecution. But I'll tell you this much, that's a damn lie about her being in school in Sacramento. I'm writing a book for Macmillan, maybe I'll tell the true story. The FBI actually put a tail on my book publisher, thought maybe he'd lead them to Patty Hearst. I'll say one more thing. I'll bet you ten thousand dollars that Patty will never be convicted."

Outside the eighteen-foot electrified fence that runs along the 8100 block of North Loop, Fred activates a small electronic box above his head and the gates swing open. He parks the car in front of Jay J. Armes' curious little mansion with its tall columns and flanking white stone lions.

A Rolls, a Corvette, and several other cars are parked in the driveway between the house and the tennis court. Gypsy, Armes' pet chimpanzee, screeches from her cage until Armes walks over and swaps her a piece of sugarless gum for a kiss. A pack of dogs hangs back, menacingly.

While the crew from CTV is hauling its equipment upstairs to the library, Armes conducts a tour of the Nairobi Village in the backyard. Armes stiffens when visitors refer to this as a "zoo," and with good reason: this place is right out of a Tarzan movie, except that most of the animals are caged. There are thatched huts, exotic plants, narrow trails through high walls of bamboo, and a lighted artificial waterfall beside a man-made lake. Though the lake is not much larger than a hockey rink, there is what appears to be a high-powered speedboat anchored against the far bank. And on the bank nearest to the house, inside a corral of zebras and small horses, sits a twin-blade helicopter. This is the chopper, Armes reveals, that he uses most often. He can have it fueled and airborne in less than half an hour. He also says he owns a jet helicopter (it's presently in Houston), a Riley turbojet, and a Hughes 500.

In the heart of the jungle, a telephone rings. Armes opens a box on the side of a palm tree and talks to someone. Then the tour resumes.

"When I was a kid," Armes says, "I couldn't even afford a good cat. I decided that when I got older and could afford it, I'd buy every animal I could find." So far he has found twenty-two different species, including a pair of black panthers from India, some miniature Tibetan horses that shrink with each generation, some ostriches, a West Texas puma, and a four-hundred-pound Siberian tiger that roams the grounds at night, discouraging drop-in visitors. Many of his prize animals, he tells the visitors, are currently grazing on his twenty-thousand-acre Three Rivers Ranch in New Mexico.

Armes opens the tiger cage and invites his guests inside. They politely decline. He smiles, having already detected the presence of fear from the movements of the tiger. The tiger seems suddenly irritable. Armes talks to the tiger and strokes its head. The tiger rears back and Armes controls it with a skilled movement of his steel wrists.

Entering Jay Armes' mansion is yet another trip beyond the fringe: it is something like entering the living room of an eccentric aunt who just returned from the world's fair. There is a feeling of incongruity, of massive accumulations of things that don't fit, passages that lead nowhere, bells that don't ring.

We wait in what I guess you would call the bar. The decor might be described as Neo-Earth in Upheaval. It is as though alien species had by some unexplained cataclysm been transposed to a common ground. Dark green water trickles from rocks and runs sluggishly along a concrete duct that divides the room. There are concrete palm trees, artificial flowers, and stuffed animals and birds. Two Japanese bridges span the duct, and the walls sag with fishnets, bright bulbs, African masks, and paintings of tigers. There is a piano in one corner, but Jay Armes does not volunteer to demonstrate that skill just now. Although neither Armes nor his wife, Linda, drinks, the bar is well stocked with Jack Daniel's, Chivas Regal, Beefeater, and two varieties of beer on tap.

In an adjacent room, what appears to be a living coconut palm floats in a tub in the indoor swimming pool. Though the pool is small, it takes up most of the room. In one corner of the room, hidden behind a thatched bar, is a washer and dryer and a neat stack of freshly laundered children's clothes.

The room behind the swimming pool is Jay's exercise room. Steps lead down to his computerized target range in the basement. After his customary two and a half hours of sleep, Jay wakes around 4 A.M., dictates into his recorder, exercises with his karate instructor, practices on his target range, has a sauna and a shower, selects one of the suits with the epaulets from a closet that he estimates contains about seven hundred suits valued at five hundred dollars a pop, has a high-protein breakfast, and calls for Fred to bring the limousine around.

"Almost every day of my life," he says, "there is some violent or potentially violent incident. I have to stay in tip-top shape." His single vice is work. "The Lord has given us a brain," he says. "We only use one tenth of ten percent of it. The rest is dormant. That's because we are lazy. I try to use as much of my brain as I can." Armes claims that he personally worked on two hundred cases last year, and that doesn't count the thousands of cases in the hands of his more than two thousand agents.

Like the other rooms, there is a disturbing incongruity to the exercise room. It's too neat, too formal.

The equipment is the kind you would find at a reducing salon for middle-aged women. It's mostly the easy stuff that works for you.

Upstairs above the exercise room is the Armes' master bedroom. Scarlet O'Hara would have loved it. Flaming red carpet, flaming red fur spread, a lot of mirrors, and the ever-present eye of the security scanner. From the video screen beside his circular bed, Jay Armes can watch any point in or outside the house.

Armes is pacing like a cat: the CTV crew is still not ready in the library. He leads the two magazine writers downstairs again, to his shooting range, where he demonstrates both the .38 and the .22 Magnum.

"Yes," he says, "I have killed people. I don't want to talk about it. It's sad . . . no one has a monopoly on life. But it's like war. Sometimes you must take a life in the line of duty. I'm guarding some diamonds, say, my job is to protect my client's property. If someone gets in the way, maybe I'll have to kill him. But I don't like to talk about it."

Then he tells of a caper in which he rescued a fifteen-year-old girl runaway from an apartment somewhere in New Mexico. He kicked open the door and a hippie with a .32 shot him three times. The third bullet struck less than an inch from his heart. There was no time for the .38. Armes raised his right arm and killed the hippie with a single .22 slug square between the eyes. "Remind me to show you a picture of it when we get back to the office," he says. Bleeding like hell, Armes drove the runaway girl back to her parents' house in El Paso. Only then did he drive himself to the hospital.

"It's funny," he says, "but when I get shot, I seem to get super strength. I know the Lord is looking after me."

When the TV camera is finally in place, Armes goes

up to the library and stands in front of a painting of a tiger, which is actually a secret door to the children's room. On cue from Heinz Avigdor, Jay Armes shows off his gun collection and tells a little story about each weapon. I had examined all this hardware earlier, so I excused myself and walked down to the bar, where I telephoned a friend.

Through the fishnet and the porthole window I could get a closer look at Jay Armes' helicopter. From appearances, it hadn't been off the ground in years: its tires were deflated and hub-deep in hard ground, the blades were caked with dirt and grease, and the windows were covered with tape instead of glass. Armes had told us that the chopper had a brand-new engine. I wondered why he hadn't put glass in the windows.

I walked back upstairs and told Armes that I had to get back to town. I made up a lie about having dinner with my old college roommate.

"Say hello to Joe Shepard," Armes said with a thin smile.

"Is Jay J. Armes for real?" I asked Joe Shepard as we devoured the *grub du jour* of his favorite Juarez hangout.

"No way in hell," Joe said. At least that was his hunch. Like almost everyone else in El Paso, Shepsy (as he calls himself) knew Jay J. Armes only by reputation. He was that mystery man in the black limo. You'd see that big sinister Cadillac glide up in front of the police station or the courthouse, Fred would pop out, look around, open the door, and Jay Armes would hustle up the steps, his head low and his hooks locked contemplatively behind his back. They had all read about Armes and seen him on TV talk shows. He lived behind that eighteen-foot electric fence way out on North Loop, in a poor section of town, in that white mansion with the never-never-land facade, next to the parked helicopter, next to the miniature lake. They had heard that wild animals roamed the estate.

Shepsy had heard, too, about the repeated attempts on Armes' life and had concluded: "El Paso must have the worst assassins in America. If I wanted to shoot Jay Armes I'd sit across the street from the courthouse for an hour or two."

Shepsy is a licensed private investigator. He showed me his card. License number A-01123-9. True, he didn't know Jay J. Armes, but he knew enough to dislike him.

"I don't want to sound like sour grapes," Shepsy said, ordering another round of tequila and beer, "but it's not that difficult to run a magic lantern show in this business. The more sophisticated a client is, the easier it is to take them. They seem to feel an obligation to understand what you're doing. The wife of Dr. —— [he named an El Paso surgeon] hired me to shadow him—I could have worked her for fifty thousand bucks, that's how sophisticated she wanted to be. But I didn't. I checked the doctor—there was nothing to it, so I dropped it.

"A good investigator will find out what a client wants to hear. After that, it's no problem to write a report. The hell of it is, there are a lot of poor people getting ripped off too. You have no idea how many poor husbands or wives will take everything out of their savings and hire a private investigator. They feel trapped, they *don't* know what's going on in their lives. . . . I guess they believe it's like it is on television."

Shepsy is forty-three, the same age as Jay J. Armes, although Armes claims to be thirty-six. Shepsy has been frequently married, and his life is constantly in danger from his current wife, Jackie, a high-spirited, free-lance nurse anesthetist who supports his unorthodox lifestyle and sometimes heaps his clothes on

the back porch and burns them. Shepsy drives a red
VW and has never owned a gun in his life.

"If I carried a gun," he said, "sooner or later someone would take it away and shoot me. If someone is
going to shoot ol' Shepsy he's damn sure gonna have
to bring his own gun."

None of Shepsy's wives, including the pretty in-
cumbent, Jackie, could get it through their heads
that he was really spending all those lonely nights
perched in a tree watching bedroom windows through
binoculars.

They had been married about four months when
Jackie hired Jay J. Armes to check out Shepsy's story
that he was flying to Albuquerque on business. She
paid Armes three hundred dollars—she's still got the
check to prove it—and he reported back by telephone. The entire substance of his report was that one
of his "operatives" followed Shepsy and, sure enough,
Shepsy had driven to the airport. He made a couple
of "mysterious phone calls," then boarded the flight
for Albuquerque, exactly as he said. Case closed. Fee
paid.

"Nobody followed me," Shepsy said. "Not in a New
York minute. I wasn't anywhere close to the airport
that night. I *drove* to Albuquerque with my clients."

Shepsy had heard all about those fantastic fees that
Jay Armes commanded, but he was skeptical. Nobody in the business charges like that—not $500,000,
not $100,000, not even $10,000. Shepsy works for $15
an hour, or $150 a day, plus expenses. One of his
larger cases popped up just that morning when a
distraught father paid him $500 to prove that his
daughter was dating a homosexual, which in fact she
was. What a price to pay for truth.

But this was a border town; the rules were a little
different. Nothing was what it seemed. So was everything. For fifty dollars you could have someone

killed. Any Juarez cab driver could arrange it. Investigators knew the rules of operating in Mexico — speak the language and have the money. They all heard about the twenty-five grand Jay Armes got for rescuing Marlon Brando's son. They believed it. They didn't believe the part about the three-day helicopter search in which Jay Armes survived on water, chewing gum, and guts, but they all knew the trick of grabbing a kid. You hired a couple of *federales* or gunsels. The problem wasn't finding the kid; it was getting him out of the country.

I told Joe Shepard what Armes had said as I was leaving. He'd said: "Say hello to Joe Shepard." I don't know how he knew I was meeting Joe Shepard.

The next night I had dinner with Joe and Jackie and some of their friends, and the entire conversation was Jay J. Armes. It turned out that Jackie had gone to Ysleta High School with Linda Chew, Armes' wife. Jackie recalled that Linda was shy and obedient, a hard worker. Jackie's friend, Guillermina Reyes, hired Armes a few months ago to substantiate her contention that the business manager of Newark Hospital was embezzling funds. Mina had been fired from her receptionist job by the business manager, but the hospital board had agreed to hear her story and she needed some hard evidence.

"This was last August," Mina told me. "I hadn't heard of Jay J. Armes at the time — I picked him out of the phone book. I went to his office and told him my problem and he said he would look into it for fifteen hundred dollars. That shook me up. Then he said, 'How about seven hundred dollars?' I apologized and said he was way out of my range, so he said, 'How much have you got?' "

Mina finally paid Armes $150, and several weeks later Armes told her, "I checked it out. This guy is clean." That was the entire report. A few weeks later

Mina and everyone else began hearing just how clean Ramirez was—the Newark business manager was arrested, charged with embezzling funds in the amount of some $21,000, and placed under $500,000 bond. Whatever the truth, Jay J. Armes hadn't exactly resembled the world's, or even El Paso's, greatest detective.

Brunson Moore, a lawyer and former El Paso JP, recalled a time when Armes had performed spectacularly in a domestic case involving a husband who thought his young wife was playing around. She was playing around all right—Armes gained entry into her apartment and produced some amazing movies. The wife's co-star turned out to be the pastor of one of El Paso's larger churches. The films were not admissible evidence, of course, but the pastor soon moved out of town.

Clarence Moyers, an attorney, had a Jay J. Armes story too. This was a couple of years ago, when Moyers was getting a divorce. Jay Armes telephoned, very familiar, very friendly, saying, "Clarence, ol' buddy, I've been out of town and a terrible thing happened to you while I was gone."

"I had never spoken to Jay Armes," Moyers said, "but suddenly he's laying it on me how his agents didn't realize what great buddies we were, so they accepted an assignment from my ex-wife to do an investigation on me. Armes said he had a stack of pictures a foot deep. He said he was sitting there right then looking at one of me in a daisy chain. I asked him what a daisy chain was, and he told me. Well, I hadn't been in a daisy chain recently, but I was still worried. Then he got to the point: he said my ex-wife had paid his agents three hundred dollars cash, so if I'd put up another three hundred dollars he'd give me the pictures and return my ex-wife's money."

Moyers instructed Jay Armes what to do with his

157

pictures and hung up. When he confronted his ex-wife later, she denied ever hiring Armes or one of Armes' agents.

There was a paradox here. Jay J. Armes' stories didn't check, yet the man was absolutely larger than life. He didn't support his flamboyant lifestyle by misleading poor receptionists or working both sides in domestic cases. The riddle of Jay Armes hung in some dark passageway; tracing it back was like looking in old encyclopedias for new discoveries. The city directory, for example, first took note of Jay J. Armes in 1957, when he should have been in California. Armes operated the Central Bureau of Investigation, named no doubt for the detective course he took in Hollywood. His office was in the Caples Building, an old seven-story warren of bail bondsmen, quicky finance companies, and ambulance chasers. The Investigators first appeared in 1963.

Joe Shepard nudged me with his elbow and motioned to follow him outside. We walked to a remote corner of the parking lot, and stood on a high ledge overlooking the lights of El Paso. Shepsy waited while a small aircraft passed overhead.

Then he said in a low voice, "The reason you're having trouble tracing Jay Armes is that's not his real name. He's really Julian Armas."

He pronounced it "Hool-*yon* Are-*mas.*"

Julian Armas was born August 12, 1932. His father was Pedro, not Jay, Sr., and his mother was Beatriz. Pedro didn't own a grocery store as had been claimed, but he worked in one. He was a butcher at the P&N Grocery in Ysleta. "He worked hard and drank his beer," recalled Eddy Powell, who used to own the store. Like Professor Max Falen, Pedro had a drinking problem.

Pedro and Beatriz Armas and their five children

were Mexican Americans. Not Italians. Not French. Julian, a friend recalled, didn't speak English until he started to school.

Records in the El Paso County Courthouse show that Julian was nearly fourteen when he jabbed the railroad torpedoes with an ice pick and blew off both of his hands. A negligence suit filed against the Texas & Pacific Railroad on December 6, 1948, claimed seventy-five percent disability and asked for $103,000 in damages, based on Julian's estimated total income for the next forty-six years. The case was dismissed. The way Armes, or Armas, tells it, he was awarded an eighty-thousand-dollar settlement, which he gave to his family. A lawyer connected with the case says Armas collected nothing.

"The boys didn't find the torpedoes beside the track," the lawyer said. "They broke into a section house. There was no evidence of negligence on the part of the railroad."

Margaret Caples Abraham recalled the day of the accident. It happened in the chicken yard behind her house. She was about seven at the time. It was her brother, Dickie Caples, who was with Julian. When Margaret and her family returned from a Saturday afternoon shopping trip, the boys were gone and the chickens were pecking on bits of flesh and small fingers. Dickie wasn't injured, but the trauma of that day still haunts him. Curiously, the Capleses own the Caples Building, where Jay J. Armes first started his detective business.

Van Turner helped Julian get fitted with his hooks. Van and Julian attended the same Catholic church and were members of Boy Scout Troop 95. They also shared a paper route. Julian operated a motor scooter specially customed with two bolts instead of handle grips, and Van rode on the back.

"I never made any money from the paper route,"

Van Turner recalled. "I never knew what Jay did with the money. I felt sorry for him."

Van Turner remembered that the other kids helped Julian with his homework. After two years of high school, Julian split for California. "When he came home seven or eight years later," Turner said, "he had changed. He was always sort of a bully, but now he was very obnoxious."

"He came back with a different attitude," said Rudy Resendez, who also delivered newspapers with Julian Armas. Resendez is now principal of an elementary school in Ysleta. "It was like he had to prove himself. He was a strange person. Nobody could get close to him. He gave the impression that he was better than anyone else."

Old friends recalled well when he returned from California. Julian, or Jay J. Armes as he now called himself, drove an old, raggedy-topped Cadillac with a live lion in the back and a dummy telephone mounted to the dashboard. He would pull up beside the girls at the drive-in and pretend to be talking to some secret agent in some foreign land.

"He told stories about all the war movies he'd been in," recalled a doctor who asked that his name not be used. "He also told the story that he had lost his hands in the war. He had his hair cut very short. He wore a hat and sharp clothes. Yes, people in Ysleta were impressed at first.

"He had another wife back then. I don't remember her name, but I remember treating one of their daughters in the emergency room about 1962. Julian [the doctor used the Spanish pronunciation, "Hool-*yon*"] said, 'Don't cry, honey, we'll watch our TV in the car on the way home.' He wanted everyone in the emergency room to understand that he had a television in his car."

The doctor, a onetime Golden Gloves champion

and a Korean War veteran, was a few years older than Julian Armas, but he recalled that "he was very active, real smart, he had his finger in every pie. No, he never played football at Ysleta, but he was a pretty good touch football player, even without his hands. He had a competitive drive even before he lost his hands.

"There are many people in Ysleta who think of him as a phony, and by most standards perhaps he is, but I don't think so, because I understand the motive behind his behavior. I have respect for Julian. For most people, losing both hands would be the end of the show; for him, it was the beginning.

"The other things, the name change and claiming to be Italian, that's compensation . . . not only for his physical handicap, which is really an asset to him now, but for the psychological stigma of being a member of the much-persecuted and -chastised Mexican American minority in Texas, which can be a problem even to the most intellectual of minds.

When you get down to it, the doctor said, Jay J. Armes isn't all that different from Julian Armas. He was always a braggart. He always demanded center stage. He always had a need to achieve, and a need to exaggerate his accomplishments. If he sold fifty newspapers, he would claim that the figure was two hundred. Even now, when he apparently has the wealth to live anywhere in the world, he built a fortress for himself located less than a mile from his place of origin. Why not one of the silk-stocking areas, you ask. Why not Coronado Hills, a section of El Paso that he openly admired?

The doctor's laugh was not sympathetic. He had a patient in the next room who manifested some of the same problems. This person had commissioned a sort of wood-carved Mount Rushmore in which his face appeared alongside Zapata, Villa, and Cortés. "The sine qua non," the doctor said, "is a departure from reality.

"Julian lives here in the Lower Valley because these are the people he needs to impress. In a better part of town the rich gringos would just look on him as another crazy Mexican."

The Catholic church that Turner, Resendez, Julian Armas, and almost everyone else in Ysleta attended still stands, as it has since 1682. It was the first mission in Texas. From the Tigua Indian museum across the church grounds visitors can still hear recordings of the ancient ceremonial chants. Long before Europeans had crossed the Atlantic, the ancestry of these people—Julian Armas' forefathers—had perfected a civilization that the flock at the Immanuel Baptist Church might not yet comprehend. This was the heritage that Jay J. Armes denied.

Almost everyone I spoke with in Ysleta who was anywhere near Jay J. Armes' age knew the story of Julian Armas. "He wasn't tough," a drunk Indian named Rachie told me, "but he was mean." Rachie recalled Julian's first job as a security officer—it was throwing Rachie and his friends out of the movie house where Julian worked. Rachie remembered how delightful it had been, shooting Julian in the head with chinaberries. Van Turner remembered that the high school PE teacher made Julian take off his hooks when they played touch football. All of the old friends remembered that Julian liked to pinch the girls with his hooks. Or heat them red-hot in the popcorn machine at the movie house. One of his pleasures was heating up a fifty-cent piece and throwing it to a younger kid. The doctor, Margie Luna, and several other eyewitnesses recounted the time he heated his hooks in the popcorn machine and grabbed Rosalie Stoltz by the arm. You can still see the burn scar thirty years later.

A few years ago when Jay J. Armes ran for justice of the peace, he failed to carry his home district of Ysleta. The prediction is he won't do much better running against Sheriff Mike Sullivan, who is also from Ysleta.

Mike Sullivan is half Irish and mostly Mexican. The people who know him think he's a pretty good man. Until very recently Jay Armes professed to think the same thing.

Sullivan made his department's criminal investigation division available to Armes and helped Armes get appointed deputy constable last August, which is the reason Armes is permitted to wear a gun and maintain a siren and a yelper on his limousine. Armes also claims to be one of three authorized Interpol agents working in the United States, but Sullivan has no knowledge of this.

Cynical talk has it that they are still friends, that Armes has volunteered his services as a stalking-horse to ward off other potential candidates. Armes did this once before, in the JP race some years ago.

Whatever the motive, Armes sounds like a serious candidate. Lately, he has been speaking to labor and women's organizations, telling how he could find Jimmy Hoffa in a few days if the price were right, and spreading bad tales about his old mentor, Mike Sullivan. He called Sullivan a "figurehead" who allows prisoners to walk in and out of jail as though it were a resort motel; who permits his deputies to beat picketers at the Farah blue jeans factory; who hires ex-cons and homosexuals; who gives his inmates amphetamines, which are "the same thing as tranquilizers, and also known as Darvon." But the most serious charge *is* serious, even by border-town standards. Armes accuses Sullivan of framing and even assassinating his enemies and credits several recent attempts on his own life to the sheriff.

At the El Paso Club one afternoon when Armes was avoiding the crew from CTV, he struck up a conversation with a banker and an architect who were talking business at the next table. The El Paso Club is one of those phony-formal, itchy, squirmy private clubs frequented by movers and shakers, a place where you're embarrassed to cough unless someone winks first. So it was that everyone in the room (except Fred, who was having lobster salad at the next table) looked up when Jay Armes began to speak of Mike Sullivan as "the first dictator in the United States, except J. Edgar Hoover." He told the banker and the architect that Mike Sullivan was arranging small cells for his enemies, and when the cells got too small, he was arranging for them to be killed.

The banker puffed on his cigar and said, "I had no idea that situation existed." Then, as though the question naturally followed, he asked, "How's the TV series coming?"

Armes told them how his producer, Leonard Freeman, had leaned on *60 Minutes* to help him get elected.

"How is the media treating you?" the architect asked.

"I'm more worried about the press than anyone else," the banker said. "If they can do it to the President, they can do it to anyone."

"Don't be surprised if a bomb goes off and blows me up," Armes said. Then he shrugged with his hooks, smiled, and said, "But that's life."

On the street outside the El Paso Club, Armes stopped to campaign with three gnarled loafers eating pecans on the curb. They didn't seem very interested. "I don't vote," an old man in a World War I campaign hat said. "I'm eighty-one. To hell with it." Armes shook his head and walked toward his waiting limo.

"Can you imagine what this country would be like if everyone had that attitude," he said sadly.

Mike Sullivan refused to talk about his differences with Armes, except to say, "I knew the kid since he used to deliver my paper in Ysleta. I liked the kid. I helped him in many ways. Then something happened and he turned against me." What happened was a disagreement over just how Jay Armes could use the El Paso sheriff's facilities. In the beginning, Sullivan had authorized his criminal investigation division to cooperate with Armes, and together they had solved some cases. Armes got the money, Sullivan pointed out, and most of the credit. From Armes' standpoint, the biggest case involved the theft of some men's slacks stored in the Lee Way trucking terminal. "We broke the case," Sullivan said, "but the kid took credit, and Lee Way was pleased. They hired him to check out a terminal in Oklahoma City where some TVs and stereos had been ripped off. I told him to go up there and work the same way he did here—work with the sheriff. Sure 'nuff, the goods were recovered. That led to even a bigger contract. He made better than a hundred grand off of that."

Then Armes became dissatisfied with Sullivan's criminal investigation division and started demanding the use of the patrol division as well. Getting Marlon Brando's son back from Mexico had been a good lesson. So had his authority as a deputy constable to serve subpoenas. Joe Shepard estimated that the right to serve subpoenas was worth at least ten thousand dollars a year to a private investigator.

"He wanted our patrol cars for cover," said Captain S. J. Palos, one of Mike Sullivan's officers. "It was the same trick he pulled when he recovered Marlon Brando's kid. Brando's attorney already knew where the kid was. Jay Armes crossed the river, hired a couple of gunsels and got him out of Mexico. There was a similar child custody case here in El Paso. He got one of our marked patrol cars to park outside the residence. After that, all he had to do was knock on the door and say, 'I'm here for the kid. My backup is parked just outside.' The rest is automatic."

Captain Palos, a retired Army colonel, said, "Jay is not a scholar of evidence. We've had to reject several of his cases because the evidence just wasn't there. It appears to me that he lives in a type of fantasy world. He reads an adventure story, and a week later he tries to relive it."

"I liked the kid," Mike Sullivan repeated. "He came back from L.A. in an old Cadillac convertible with a dummy telephone, all fired up to be a private detective. I told him then, 'You do that work just like you do anything else: you take care of business, you do it by the book.' I said, 'You'll be living off human suffering, you had better stay on a straight line.' "

I asked Sheriff Sullivan about the submachine gun that Fred the bodyguard carries. Sullivan told me it was an M-1, hammed up to look like a submachine gun. A hype. Just like the helicopter at the side of the house. The same prop rusted years ago in front of Kessler Industries until Armes acquired it and had it shipped to his place.

Captain Palos had an explanation for Jay Armes' boast that he employs more than two thousand agents around the world, six hundred of them in the El Paso office. There is an association of private detectives with about that number of members. They can all claim each other. "There are about four hundred thousand police officers in the United States," Palos said. "Sheriff Sullivan, as a member of the National Sheriffs Association, could claim all of them as agents. I seriously doubt if Jay's got two agents in El Paso, let alone six hundred. I have never seen them as long as I've been here. Put a pencil to it and figure up how much six hundred full-time agents would cost a year."

I did, using the mythical poverty line as a pay base, but the figure was so ridiculous I threw it away.

If this were a real detective story it would now be time to confront the suspect, and with him the reader. It would be the place to pull in all the facts and discard all the red herrings and wrap the whole package with a red bow. But there won't be any neat red bows, because the true story of Jay J. Armes lies buried beneath the rubble of twisted stories, mistaken dates, and transposed facts: we may never know the true story, but it has little in common with what *Newsweek* and *People* and other periodicals printed, or with the B-grade plots and grand mystique that Armes projects for himself. The real story is of a Mexican American kid from one of the most impoverished settlements in the United States, how he extracted himself from the wreckage of a crippling childhood accident and through the exercise of tenacity, courage, and wits became a moderately successful private investigator. There is more sympathy, drama, and human intrigue in that accomplishment than you're likely to find in any two or three normal studies of the human condition.

Who really understands the agony of Julian Armas? He wanted much more: he wanted the hands and blue eyes of his self-portrait, he wanted to be in the movies, he wanted his life to be *like* the movies. Maybe he didn't see the right movies. Maybe they didn't show them in Ysleta, or maybe he wasn't paying enough attention to see that the audience eventually woke to reality. What makes the story of Jay J. Armes, AKA Julian Armas, so difficult to tell is precisely the Hollywood mentality in which nothing is what it seems, in which everything is an illusion.

There is no recourse then but to pare away the mis-statements and exaggerations and attempt to fill in the blanks, but first I want to point out that I did not go to El Paso for the purpose of exposing Jay J. Armes. I had never heard of him until two days before I arrived, a bewildered guest, at his home. I hadn't read any of the magazine articles or seen him on any of the TV talk shows or even heard the mention of his name, although I soon discovered that half the kids in El Paso and even Austin knew him as that dude in the hooks who can do karate. The reader has discovered Armes the way I discovered him, and if the first part of this story overwhelms you, imagine what it did to me.

As the reader may have guessed, they never heard of Armes/Armas at UCLA. They never heard of Armes/Armas *or* Professor Max Falen at NYU. If this classic father figure, this teacher who first recognized his student's talents and took him into his own home, really is employed "as a sort of visiting fireman" in Armes' Los Angeles office, then he too has a serious handicap. Neither Falen nor the office is listed. Neither Falen nor Armes has a California detective's license.

The Federal Aeronautics Administration never issued a pilot's license to Armes or Armas. The Academy of Motion Pictures has no record of a film entitled *Am I Handicapped?*, starring Dana Andrews or anybody else. Old friends speculate that Armes may have made some technical films illustrating expert command of hooks, but no one knows for sure. He did appear in one episode of *Hawaii Five-O* as a heavy named Hookman, but some people who know Armes and have heard the sound track believe the voice is dubbed. Armes claims the Library of Congress selected that episode as the "best show ever on TV," an award the library has never made nor has any intention of making.

CBS isn't filming *The Investigator*, as the El Paso *Herald-Post* reported on November 29, 1976. That film crew that everyone supposed to be from CBS was a crew from Chicago doing commercial work for a toy company. A spokesman at CBS acknowledged that the series was a hot project of producer Leonard Freeman. But Freeman, the man Armes was repeatedly calling while I was there, died almost two years ago. The dog-eared script on Armes' desk is owned by Lorimar Productions, but it is not an active project. It is one of hundreds of scripts mildewing in Hollywood.

There is a staff memo making the rounds at *60 Minutes* suggesting a story on Jay J. Armes, but no decision has been made. Whatever the decision, it won't help Armes to any election victory in January. The Democratic primary isn't until May, of course, and the general election is in November, as always. The wonder of it all is that apparently Armes himself is so wrapped up in his own myth that he doesn't realize what damage an investigative TV show like *60 Minutes* could do to him.

There was, to be sure, a dramatic Mexican jailbreak using a helicopter, which inspired the Charles Bronson movie *Breakout*. The only authoritative account of it, *The 10-Second Jailbreak*, does not mention Jay J. Armes. Armes takes credit for this oversight: he claims that the pilot who got the publicity was a soldier of fortune from Jamaica whom Armes hired to take the heat off himself. Otherwise, Armes says he would be arrested the next time he put a foot over the border and be forced to serve out the remaining years of the sentence. Who knows?

Law officers in El Paso believe that Armes did bring Marlon Brando's kid out of Mexico, though they believe the circumstances were considerably less

picked up a purchase option a few years ago.

It is true that Jay J. Armes drives around El Paso in the damnedest black limo you ever saw, armed to the teeth. That pistol in his hook is the real McCoy; I watched him fire it. So is the loaded .38 on his left hip. Fred's "submachine gun" might technically qualify as a submachine gun: anyone with a knowledge of weapons can rig an M-1 with a paper clip and make it fully automatic.

Of all those incredible tales, at least two are fairly accurate, and they probably say more about our junk-commodity society, counterfeit-hero mentality, and burned-out consciences than all the fantasies and delusions of a poor boy from the Lower Valley.

The Ideal Toy Corporation is marketing a series of Jay J. Armes toys, designed along the line of the highly successful Evel Knievel series. "It's what we call our hero action figure," Herbert Sands, vice president of corporate marketing, told me. "Batman and Robin, Superman, that sort of hero, but like Evel Knievel, Jay Armes is a real live super hero doing what he really does." There will be Jay J. Armes dolls with little hooks for hands, Jay Armes T-shirts, a Jay Armes junior detective game. That film crew that the El Paso *Herald-Post* reported was shooting "The Midget Caper" with Armes and Mike *(Mannix)* Connors in November was in fact doing a trade film for Ideal toys.

And Macmillan Publishing Company of New York does have a contract for the Jay J. Armes story. I talked to Fred Honig, executive editor of the general books division, who got the idea for the book after reading the article in *Newsweek*. Honig immediately flew to El Paso and arranged the deal. He wouldn't confirm the price, but the contract I saw in El Paso revealed that Jay Armes would receive about a fifteen-thousand-dollar advance, and an extra-large

dramatic than the tale Armes spins. I saw a photograph of Armes and Brando, both exercising large
smiles, but I also saw a photograph of Armes and
Miss Universe. I couldn't reach Brando for his version. The UN Plaza jewelry caper, which came after
Armes' recent spate of publicity, appears genuine, but
there is no way to check the other claims—the Interpol connection, the third-degree black belt in karate,
the glider caper in Castro Cuba, or the friendship
with Howard Hughes; for that matter, Armes could
have easily said he was a CIA agent or a UFO carrot
farmer.

As for the obvious question, where does Armes get
all that money if he's not a big-time operator, I didn't
see evidence of that much money. When you check
the El Paso city tax records, Armes' "nine-acre estate"
turns out to be 1.24 acres, although he does own 1.5
acres of adjacent property, as he claims. Most likely
the net value of his estate is considerably less than the
$1 million figure quoted in *Newsweek* (or the $1.2
million that he told me). The estimated replacement
cost that appears on the city tax real estate card is
about $50,000. Armes paid real estate taxes last year
of $476.13.

Armes probably did earn a nice chunk for the Lee
Way security job, and there is convincing evidence he
collected on an eighty-thousand-dollar settlement
from a bizarre lawsuit against the American owner of
a Juarez radio station who hadn't paid Armes for his
work in Mexico. Armes' friends trace a big part of his
personal wealth to his friendship with an eccentric
and reclusive multimillionaire named Thomas Fortune Ryan, who has supposedly cut Armes in on some
lucrative real estate deals. The Three Rivers Ranch on
the backside of White Mountain in New Mexico,
which Armes claimed to own, is in fact Thomas Fortune Ryan's reclusory, although Leavell Properties

171

break on royalties.

I asked Fred Honig for his impressions of Jay J. Armes.

He told me, "Here in New York we always think of someone from El Paso . . . in the wilds, you know . . . we think of them as being fairly unsophisticated . . . fairly unknowing of what's going on. But this man is fascinating. Very quick, very intelligent, able to grasp problems and solve them."

Yes, I thought, *that sounds like Jay J. Armes.*

January 1976

Postscript

Jay Armes became considerably less talkative after this article appeared in *Texas Monthly*. He even tried to block publication with a court injunction. "I spent three days hiding from the process servers while we got the thing mailed and the injunction lifted," publisher Mike Levy recalls. Armes threatened to sue, but he never did.

People in El Paso remain reluctant to talk about Armes, but they still read about him from time to time. The court awarded an El Paso woman a large amount of cash after she sued Armes, claiming he chased her down a major street at speeds in excess of one hundred miles an hour.

The most poignant story, though, happened when Armes and syndicated columnist Jack Anderson and two others founded a new magazine, in September 1981, called *The Investigator*. Anderson forgot to investigate his partner, however. While Armes was doing a promotional tour, reporters at the Washington *Post* and the Cleveland *Plain Dealer* dug out the old issue of *Texas Monthly* and confronted Armes and

Anderson with the allegations. Anderson had never read the story, though he recalled reading stories in *People* and *Newsweek*. When a *Post* reporter read part of my story to Jack Anderson, the respected dirt-digger said the alleged facts about Armes were "cheap and sordid." "If that's true," he said, "I don't know what I'd do."

Armes claimed that *Texas Monthly* wanted him out of the sheriff's race and sent me to El Paso to "do a hatchet job." He also claimed that the El Paso *Herald-Post* contradicted everything *Texas Monthly* printed. As records at the *Herald-Post* prove, Armes himself produced at least one "minor character" who told the newspaper his quotes were used out of context. But they weren't; the same person signed an affidavit *before* publication, swearing to the authenticity of his quote. He didn't question the context then, and nothing was changed. Since Armes was looking over his shoulder while he talked to the *Herald-Post,* I suspect he might have had additional thoughts due to his influence.

Shortly after this uproar, Jack Anderson removed the private detective's name from the magazine masthead, then pulled out of the project entirely.

8

Border Towns

It has been a long, hot, very dry drive from Austin
and I am in no mood for restraint or the preachings
of the chickenhearted. For the last hour or more, as
we dropped like doughballs into the sizzling delta of
the Lower Rio Grande Valley where the great sky is
master, I have been listening to Billy Joe Shaver singing "Ain't No God in Mexico," contemplating how
that border-crossing feeling does for sure make a fool
out of a man. What can I say? It makes you want to
whistle. To understand, you have to feel twenty years
old, and a ten-dollar bill has to feel like a hundred.
You have to crave cheap liquor, cheap sex, and cheap
thrills, and you need a passion for anarchy and a
blind spot for trouble. An international bridge is
always an invitation to fantasy—that is why, on the
American edge of every bridge, there is a discount
store where poor Mexicans can glut themselves on
plastic and polyester, and on the Mexican side there

is a money exchange where Americans can make believe that pesos come from orchards. Soon, my bridge and I will be reunited.

I am drinking at the well-padded bar of Brownsville's Fort Brown Inn, overlooking the resaca that centuries ago was the riverbed of the Rio Grande, waiting while my traveling companion, M.S., showers and changes into something that will make her look like a Mexican field hand.

While I wait, I peruse the day's headlines. A captain in the Mexican army has been arrested for attempting to smuggle ten thousand rounds of ammunition into his own country. And Henry the Peacemaker is, they say, negotiating a deal for the exchange of prisoners with Mexico. Also, Mexico has discovered giant oil reserves.

"Something is afoot," I observe as my traveling companion joins me. "Something always is on the border," M.S. replies.

Yes, but it takes the hard practiced eye and hedonistic perception of an old river-runner to know just what. Like the river, political power is mindless and arbitrary. Take, for example, the case of the unfortunate Matamoros army officer. In other times, he would be a hero, a subject for monuments—he may be yet. Smuggling can be the ultimate heroic act when committed in the name of a cause, in his case the continuation of the Mexican revolution, which has been maintained in varying degrees against a succession of tyrants ever since the 1790's when the Holy Office denounced Father Hidalgo for reading forbidden books. An honorable profession, smuggling. It is only when politics shift that it gets a bad name. Or take the case of the miserable wretches that Henry the Peacemaker is attempting to spring from the dungeons of Mexico: most of them were put there with the aid and insistence of the drug enforcement agencies of the United

States government. Yesterday's refuse is today's humanitarian pursuit.

Even the oil discoveries have the thoughtless ring of history. It was right here at Fort Brown, maybe on the banks of this very resaca, maybe under this very table, that the expeditionary army of General Zachary Taylor camped, foreshadowing the Treaty of Guadalupe Hidalgo, by which the U.S. grabbed for herself half of the territory of Mexico, thus fulfilling Manifest Destiny and grinding the Mexican nation forever under the boot heels of Uncle Sam. Or so it was written. Maybe all that will change. Maybe in fifty or one hundred years, wetbacks will have blue eyes and wear Willie Nelson T-shirts.

Brownsville, and its larger, more sinister sister city, Matamoros, are the southernmost points in the twelve-hundred-mile river border separating the two countries. A perfect place to begin our personal exploration of border towns. So it is that I now feel the exhilaration. We are traveling in M.S.'s brand-new Buick with the air conditioner and tape deck; I have three hundred U.S. dollars in my jeans, a good map, some books, some names and addresses, and time enough to kill four men my size. What is more, M.S., my comely, enterprising research assistant, is a woman who never backs away from a dare or underestimates the therapy of a cheap thrill. On the first page of my notebook, under the notation about the great sky, the sea meadows, the endless fields of okra, onions, fruit and grain, and the very tall, very slender palms that stand like formations of dark flamingos, I record the words of some old river desperado whose name is long forgotten: "We love living more than we love life."

Travel editors and border samplers will tell you that the best place in Matamoros to eat and drink is a spot called the Drive-Inn. They will tell you about the elegant dining room with chairs that make you disappear, and about waiters in tuxedos, linen tablecloths, wild-game dinners and flaming desserts, about the dance floor with revolving lights where coiffured women outfit their young sons in blazers and white shoes and make them lead while a Mexican orchestra very heavy on violins and organ renders such traditional numbers as "Baby Face" and "I Left My Heart in San Francisco." All I can tell you is, the joint is phony and ridiculously overpriced—dinner for two is about twenty bucks—the drinks are watered, and the waiters resemble something Mexico might manufacture and export to France.

The Texas Bar on the *zocolo* (central square) is a moderately good spot—at least the waiters ignore you. You can get cheap (forty-five-cent) tequila and a good shrimp cocktail down the street at the Mactezuma, a gay hangout. By far the best place we found in Matamoros was Los Portales on the Victoria Highway a few miles from the center of town. Los Portales specializes in *carnes al carbon* (charcoal-broiled meats), and on a warm evening you sit on the patio under willows and blooming oleanders, enjoying good mariachis. The clientele is mostly Mexican families. The family unit hasn't yet dissolved in Mexico and you can frequently see three or even four generations knocking down beer and *cabrito* while little kids in Zorro masks scramble at their feet.

Owner Everardo M. Gonzalez, a courtly old caballero, retains the trappings of his Indian ancestry: authentic oxcarts, Mexican charro saddles of hand-tooled leather and cured mesquite core, and a large black-and-white portrait of Zapata. Any taxi driver can find Los Portales, or for a couple of pesos you can grab a maxi-taxi (VW bus) out south Sixth Street. Just watch for the oxcart, or the maddening smell of charcoal-broiled meats.

178

There was a wedding reception going on at the pavilion next door, so after dinner we wandered over and joined the fun. The bride wore one of those storybook gowns you see in the shop windows of Mexico—Mexicans are very big on weddings and funerals. Mexicans are also excessively generous, and those who have tasted upward mobility are ludicrously class-conscious.

"Did I ever tell you the story of the portrait of the wife of the Telephone Pole King of Durango?" I ask M.S. as we drink tequila and watch the bride and groom pose for pictures. "I never actually met the lady, of course, but I attended a Christmas party at her home a few years ago. Crazy Dennis Hopper was in Durango making a film and he had rented out the mansion of the Telephone Pole King."

"How did he get appointed Telephone Pole King?" M.S. asks.

"I'm coming to that. It was a very grand home. It was like a time warp—something out of the fifties, a grand piano, and gardenias floating in the swimming pool. You really expected to see Esther Williams and Ricardo Montalban waltzing across the patio. Anyway, the portrait. It hung in the most prominent spot on a prominent wall of bad paintings. The dear lady was portrayed as a veritable *madre de Mexico*, a heroine of epic stature, superimposed over Aztec pyramids, the eagle and the serpent, Father Hidalgo, Benito Juarez, every legend and symbol of the country's struggle. That was how the wife of the Telephone Pole King chose to have herself portrayed.

"The so-called Telephone Pole King made his fortune planting telephone poles along the mountain highways outside of Durango. Of course there were no telephones way out there, and there was no wire between the poles. But if the government ever got around to it, the poles were waiting."

"What did the Telephone Pole King do before he sold telephone poles?"

"Sold shoes," I tell her. "Mexicans are very big on shoes. The two most prominent buildings in any Mexican town are likely to be the cathedral and the Canada Shoe Store."

We were the only two people in the pavilion wearing Mexican sandals. But it was okay. We were from *el otro lado* — the other side.

On the *zocolo*, near a Mexican discount store called Mas Mas Mas, we run across Tim Perez. Or rather he runs across us and refuses to go away. Tim Perez is a professional tour guide and insists on taking us to some overpriced rock joints in the *Zona Rosa* — pink zone. Tim is a pleasant, gregarious man in his late sixties. He speaks good English and claims to have friends in all fifty states.

Tim tells us that he has never met a man he doesn't like. He also tells us: "You must understand, women are the true heroes of Mexico — of the revolution." Tim says we should relax, have some fun. M.S. says she thinks it would be fun to dance with that slender Mexican boy with the turquoise necklace and the shirt unbuttoned to his waist. Tim has a brief coughing fit. He takes off his service hat and fans himself.

"Don't worry," he tells me as we watch M.S. approach the soon-to-be-amazed young Mexican. "He's . . . how do you say . . . queer."

While M.S. is showing her partner around the dance floor, Perez tells me his life story. He was born in Guadalajara, which he constantly refers to as "the second-largest city in Mexico," as though its size is one of the largest factors of his life. "My mother was the greatest person who ever lived," he says. His oldest brother was a conscript in the army of Carranza, a onetime sidekick of Pancho Villa who lost his revolutionary zeal once he got to the palace in Mexico City. Perez doesn't remember his father too well because he was still a baby when his mama gathered up her cooking pot and children and followed the older brother to war. "That was the custom of that time," Perez tells me. "We lived some in Veracruz, but mostly we traveled with the army, chasing Villa and the revolutionaries." When Carranza was murdered in bed by one of his own officers, Mother Perez took her brood to Matamoros where there was work harvesting. She died 26 years, 10 months, and 8 days ago, Perez says sadly. She is buried next to his oldest brother. Perez visits the graves every single day, sometimes bringing fresh plastic flowers.

"Your revolutions," I tell him, "are infamous for their irresolution."

"The revolution was like the children's game—king of the mountaintop," Perez tells me. "Whoever is on top makes the rules. Somebody has got to make the rules. What's the difference?"

"It was a helluva problem for the United States, your revolution. We never knew which side to back."

"It was like your Vietnam," Perez observes.

"It still is," I tell him.

"I am old now," he says. "I don't want another revolution. Revolution is murder. Many men die, and nothing changes so much. We should all be friends. We should all love each other."

"Mexican guys are the greatest dancers in the world," M.S. says as she rejoins the table. "That's about *all* they are."

Perez presents us with a bill of twenty dollars for his services, which I calculate have cost us twice that much again in bad drinks and cover charges. Perez insists on seeing us to a taxi. He gives the driver a tongue-lashing in Spanish, then tells us: "He will take care of you, don't worry."

I wake with a boss stud-bull monster Mexican tequila hangover and wonder where went the boy I once knew? Border-town Mexico is like I remember. Only it's not. Or I'm not. Something has changed. I prefer to think it's Mexico.

M.S. is already poolside, boiling under a sun that may be great for cotton and citrus but is intolerable when applied to the human body. I take a quick look around the Fort Brown Inn, which is billed as "21 acres of Tropical Paradise." In my notebook I write: "Pestilence . . . floods . . . famine . . . fine, pale sand that sticks to your teeth . . . inhuman heat . . .giant killer shrimp." In Paul Horgan's monumental two-volume history of the Rio Grande, *Great River*, there's a marvelous exchange between one of General Zachary Taylor's bedraggled officers and a fresh replacement just shipped down from the East. The replacement asks the veteran if those could possibly be fleas crawling through his hair, and the old officer replies indignantly: "Fleas! Do you think we are dogs who go about infested with fleas? These are lice!" I ask the woman desk clerk in the inn lobby to direct me to the ruins of old Fort Brown, and she says I'm standing on them.

There are, I learn later, several existing buildings from the old fort across the resaca on the campus of Texas Southmost College. Citizens on both sides of the river have a passion for recycling history. There is, for example, a little locomotive repainted red, white, and blue in honor of the Bicentennial in a small park near the hotel. A Chamber of Commerce sign explains that this is Old Number 1, the very locomotive that made its first international run in 1873. A trademark still visible on the belly of the old puffer claims it was built in Philadelphia in 1877. History has been economized. History has been reduced to black and silver markers telling you that under this tree General Zachary Taylor encamped. There is nothing about the true settlers of the Lower Rio Grande—the bankrupts, the bandits, the escaped criminals, the army deserters, the gamblers, swindlers, exploiters, and armies of occupation.

Across the shallow, muddy river, I retrace my wayward steps, dodging the demolition derby traffic along the narrow streets of Matamoros. It is Saturday afternoon and the streets swarm with campesinos (farmers or country people) and their families. The heat has driven most of the gringos indoors, on their own side of the river. I observe the curious mixture of 1950's modern and colonial architecture, the beautiful tiled sidewalks, the surprising number of handsome wood frame buildings, the hustlers and beggars and thieves. Pat Crowe, a friend who grew up in Brownsville, had told us, "The attitude toward property is completely different here. If you need something, or even if you don't need it but would like to have it, it is socially acceptable to steal it." Ford pickup trucks are a popular item among thieves. This is not because of some intrinsic quality developed in Detroit, but because Ford ignitions are quickly and easily interchanged. Old Henry sure knew what he was doing when he invented "a car for the people." The police department of Matamoros fences the hot pickups, or that's the story that goes around. Another local scam, Pat told us, is spare parts. Mexico literally runs on spare parts. Having miraculously avoided the disgrace of a junkyard along some U.S. interstate, the expatriate vehicles of America find long and useful service in Mexico, where a piece of baling wire is worth ten trips to the dealer. Mexicans like anything loud and faster than a burro, but they especially love trucks. They decorate their scabby trucks like they decorate their homes and churches and graveyards— with fringe, ornaments, and holy objects.

Of course the two biggest scams anyplace on the river are guns (going south) and dope (going north). The products are endemic and interchangeable. A Browning automatic rifle is worth a pound of cocaine. Several times each week the river spits up the body of a poor smuggler or unscrupulous dealer, gunned down in an unexpected moonlight encounter.

Munching a slice of fresh watermelon purchased from a sidewalk vendor who also played marching songs on a portable handcrank organ, I find my way back to the Teatro Reforma, an old theater building that Perez had pointed out. The wonderful old building was supposed to be the city's tribute to the emperor Maximilian and his power-mad wife, Carlota, but the royal couple never showed. That would have been about 1865, I calculate. What a fiasco. On one side of the river, the Union was chasing the Confederacy, and on the other side Maximilian's fancy-pants French army was chasing the roving government-in-exile of Benito Juarez. Caught in the middle of this insanity was the port city of Matamoros. Matamoros is known as "thrice heroic," having been burned by three different invading armies.

As I cross the bridge again, I am aware of the enormous amount of cargo being moved at a given moment. In the exact middle of the bridge a Mexican boy sells American cigarettes for two bucks a carton. An old Mexican woman has stopped to rearrange some articles in her American grocery sack.

My God, is that Alpo dog food I see? For her *esposo*, perhaps.

Sunday . . . En Route to Reynosa

I'll tell you up front about getting busted. It happened at the American customs station on the international bridge at Progresso, a hot, dusty town of no distinction halfway between Matamoros and Reynosa.

There is only one reason an American would stop in Progresso, and that's to eat at Arturo's. Arturo's is what the Drive-Inn is cracked up to be, a really first-class family-style restaurant, featuring a wild-game dinner and *carnes al carbon.* Prices are high, but prices are high everywhere. Kiss good-bye the myth of the cheap Mexican border town.

Inspector Reynaldo of U.S. Customs must have spotted us fifty yards away. Two smiling gringos in a new Buick. No liquor to declare. No Mexican pottery. Just taking in the sights, heh? He had us open the trunk and he went straight for the only suitcase with a lock. It was uncanny: it was like he had built-in radar. Inspector Reynaldo rammed his fist straight through M.S.'s carefully folded lingerie to a cardboard box clearly labeled backgammon.

"Mother of Christ!" I said as he opened the box. "Where did that come from!"

I could see from his expression that Inspector Reynaldo was wondering the same thing.

The inspector treated us with the cordiality reserved for truly master criminals. He took a long time to weigh the marijuana. It came to forty-eight grams, less than two ounces. That puzzled him. He telephoned for a female customs agent, then they gave us both an amazingly thorough body search. They went through every piece of luggage as though they were inventorying the estate of Howard Hughes, then they started on the car. Finally, Inspector Reynaldo stepped back, shaking his head.

"I don't understand," he said. "Where is the rest of it?" "There ain't no rest of it," I told him. For the better part of an hour M.S. and I had been sitting in the customs office looking at a portrait of Gerald Ford with his arms crossed resolutely and that dumb cartoonist's grin on his face, wondering why God made some of us more stupid than others.

"This is all too simple," Inspector Reynaldo said, pacing about like Peter Sellers in *The Pink Panther*. "You have less than two ounces of marijuana . . . I don't understand. Why? It's too simple. What are you trying to pull on me? I want an explanation."

"Gringo *estúpido*," I said. "Who else would smuggle Austin grass into Mexico, eat lunch, then smuggle it back?" If I hadn't been so busy feeling sorry for myself, I would have felt sorry for Inspector Reynaldo. You could read his mind. *Duped again.* Here he was, the scourge of the Progresso bridge, squandering his time with two five-and-dimers while the real load, probably an eighteen-wheeler hauling fifty thousand pounds of high-grade cocaine, slipped through with its terrible cargo.

After checking with the Drug Enforcement Administration in McAllen, which ascertained that we were indeed small fish not worth frying, the inspector "handled it administratively." That is, he seized our marijuana and our brand-new Buick. Then he read us section 618 of the Tariff Act of 1930 and allowed us to reclaim the car for $200 cash, which we had to send for.

But, God, I'd do it all again just to have a snapshot of Inspector Reynaldo's face when M.S. finally handed him the money and asked could she please have her favorite roach clip back. That of course was out of the question, but the propriety of the question greatly disturbed Inspector Reynaldo.

It was late that afternoon when we again crossed the bridge, this time at Reynosa, the most Mexican of border towns owing to the fact that the only thing on the Texas side is the discount store crossroads called Hidalgo. We purchased a cheap bottle of palm rum and checked into the Hotel Amelia to wash away our despair. The Amelia is your traditional Mexican hotel, which is to say the toilets don't flush and the showers are carefully engineered to flood the bathroom.

"How do you feel about your goddamn border now?" M.S. asked. I ignored the question. I was trying to work the air conditioner, but the knob fell off in my hand.

"Did you know that in Mexico they train engineers to design things that don't work?" I said, drinking palm rum from the bottle. "It's a fact. The economy of Mexico is totally dependent on repairmen. It would therefore be catastrophic if anything worked."

"Yes," she sighed. "It would be a miracle."

After a delicious meal of tacos purchased (eight for one dollar) from an ingenious street vendor of gourmet stature, we decided to take in the *zona roja*—the red-light district. In larger cities like Matamoros and Nuevo Laredo, the *zona roja* (AKA Boystown) is located in walled fortresses four or five miles from the center of town. The difficulty in escorting an American woman to the *zona roja*, aside from the obvious, is that taxi drivers absolutely refuse to be a part of such foolishness. Reynosa's red-light district, however, is located near the *zocolo*, and with some instructions from our friend the gourmet taco vendor we found it on our own.

There is a sinister low-life aura about any Mexican whore district—again, there is that time warp, only now you're in the thirties, you're in the Foreign Legion and cutthroat Arabs are bellying across every rooftop. But the *zona roja* in Reynosa is Mexican Dogpatch, the flash of a twisted libido swooping low, devouring sweet children in choir robes. We walk along a cratered, flea-bitten street of neon bars with names like Chinese Palace, ignoring indifferent glances of taxi drivers, pimps, shoeshine boys, and hookers in blonde wigs and tight dresses who mingle on the sidewalk against the oppressive heat inside. This is the main street, the showcase. The low-rent street, which intersects it, is pure Swine Alley — the central feature being rows of barrackslike rooms where ratty old hookers sit in open doors framed against naked light bulbs and lumpy beds and pathetic personal garnishings such as teddy bears and pinups of Mexican movie stars and radios with broken plastic cases. A brightly lighted club called Ciro's reminds M.S. of where they used to hold FFA dances in Oklahoma, so we stop in for a couple of beers.

"It *is* like an FFA dance," M.S. says. "Look, the girls sit with their backs to the walls, waiting for the men to ask them to dance. That poor fat girl. I'll bet no one ever asks her to dance. All the men look like farmers and cowboys. Look how they hold the women — almost at arm's length."

The campesinos drinking beer at rough wooden tables pay us no attention: whatever we are up to, it is none of their affair. I am concerned that maybe the hookers will consider M.S. a threat, but that is not the case. A nice-looking young woman even asks her to dance.

At the Chinese Palace, we meet a bright young Mexican pimp named Pancho, who speaks good English and tells us that he is from a prominent family of Mexico City drug dealers. By now we feel comfortable, even euphoric. Pancho tells the girls that I am a writer, and soon they are clustered at our table, writing their names in my notebook.

M.S. shares the popular assumption that most Mexican whores are poor farm girls kidnapped and forced into a life of slavery, but Pancho tells her that is not necessarily correct.

"They are not slaves," he says. "They can go away. Only they don't have no place to go. It is not a bad life for a young girl. They make sixty, seventy dollars a week, sometimes more, and they are protected."

"What happens when they get old?"

"What happens when any of us get old?" Pancho asks rhetorically.

Monday . . . Laredo–Nuevo Laredo

Feels like the first day of summer. Driving north on Highway 83, paralleling the river; the terrain changes from tropical to shimmering desert. White Brahmas stand motionless among mesquite and chaparral.

We stop at the old river port of Roma, once a haven for smugglers and bandits. Here the river is wider, cleaner, better defined. I am interested in tales of an infamous outlaw of the 1860's, one Abram Garcia, AKA the White Cavalier, but nobody in town ever heard of him. I'll bet their great-great-granddaddies did. Garcia rode a snow-white stallion, dressed in tight velvet trousers and short jackets of gold and silver thread, and carried enough weaponry to pulverize a mountain. It was the White Cavalier's pleasure to watch grown men dance. He encouraged them by shooting at their feet, and when the dance had ended he ordered them stripped and whipped to death.

With the exception of an old (1840) Oblate Fathers mission now occupied by a small museum, the citizens of Roma fairly well ignore the ruins of their hot little village. But you can walk along the north bank of the river and get an idea how it was. Pulques Cantina still exists, after a fashion. I'll bet the White Cavalier had some big times in there. The store of Manuel Guerra stands, its ancient hand-cast brick walls, great hand-carved, weathered doors, and weed-choked courtyard preserved by the Texas Historical Society. The descendants of Manuel Guerra now operate an export-import business from a modern, aluminum-sided office and warehouse across from the old store.

An item in the museum catches my eye. It appears to be the ammunition belt of a dead-solid drinker — three holsters shaped like whiskey bottles hanging from a broad leather strap. No one in the museum can account for its purpose. I'll bet the White Cavalier could figure it out.

We stop south of Laredo to inspect the well-preserved ruins at San Ygnacio, and an hour later we are secure in the arms of the twentieth century, in a large, cool, elegant room at La Posada Motor Hotel, overlooking the river and Mexico. La Posada is a hotel for your low-range fat cats from both sides of the river. I mean, Laredo ain't Cozumel or even Acapulco, but layouts such as La Posada do offer maximum creature comforts for what M.S. calls "your basic trader class." In the bars, and at poolside, Mexican and American wives practice their bilingual proclivities (*"Que niños usted?"*) while their husbands make deals. The corner of the hotel behind the swimming pool was for a brief time in 1840 the capital of the Republic of the Rio Grande, a breakaway confederation of federalists opposed to the despotic rule of Santa Anna. There were *seven* flags over this part of Texas.

Because its streets are narrow and loud and smell like motor fuel, Nuevo Laredo is considered by purists as your most faithful border town. It is busy in that maniac, turbine, move-your-ass-outta-my-way fashion that Juarez, Durango, Monterrey, and other much larger Mexican cities are busy, yet it is small enough to cover on foot. With the exception of the *zona roja* and several good restaurants, any place worth visiting is within walking distance of the bridge. The Cadillac Bar, where the Ramos gin fizz is a tradition worth sampling. The *zocolo,* where horse-drawn carriages wait to show tourists the sights. The market.

The Plaza de Toros has, unfortunately, been demolished—the nearest bullfighting plaza is in Monterrey, a two-hour drive into the interior.

The best eating place in Nuevo Laredo (maybe the best in Mexico) is Jorge 'n Charlie's Laredo Grill, a couple of miles out the Monterrey highway. It's a modern place, but the walls are plastered with old photographs and newspaper reproductions illustrating the history of Mexico—six revolutionaries hanging from a single tree, Villa puffing a joint, Villa and Zapata posing like Aggies in the National Palace, an unidentified man in a black suit grinning and having a smoke in preparation for his final performance before a firing squad. Everything on the menu is worthy of attention. Only an idiot would fail to sample the oysters *diablo, madranzo,* and *cardenas*—for $3.60 you can try all three dishes. Order oysters 4-4-4. The lime butter steak or garlic-battered shrimp with mustard sauce will reduce the most jaded connoisseur to a slobbering swine. The waiters are attentive and have a sense of humor. After dinner they serve a complimentary white russian and a dish of lollipops. There is also a wheelchair, in the event you have difficulty returning to your car.

In the heat of the afternoon we escape the insanity by retreating to the bar of the Hotel Reforma. Until recently the Reforma bar was a place of quiet dignity where old waiters with limps recalled the days of the quick getaway and young matadors talked of going in high and clean over the horns. It is still a good place to watch the traffic along Avenida Guerrero, but the linen tablecloths have been replaced by textured vinyl ones, the lighting is fluorescent, and the old ceiling fans have given way to central air conditioning. The waiters skip lively now, and the only customer who could possibly be a matador wears a baseball cap turned sideways. On the avenue there is a monster traffic jam as an eighteen-wheeler that has made an illegal turn attempts to back up against the flow of traffic. Another eighteen-wheeler that is pinned up in traffic blocks the way. Soon the two drivers are on the sidewalk, shouting and waving their fists. A thousand horns blast a raucous concert.

"What do you suppose are in all those trucks?" M.S. asks wistfully.

"Mexico," I tell her. "They are hauling it away."

"I'll bet they can sell it in the U.S.," she speculates.

"I'll bet you're right," I say.

Sometime after midnight, when M.S. is sleeping, I walk back across the bridge and take a five-dollar taxi ride to the *zona roja*—Boystown. I have a tequila in all the old places. Papgoyas, the Savoy, the Club Miramar, the Marabu. But the thrills are not cheap. They're not even thrills. In one final foolish gesture I trade my watch for a hooker's black lace bra. In my present condition, it seems like the perfect gift. But halfway across the bridge, returning to the hotel, I throw it into the Rio Grande and watch it float toward the sea.

Tuesday . . . Eagle Pass–Piedras Negras

Sixty miles north of here, in the Del Rio–Acuna–Amistad Lake region, the highway will desert the river, leaving it to its wild, reckless meanderings down through the Big Bend, then north again along the Chihuahua wasteland all the way to El Paso and Juarez. It's almost a symbolic gesture, an act of ultimate revulsion, as though the course of civilization was not yet prepared for such hostile terrain or arbitrary tricks of nature.

There are still a few small falling-off places where a visitor can stand on sheer cliffs and look across into the wilderness of a foreign land. One of these is the Texas ghost town of Langtry, Judge Roy Bean's old hangout, inhabited mainly by rattlesnakes and vinegarroons. There are, of course, the spectacular canyons of the Big Bend, which a motorist can reach by zigging and zagging among mountain peaks and through moonscape gaps that make the planet Mars look like Sunday at Fair Park. And there is the hellhole of Presidio-Ojinaga, best viewed on the TV weather map.

But it is hundreds of miles now before the highway and river make their peace just south of El Paso.

Since I have been to Juarez many times, and have no intention of going again just now, I will offer two suggestions: (1) stay out of the *zona roja*, unless your pleasure is getting robbed and/or beaten about the head; (2) eat at least one meal at Julio's Cafe Corona, where the *caldillo* (a fiery Mexican stew) is unexcelled. With its purple mountains and thin desert air, El Paso–Juarez is the most scenic of the river border towns, and almost the most sinister. This is a land and a law unto itself. Until the Mexican government cracked down, Juarez was a popular spot for quicky gringo divorces. Now it's a popular spot for contacting hit men or big league drug czars. If I had to pick just one border town for those hedonistic qualities mentioned at the beginning, I would pick Juarez. If I had to pick five, it wouldn't even be on the list.

Five days into our adventure along the river of latent desire, I feel this ambivalence: my soul cries *more*, but my head answers *never*.

Where the highway from Laredo to Eagle Pass–

Piedras Negras bends away from the river, we are stopped by U.S. immigration officers searching for aliens. They are attempting to break the back of a smuggling ring specializing in human cargo.

"What they do," an officer tells us, "is lower them with ropes from the old bridge to a place where they can wade ashore and cut through the U.S. customs lot without going through immigration. They charge the Mexicans about three hundred pesos each [twenty-four dollars]. We figure sixty-five or seventy make it across each week."

"Why can't they just walk across the bridge like everyone else?" M.S. asks.

"Some of them are either too poor or too disreputable to get a bridge crossing card," he explains.

"We must have crossed a dozen bridges," M.S. says, "and we didn't have any kind of card. It doesn't seem fair."

I implore the immigrations officer to ignore this last demented remark, explaining that my traveling companion has a fever but will no doubt be all right as soon as I can get her to a Dairy Queen. The officer understands. His quarry would not be dressed like Mexican field hands, driving a new Buick. We thank him and are quickly on our way, but I am still wondering about those aliens out there in the brush, alone in hundreds of square miles of desolation. I don't know where they think they are going, but they won't like it when they get there. Could it be that they are going nowhere, that the adventure is the trip itself?

As we pass through Carrizo Springs and the road bends back toward the river, I write in my notebook: ". . . beautiful desolation of the great ranches . . . except for the highlines and fences, the land is much like the Comanches found it centuries ago when they first crossed the river just south of Eagle Pass."

After the bedlam of Laredo, there is a healing tranquillity about Piedras Negras. The north bank of the river was the site of Fort Duncan, one of the chain of river forts established to ward off smugglers, bandits, and bad Indians, but the only "battle" that Paul Horgan records in his history of the river took place in the 1850's when an American hoodlum named Callahan crossed the Rio Grande in pursuit of some Seminole Negro slaves who had escaped. Callahan and his raiders never recovered the slaves, but they did pause long enough to loot Piedras Negras, and the soldiers at Fort Duncan covered Callahan's retreat. Perhaps the serenity that we feel now can be attributed to the easy, laid-back, compromising attitude of the early settlers. Although the citizens of the Texas side had little sympathy for the Confederacy (they voted overwhelmingly against secession), immense shipments of Confederate cotton crossed here and were transported by land to the Mexican seaports of Matamoros and Bagdad. When word reached the river that the emperor Maximilian had been captured and executed by firing squad, they threw a memorable party in the customs house at Piedras Negras.

In the late-afternoon shadows we stroll the narrow, pastel streets, eating ears of buttered corn. Lovers, drunks, and loafers share the concrete benches of the *zocolo*. The local movie house, Cine Rodriguez, is featuring a film about a mad professor who gets his jollies bolting naked blondes into chastity belts. An ancient campesino with a silver-and-velvet-trimmed carriage and a horse that may have been left here by Cabeza de Vaca tips his hat and offers us a ride. There is a sign on the side of the carriage. It says, in English: "BACK FROM MOON—WELCOME." A boy is selling tickets to the bullfight in Piedras Negras.

We wander through the cluttered, low-key back streets of the market, pausing to inspect an amazing variety of medicinal herbs.

"If we could only read Spanish," I tell M.S., "we would realize that we have landed in a veritable dope fiends' Garden of Eden. I've read that there are something like forty-seven hallucinogenic plants growing wild in this part of Mexico."

"*Para la mala digestion?*" M.S. says, reading the labels. "*Gripe . . . hemorragia . . . rastornos . . . mestruales . . . devildad sexual?* What does it mean?"

"I'm just guessing," I tell her, "but it probably means it will get you high or kill you."

We had already determined to do a quiet dinner and early bed, but now we're chasing tequila with *sangrita* (a flavorful nonalcoholic drink composed chiefly of hot chilies and orange, lime, and tomato juices; not to be confused with wine-and-brandy-based *sangría*) at a fancy joint called Las Roches, overlooking the river.

A number of drinks later we are dining and dancing at the Moderno Restaurant, an authentic fantasy land of leaded onyx tables, plastic zebra-striped seats and genuine American toilet paper. The owner, Raul de los Santos V, a splendid figure with a Gable moustache and a loud sport coat, tells us that he can supply anything our hearts desire.

"I have many friends," Raul says. "Not just in Mexico. On both sides. You tell me your troubles, I will take care of them."

In the company of Raul de los Santos V and Manuel D. Sanchez, owner of the A-1 Plumbing Service in Uvalde, Texas, we hit every bar in Piedras Negras. Sanchez' wife carries a sack of coconut shells in which bartenders can prepare her favorite drink of rum and fruit juice. Sanchez tells us proudly that though he has only a third-grade education, he is the plumber that Governor Dolph Briscoe normally calls in an emergency. Sanchez and his wife drive to Piedras Negras about once a week, "to get away from the kids and the telephone and have a damn good time." And by God we are, we are having a good time.

"I ain't no Meskin," Sanchez proclaims at one point, "I'm an Arapaho. You call me a Meskin again, I'm gonna pick up my hoe and . . ."

We are laughing and falling out of chairs. Me and Sanchez take an oath of blood brotherhood. We even attempt to cut our wrists with a kitchen knife. Fortunately, we are too drunk.

"I don't know about you," I blather as they pour us out in front of our motel just before dawn, "but I ain't ever had a better time."

"I can always tell," M.S. says. "About midnight you get that wild look and start talking like the Frito Bandito."

Wednesday . . . Garner State Park

Spent the entire afternoon on the banks of the Rio Frio, in the shade of a granddaddy cypress. There is no word in any language for this kind of sick. I am shivering and sweating like a pig, and my hand is shaking so badly that I am having to dictate these notes. I have a terminal overdose of Mexican border towns. I will die here, and now.

"What shall I write?" M.S. asks.

"Just repeat the first line," I say, shutting my eyes. "Tell them we love living more than life. Only make it past tense. *Loved.*"

"Are you sure?" she asks softly, tenderly.

"Just as sure as I'm gonna die."

August 1976

Postscript

I read recently that some high-minded city officials shut down the *zona roja* in Matamoros, and that similar areas of pleasure in other border towns are being threatened. Some people have no respect for tradition.

Incidentally, M.S. (it stands for Main Squeeze) is now my wife, AKA Phyllis. She tells me we paid the narcs *three hundred dollars* (rather than two hundred dollars, as I reported) to recover our car at the Progresso bridge. She's still unhappy they wouldn't return her favorite roach clip. I'm still unhappy with the editors at the Dallas *Times Herald* who refused a two-hundred-dollar line item in my expense account, labeled "busted."

I still love border towns.

9

The Death of
A Ranger

When Texas Ranger Bobby Paul Doherty looked out of his kitchen window and saw patches of snow, he thought about the firewood he hadn't cut on Sunday. He had promised his wife, Carolyn, that he and Buster would do it right after church, but there had been a meeting of deacons, then the telephone call from the Denton sheriff's office saying the drug raid was set for that afternoon. Sunday had been a day of prolonged frustration. The drug raid hadn't gone down after all. He didn't know why. That's the way it was with dope dealers. You could work for days or weeks setting it up, then the whole show could fold at the whim of a dealer or the duplicity of an informant.

There was only one thing in this world that Ranger Bob Doherty hated worse than dope, and that was dope dealers. He was a fanatic on the subject. "They call us Mr. and Mrs. Redneck," Carolyn had joked to friends. Carolyn certainly did not approve of drugs, but she was not vehement about the long hair and beards and weird lifestyles that her husband automatically associated with major crime. "In his line of work," she said, "he had to think that way." Even out in Azle where they made their home, well away from the degenerate streets of Fort Worth where a school kid could score a lid of grass as easily as he could buy a soda pop, drugs occupied an alarming share of school-yard conversations.

All that talk about *victimless* crimes made Bob Doherty sick. Someone always got hurt, someone other than the person using the drugs. "You ask them if they think drugs are a victimless crime!" he had told his seventeen-year-old daughter, Kelly, on the morning that she was to attend a high school assembly conducted by three former addicts. The Ranger had told his sixteen-year-old son, Buster, about the time, only a few months before, when he had kicked in the door of a gambling den, crashed through a hole in the floor, and landed dead center on a homemade bomb placed there to destroy evidence in the event of just such a raid. If the bomb had exploded, the entire Doherty family would have been its victims. Only a lawman knew what it was like below the surface of a drug culture. It was like his old friend Dwight Crawford, captain of criminal investigation for the Denton County sheriff's department, had said so often: "Bob, it's a sewer down there. Dark tunnels leading off in ever' what direction." That's why they had all been so frustrated on Sunday. They had an opportunity to explore a few of those tunnels, but someone slammed the door too soon.

Now it was Monday, February 20. It was the official state holiday for Washington's birthday, but for Ranger Doherty it was just another morning for wondering if he would ever find time to cut the firewood.

This was no mere ceremonial task like trimming the Christmas tree or painting the porch. Their house was heated entirely by woodburning fireplaces. Bob and Carolyn Doherty had built their handsome white brick home on an isolated three-and-a-half-acre plot that had been part of her daddy's dairy, and though it contained many modern conveniences, the center of their family life was the den with its large fireplace. The den was the Ranger's favorite room, the place he kept his collection of handguns and the antique rifle that was supposed to have been used by one of General Custer's troopers. The stone fireplace reminded Bob Doherty of times past, times he had only read about: when old-time Texas Rangers lived on parched corn, jerky, and brackish coffee, freezing on some desolate plateau and ranging hundreds of miles alone on horseback to protect life and property from Indians, Mexican bandits, and other desperadoes. The Ranger had told Carolyn on many occasions: "Honey, I think I was born a hundred years too late." But he was still a Texas Ranger, and it was far and away the proudest fact of his life.

It was not yet 8 A.M. when Captain Dwight Crawford telephoned from Denton. "Mary Nosser claims Baker tried to kill her last night," he said, while Bob Doherty listened without comment. "Says Baker tried to overdose her with some heroin mixed in a Coca-Cola. Sounded like they had *some* party."

Bob Doherty hung up and grabbed his white Stetson. Carolyn met him at the front door with his briefcase. Everything else he would need was in the trunk of his car. "I'll be home as soon as I can," Doherty told his wife. In the eighteen months that he had been a Ranger, Doherty had told his wife good-bye every morning with almost the same words, and Carolyn seldom asked the question that was on her mind— when did he intend to slow down? It had been four years since their last vacation and almost two years since his last full day off. "The kids and I weren't jealous of his job, but we were jealous of his time," she would admit later. "But Bob wanted to be a working Ranger, and we knew he would slow down when he felt he was able." The only times Doherty's family could be certain he would be with them was when Buster's Azle High School team played football. The Ranger, who had been a football player himself, never missed a game.

Carolyn stood on the porch under the graceful Spanish arches and watched as her husband strode through the patches of snow to his car. The arches had been his idea. Someday, he had said, he would hang a hammock here and watch the sun do its work. She suddenly remembered something. "Remember the deacons' meeting at the church tonight," she called out. "I'll try to make it," he said. She watched him turn his car and head out the driveway.

On his way to Denton, Bob Doherty thought about Mary Nosser. If Jimmy Baker really had tried to kill her, then it was likely that the whole deal was off. The Ranger and Dwight Crawford had been working for weeks to land Jimmy Baker; Nosser was their bait. The case had developed when Nosser's boyfriend, Kenneth Ray Bunyard, called Dwight Crawford to his cell in the Denton County jail and suggested a deal. Bunyard and Baker had once been partners in a drug operation, but they fell out and Bunyard was later arrested and charged with stealing cocaine from a local hospital. In return for certain considerations that were never made public, Bunyard fingered Jimmy Baker as "a heavy dealer of marijuana, cocaine, and speed in the Gainesville-Denton area." Since Baker didn't live in Denton County, Crawford asked Ranger Bob Doherty for assistance. A big part of a Ranger's job is to assist local law enforcement agencies, especially in cases where more than one county is involved. Mary Nosser agreed to set Baker up for a marijuana buy, but they also would need an undercover agent to act as the customer. Ranger Doherty telephoned the Department of Public Safety (DPS) Narcotics in Austin, and agent Ben Neel was dispatched to Denton on special assignment. Neel, a shaggy-haired forty-one-year-old agent who looked like an aging hippie, posed as "Steve McCloud," an ex-mafioso heroin dealer from St. Louis. Nosser had already convinced Baker and his wife, Linda, that "McCloud" was a trusted contact from her own days of street dealing in St. Louis, and Baker had agreed to sell him fifty pounds of grass. The shipment had arrived over the weekend, but Baker and some of his friends, including Mary Nosser, had decided they would rather party than work, so the meeting with "McCloud" never took place. Maybe Baker had seen the setup and really had tried to kill Nosser, or maybe in the paranoia of the heroin party Nosser just thought so. Either way, it could jeopardize weeks of undercover work. This was a side of Bob Doherty's job that the public never understood and that made it even more frustrating. The Ranger knew about those dark tunnels that Dwight Crawford described. He knew that without a few breaks they went nowhere.

The break came late Monday afternoon. Apparently the episode with the heroin hadn't been serious, because Mary Nosser called Captain Crawford and said, "He's ready to do the deal tonight."

They moved into action. Crawford arranged for two rooms at the local Ramada Inn, room 154 for "Steve McCloud" and room 155 for his raiding party of cops. By the time Mary Nosser delivered Jimmy and Linda Baker to room 154, the trap was set. Agent Ben Neel, posing as the dealer from St. Louis, was alone when he opened the door, but listening at the unlocked door of the adjacent room were four heavily armed lawmen—Ranger Bob Doherty, Captain Dwight Crawford, and two of Crawford's deputies, Bailey Gilliland and Ron "Tracker" Douglas. From the opening conversation, Doherty and Crawford could tell that things were not going as planned. Baker had agreed to bring fifty pounds of marijuana but showed up with only one pound. "I thought you'd want to taste it first," he told Neel. Neel would testify later that he "simulated" smoking the grass, then gave his approval. Baker telephoned a friend, Joe Fultner, who was supposed to bring the remaining forty-nine pounds. Neel sent out for beer, and while they waited for the full shipment they drank, passed joints, and listened to Neel's concocted tales about his Mafia and heroin-dealing days in St. Louis. When Joe Fultner arrived about an hour later, Doherty, Crawford, and the two deputies burst into the room and made the arrests.

Crawford took charge of the sack that Fultner had delivered. "There's only nineteen pounds here," he said—twenty counting the sample Baker brought. Baker told them that was all he could get.

There are two versions of what happened next. According to Ben Neel: "I told Mr. Baker that if he would assist us in going ahead with the entire fifty pounds . . . in other words, by getting the remaining thirty pounds . . . I would advise the district attorney that he cooperated." Baker then told the lawmen that he had a friend named Greg who lived in the country and might be able to fill the order. But Jimmy Baker's version was different: "It was already known that I was going to get the next shipment from Greg and they already knew it and they knew where his house was and it was just a matter of time. They were going out there anyway." Linda Baker added one more detail. She said: "One of them told Jimmy that if he didn't cooperate, he wouldn't ever get to jail alive." All parties agreed that Baker then telephoned Greg Ott, a twenty-seven-year-old honor graduate student at North Texas State University, and arranged to bring his pal "Steve" to Ott's place in the country later that night.

While Dwight Crawford returned to town to book Linda Baker and Fultner and to secure another fourteen hundred dollars in "buy" money, Neel and the deputies finished the beer and planned the raid. To Ranger Doherty it was like a military operation, but deputies Gilliland and Douglas looked on it more as a possum hunt. They gave the impression they had been waiting a long time for some real action. Sometime before Crawford returned with the buy money, DPS narcotics agent Don Jones joined the party at the Ramada Inn. Jones apparently wasn't expecting a raid because he didn't bring a gun. Neel loaned him one.

It was about 11 P.M. when a pickup truck with a camper on the back turned off Hickory Hill Road, near the tiny Denton County community of Argyle, and headed up the long, curving blacktop of Twin Pines Ranch. The ranch was primarily a place where wealthy girls stabled their horses and took riding lessons, but there were several rent houses on the property, including the small frame structure where Greg Ott had lived for about four years. Jimmy Baker, who was now in the uncomfortable role of informant, rode in the cab with Ben Neel. Hiding under a blanket in the camper were Ranger Bob Doherty, Captain Dwight Crawford, agent Don Jones, and the two deputies. None of them were wearing uniforms, although Crawford had a Denton County sheriff's department emblem on either shoulder of his quilted, fur-collared jacket. Bob Doherty still wore the brown Western-cut jacket he had put on before he left home, but he had replaced his Texas Ranger Stetson with a red baseball cap and, according to the testimony of the other officers, now displayed his Ranger badge over his left chest pocket. Even in the light of a nearly full moon the five men must have looked more like duck hunters than lawmen.

Jimmy Baker had told them that Ott kept his goods in the barn behind the house. Agent Neel, the expert in these matters, formulated this plan: Baker would take Neel inside and introduce him as "Steve Mc-Cloud" (Neel even carried an out-of-state driver's license issued in that name), and they would begin negotiating a deal. Neel would accompany Ott to the barn, and when they returned to the house with the marijuana, Neel would leave the kitchen door open as a signal for the raid to commence. Things went as planned up to that point.

What happened in the next ten to fifteen seconds could have passed for a Keystone Kops comedy if it hadn't ended so tragically. As Ranger Doherty was leading the raiding party out of the back of the camper, the swing-up overhead door dropped and hit him in the back, rendering into the crisp winter night a dreadful noise. The Ranger grabbed his shotgun and ran toward the northwest corner of the house. Dwight Crawford, the second man out, followed Doherty. Crawford would testify later that as he ran along the edge of the house he twice shouted, "Police officers!" Agent Don Jones was the third man on the ground, and he ran straight toward the door that Neel had left open, the door leading to the kitchen. Deputies Bailey Gilliland and Tracker Douglas got tangled in the blanket and were slow getting out of the camper. Tracker, who got his nickname because of his distinctive Indian features, would testify that as he was climbing down he glanced at the kitchen door and saw the figure of a man. "I told Bailey to be real careful, somebody was gonna get blowed away," he recalled. Both deputies would testify that they heard unidentified voices inside holler, "Drop the gun or I'll kill you!" and "He's got a gun!" followed by two gunshots several seconds apart.

Ben Neel, Greg Ott, and Jimmy Baker were in the back bedroom examining the marijuana when they heard the noise of the camper door falling. Neel testified that Ott hurried to the kitchen door and looked out. From Ott's point of view it must have been a terrifying sight: five heavily armed strangers in hunters' clothes climbing from the rear of a camper. Ott ran back through the middle room and toward the beaded curtains leading to the living room, passing very close to the bedroom door where Neel was still standing. Ott had a pistol in his hand, and by now Neel had drawn his own .45. Neel testified: "I stepped out into the doorway of the bedroom and I hollered in a real loud voice just right in his face, 'Police officer! Drop the gun!' He . . . started toward the doorway [to the living room]. . . . Again I yelled, 'Police officer! Freeze!' "

Just as Ott was about to disappear through the beaded curtains and into the living room, Neel fired at Ott and missed. Ott, gun in hand, was headed toward the living room door at the northwest corner of the house.

Outside the northwest corner of the house, Ranger Doherty and Deputy Gilliland heard Neel's shot. Gilliland leaned across a pile of firewood and tried to see through a window curtain. Ranger Doherty positioned himself directly in front of the living room door, crouched slightly, and kicked it open. At the exact second that the Ranger's boot smashed into the door, a bullet fired from inside the house passed through the door and hit him above the right eye. Bob Doherty fell straight back, staining the snow with blood. He never saw the man who killed him.

Telephone calls in the middle of the night never bothered Carolyn Doherty. But for twenty years she had lived with the dread of a knock at the door. "I knew if I heard a knock in the middle of the night and I opened the door and a lieutenant or sergeant was standing there . . . I knew Bob would be dead." But on the night of February 20, there was no time for official courtesy. Bob Doherty was unconscious but still showed vital signs as the ambulance raced from Denton to John Peter Smith Hospital in Fort Worth, escorted by maybe a dozen police units sealing off traffic in every direction. Police radios all over North Texas crackled like leaves in a storm.

It was sometime after 11 A.M. when Carolyn Doherty answered the phone. Ranger Tom Arnold, calling from Arlington, told her, "Carolyn, I hate to tell you, but Bob's been hurt."

"How?" she asked.

"Gunshot," Arnold said.

She didn't want to ask the next question, but she had to. "Where?"

"In the head region," Arnold said.

He said he was coming to get her, but Carolyn told him there was no time. She hung up, amazed at her own calm. She telephoned her preacher, Jesse Leonard; then her mother, who lived next door; then Charlie Stewart, chief of the Azle police department. The calls had awakened Kelly. "Your daddy's been shot," Carolyn told her daughter. "Don't wake Buster till we see how bad it is." Carolyn's father arrived from next door to stay with the children. In a matter of minutes Carolyn, her mother, and the preacher were passengers in Chief Stewart's police car, screaming toward the hospital in Fort Worth. At every traffic light there was a city or county or state police vehicle sealing off traffic. *Nobody but another policeman could understand,* Carolyn thought to herself. *It's a brotherhood.* The crackling of the police radio gave her a block-by-block account of her husband's race against death.

Carolyn is a large woman with a gentle face and, by her own admission, could "cry at the drop of a pin." But no one this night would see her tears. All the way to the hospital, all she could think was, *Isn't it odd how things turn out?* Carolyn and Bobby Paul Doherty had been sweethearts since they first met in the early fifties at Lake Worth High School, not more than a mile from where they lived now, and yet they had come so far. Bob Doherty was an all-around athlete in high school, good enough to win a football scholarship to Lamar Tech in Beaumont. He lasted only that first year. She remembered: "Beaumont was a long way from Lake Worth. He tried it, but after a while he came home to be close to me." Even in high school Doherty had talked about becoming a Texas Ranger. But that seemed an impossible distance from where they were when they got married in 1957. Maybe if he had stayed in college. But things turn out. Doherty worked for a while at General Dynamics in Fort Worth and served as a volunteer fireman and reserve police officer in Lake Worth, all the time waiting for word on his DPS application. Today it takes a minimum of sixty college hours for an applicant to be admitted to the Department of Public Safety Academy, but in those days it was easier, and she remembered their jubilation when he was finally accepted in 1958. "We didn't have much money then," she recalled, "and yet things were so good that sometimes it scared me."

For his first five years as a DPS trooper, Doherty was stationed in Wharton. Carolyn recalled how happy she had been when she heard they were transferring to Gainesville, much closer to home, but now there was a lump in her throat as she remembered how the vacancy came about—a DPS trooper had been shot to death. In 1969 they were transferred to Fort Worth and built their home in Azle. Even then she had mixed feelings. Doherty had already decided to apply for the Rangers, and Carolyn knew that when he was accepted he would likely be stationed in another part of the state. Both children were established in school now—Kelly was an honor student and Buster a promising young middle guard on the football team. It would be very hard to move again. Sitting in the front seat of Charlie Stewart's police car, Carolyn almost cried when she recalled that day in 1976 when Bob suddenly asked: "If you could have two wishes, what would they be?" She had answered immediately: "For you to get promoted to the Rangers and for us to stay here." Bob had smiled and told her: "You guessed it." Bob's career prospered, and they settled into their house. So things turn out, but in such odd ways.

Charlie Stewart's police car arrived at John Peter Smith Hospital just ahead of the ambulance. Carolyn waited at the emergency room door. "My first thought," she said later, "was, Lord, don't let it be serious. Then I saw them bringing Bob in and I knew it was too late. My next thought was, Lord, give me strength to accept what will be." By now the emergency room was swarming with every variety of cop. It was only a few minutes before Ranger Captain G. W. Burks, Doherty's commanding officer, took her aside and said, "Carolyn, he's gone."

"It's funny the things you think to say at a moment like that," she recalled. "I asked if Bob had ever been conscious. He said no. That's what I wanted to hear. I asked if they got the man who did it. He said yes." Someone gave her Bob's briefcase. She almost felt like a trespasser opening it. The briefcase contained a number of unanswered letters postmarked from all over the state. One was a note from Roy D. Tavender of Texas Refinery Corporation thanking the Ranger "for signing all those Gunslinger Awards." Taped to the inside lid of the briefcase was a card titled "The Ranger's Prayer." At the top of the card was a picture of a machine gun. Carolyn's mother was crying, and the preacher looked like he was experiencing Judgment Day, but Carolyn Doherty was thinking, *I'm glad he didn't get killed going to the grocery store. He hated to go to the grocery store.*

When Carolyn picked up the newspaper the following morning, there, staring at her, was a picture of the accused killer, Greg Ott. His hands were cuffed across his chest and through the wild nest of long, black hair and scrubby beard his eyes burned with a terrible light. It was impossible to look at the picture without thinking *Charles Manson.* How strange, Carolyn thought, that she felt no bitterness, no hatred, just a permanent sense of loss. But she said to herself: *This man is everything Bob was against.*

No one in Fort Worth could recall a funeral quite like Bob Doherty's. The Lakeside Baptist Church where he was a deacon was too small, so the service was held at the Rosen Heights Baptist Church. A crowd estimated at two thousand filled the church and its auxiliary chapel. Hundreds more waited outside. Letters and flowers and telegrams came from all over the world. Dolph Briscoe was expected but didn't show. Attorney General John Hill was in prominent attendance. DPS Director Colonel Wilson Speir was there, as was the largest gathering of Texas Rangers anyone had seen since the dedication of the Texas Ranger Hall of Fame in Waco. Outside the church about 350 uniformed lawmen, representing departments as far away as Texarkana and Houston,

Frank Hamer, A. Y. Allee, and Bill Wilson, along with Clyde Barrow's Colt revolver and Bonnie Parker's sawed-off shotgun. The curator of the museum has asked Mrs. Doherty for her husband's .45; he hasn't yet requested Greg Ott's .38, but it is not unreasonable to think that someday he might. Some of the exhibits have nothing specifically to do with the Texas Rangers, but they do glorify the code and legend of the West, of which the Rangers no doubt consider themselves the custodians.

There was hardly any law in Texas when Stephen F. Austin created the Rangers in 1823, so the Rangers made their own. Their mission was to protect the lives and property of Anglo settlers and businessmen against Indians and other renegades unsympathetic to the white man's ways, and legal disputes were often as not settled on the spot with a Colt revolver. An anonymous outlaw once remarked to old-time Ranger W. M. Green, "It is easy to see a graveyard in the muzzle of a Ranger's gun." Back around 1880, in an operation that became known as the "Red Tide," a Ranger sergeant working undercover took crude photographs of outlaws and might-be outlaws along the border, then dispatched fifteen Rangers to "remove from circulation" anyone resembling the men in the snapshots. In a few weeks some one hundred "outlaws" were buzzard food.

In the early days the Rangers were a military organization, but one with a special mission. Walter Prescott Webb wrote: "The Rangers were Indian exterminators; the soldiers were only guards." They also played a special role on the Mexican border, continually reminding those Mexicans living north of the Rio Grande that the *tejanos* had won the Battle of San Jacinto. On one memorable occasion, a few Rangers invaded Mexico, attacking a heavily armed rancho to regain some rustled King Ranch cattle. Early Rangers lined the parking lot in an honor guard. It had been forty-seven years since anyone had killed a Texas Ranger in the line of duty.

Forty miles north of Fort Worth, in the quiet college town of Denton, Greg Ott was being charged with capital murder and held without bond. Ott's face was badly swollen and his ribs were bruised. He had been handcuffed facedown on the floor when Bailey Gilliland jerked him up by the hair and held him for Tracker Douglas, who said, "You won't forget this Indian!" and smashed Ott between the eyes with his fist.

The folktale of "one riot, one Ranger" is the perfect example of the Ranger legend, because it probably never happened. Like their nearest counterparts, the Canadian North West Mounted Police, the Texas Rangers were too wild and improbable for most history books, so their exploits had to be reconstituted for general consumption. So mystical is this branch of law enforcement that when a woman friend of mine read that a Texas Ranger had been killed she automatically assumed he was a baseball player. The "one riot, one Ranger" parable apparently refers to an incident in 1906 when Captain Bill McDonald faced down a group of twenty black U.S. Army soldiers at Fort Brown. But what McDonald said on another occasion probably speaks more accurately of the Ranger mentality, past and present: "No man in the wrong can stand up against a fellow that's in the right and keeps on a-coming."

The museum at the Texas Ranger Hall of Fame in Waco commemorates the legacy of violence and celebrates the myth of the "fellow that's in the right and keeps on a-coming." Almost all the museum exhibits are firearms once wielded by famous lawmen or equally famous outlaws. There are a number of guns used by famous Rangers like Lone Wolf Gonzaullas,

like Rip Ford and Ben McCulloch would charge a band of Comanches or confront an angry mob single-handedly, but as the Indians vanished and the border settled down, the Rangers had to adopt a new role. Some say they were never the same once they exchanged their horses for automobiles, once they became just another breed of peace officers, constrained by bureaucrats and red tape. They couldn't *be* the law anymore; they had to serve it.

Throughout their history, the Rangers have always found it easier to handle Indians than politicians. This was particularly true from the turn of the century until Governor James Allred instigated sweeping reforms in the state police force in 1935. Until 1935 the Rangers *were* the state police, operating under the direction of the adjutant general. These were times of world war and revolution in Mexico, of Prohibition and oil boom towns, of political corruption and pitched battles between ethnic groups. And there was turmoil within the Ranger service itself. In those days governors would replace key Rangers with favored lackeys and stooges. The fabled Ma Ferguson discharged the entire Ranger service and replaced it with 2300 "special" Rangers, some of them ex-convicts and others getting ready to be. A legislative investigation in 1919 charged Rangers with crimes ranging from murder to being in the pay of German spies. One of Allred's first tasks was to cancel all "special" Rangers and to establish new criteria for special commissions not to exceed 300, a legal quota that still exists. Special Rangers (there are about 170 of them today) are mostly agents hired by railroads, cattle ranches, and oil companies, though some of them are merely good ol' rich boys who get pumped up when they pin on a star.

Although Allred's reforms created the modern agency called the Department of Public Safety and placed the Rangers under its direction, it did not impede the power of a governor to use the Rangers for his own purposes. As an intimidating arm of the governor, Rangers have been called on to break strikes, suppress minority groups, and generally chill political dissent. This practice seemed particularly blatant in the sixties. When John Connally was governor, the Rangers built a reputation for brutalizing Mexican Americans in the Valley. The first incident was in 1963 when Crystal City's majority emerged and elected all Mexican Americans to the city council. Under the command of Captain A. Y. Allee, Rangers were sent to "keep the peace," which Allee apparently proceeded to do after his own fashion. He was later charged in a civil suit with cursing at Mayor Juan Cornejo and then banging his honor's head against the wall six times.

But the bad blood in Crystal City was tame stuff compared to Starr County, where in 1967 the United Farm Workers were attempting to organize labor. Connally sent in the Rangers after protesters burned down a railroad trestle, stopped a train by lying across the tracks, and defied state laws against mass and secondary picketing. Whatever his original intent, the effect of Connally's order was to break the back of the UFW's attempt to organize. Various Rangers were accused of smashing demonstrators in the face with shotguns, demolishing union cameras and exposing film, threatening to drown a UFW organizer, and in at least one case, dangling a union man alongside a railroad track with his nose inches from a fast-moving freight train.

As in Crystal City, the villain of the Starr County war was A. Y. Allee. The captain was a gruff old veteran of Ranger wars dating back to boom town campaigns. He was truly carved out of the best Ranger tradition, which critics thought was precisely his

215

problem. As the old captain told a *New York Times* reporter, "Those people, by George, started to picket fifteen to twenty at a time. They didn't work and didn't want to. They said they wanted to be arrested, and, by George, I accommodated them!" No Ranger in modern times (if ever) has received the heat Allee did over the Dimas incident in Starr County. Magdaleno Dimas was a UFW organizer with a long police record and heavy Teamsters backing, none of which made him the type of person A. Y. Allee would take to lunch. After several minor skirmishes, the captain chased Dimas home, kicked down the door, and whacked poor Magdaleno across the chops with the barrel of his shotgun. For this Allee was required to stand up before a special three-judge federal court in Brownsville and explain his actions. Allee said he was only doing his job. In an attempt to portray Allee as a racist killer, a union attorney kept accusing the old captain of disliking Dimas.

Allee reminded the court that Dimas had a highly unsavory police record. As to the charge that he tried to kill Dimas, Allee responded: "I could have killed him if I wanted to, but I didn't want to kill him. Didn't want to hurt him. I could have shot him three or four times before he got in that door if I was that kind of feller. I didn't want to." When the union lawyer pressed on with his belief that the captain had tried to kill Dimas, Allee snorted, "If I wanted to *kill* him, I'd probably take a little Bee Brand insect powder and kill him. Hell, it won't take much to kill him." Allee took the heat for Starr County, but the real villain was the secondary picketing law, which in 1972 was found to be unconstitutional.

As a practical as well as a public relations matter, a Texas governor would have to be faced with a very serious labor riot before calling in the Texas Rangers today. "The tendency now is to use uniformed people at labor locations," says Colonel Wilson Speir, choosing his words carefully. "Some people felt the Rangers misused their authority in the Valley incident. But remember, Texas had a law against secondary and mass boycotts. Later, the federal courts threw the law out. Therefore, we are no longer required to enforce that law."

It is the job of the Texas Rangers to investigate major crimes, make arrests, and assist local law enforcement agencies. Though the Rangers are the crème de la crème, they are only one of four services within the DPS Criminal Law Enforcement Division. They are not even the largest. The Legislature currently authorizes 94 Rangers, compared to 124 narcotics agents, 50 criminal intelligence agents, and 22 motor vehicle theft officers. Still, the Ranger badge is the highest honor accorded to a lawman in Texas. Something like eighty percent of the current Rangers came up through the DPS ranks.

Each year the DPS receives about three hundred applications for Ranger service, of which maybe a third qualify to take the entrance exam. An applicant must be between thirty and fifty, have at least sixty hours college credit and eight years experience in law enforcement, and possess a spotless record. Of the hundred or so who qualify to take the written exam, only the top thirty appear before the Oral Interview Board. Of the thirty, maybe three or four will be certified as "eligible." Last year there were three eligible applicants and two vacancies. "We're probably the only police force anywhere that doesn't recruit," says Captain Bill Wilson, a former University of Texas football player who is supervisor of the Ranger service. "We're kinda proud of that." Four of the ninety-four Rangers have Spanish surnames, but there has never been a black Ranger, much less a female. "As far as I know, we've never had a woman applicant," says Speir.

Rangers are paid the same salary as Highway Patrol sergeants, $1302 a month. They are furnished with a .357 shotgun. They get a $500-a-year clothing allowance. Except for the Stetson and boots, there is no official Ranger uniform. In the sixties Rangers were required to own a gabardine suit for ceremonial purposes, but that requirement was dropped. Most Rangers these days prefer leisure suits. A Ranger's proudest possession is his badge, traditionally made from a Mexican five-peso piece. The origin of this practice is not clear, but in the old days Mexican silver was soft enough to cut easily with a knife, and taking a five-peso piece from a Mexican was no great chore for a Ranger.

Given all this tradition and mythical status, you have to wonder what Ranger Bob Doherty was doing messing around with a nickle-and-dime marijuana bust. Captain Bill Wilson told me, "He had initiated the case himself, using information he got from a man in jail. It was just good, sound police practice is what it was. One fellow led him to the other fellow."

But was it sound police practice to surround that farmhouse in the middle of the night unannounced and wearing civilian clothes? They could have easily come back the next day or, better yet, grabbed Greg Ott on his way to class. The Texas Rangers made 1764 felony arrests last year, and in no case that anyone could remember had it been necessary to act like they had Machinegun Kelly trapped in an attic. Captain Wilson reminded me, "Any narcotics dealer who carries a gun has got to be considered a major criminal." But Greg Ott was no major criminal, not until Bob Doherty was dead. What compounded the tragedy of February 20 was that it never should have happened.

If someone had walked into the philosophy depart-

ment at NTSU on the morning of February 21 and announced that God had caught his fist in the soft drink
machine, it would have made more sense than the
news that Greg Ott was in jail charged with the capital murder of a Texas Ranger. One of the women
quickly charted Ott's biorhythms and reported that
he was in triple crisis. She could only wonder about
the dead Ranger's biorhythms. Everyone knew that
Ott dealt a little weed, that was no big deal in a college town, and of course he was a trifle weird, as were
most of his friends. "You see a slice of strange people
in any philosophy department," Professor Pete
Gunter said. "But I'd have to say Greg was less kinky
than most. He was the last person in the world I
would have expected to shoot someone." They were
already speaking of Ott in the past tense, as you do
when anyone's life has changed irrevocably. *A Texas
Ranger.* Unbelievable!

In his seven years of college Ott had been a fairly
good student, and in the last year or so an exceptional
one. He had graduated summa cum laude with a psychology degree the previous December. Now he was
heavily involved with Heidegger, existentialism, Zen,
and Buddhism. There had been an occasional girl
friend (he was married once briefly), but Ott stayed
pretty much alone, living in the country with his cat
and his books and his leather-working equipment.
His place, which he rented from Twin Pines Ranch,
was a shanty onto which he had added two rooms,
more than doubling the original size. In a workshop
near the house, Greg and his partner Ron Mickey
made belts, purses, vests, whips, and other leather
goods that they peddled around campus.

Greg had had a bad time a few years before. He had
been hooked on heroin, but now he was clean and
gave every indication of staying that way. His friends
seemed to think he had pulled himself together in re-

cent months, and they were happy for him. But the heroin had permanently damaged his liver and he confided to friends that he didn't expect to live long. "The thought that he might be dying made it hard for him to get close to anyone," said Shirley Smith, who had dated Ott for about a year.

As a dealer of marijuana, Ott was small onions. He never had much money. If there is such a thing as grooving on poverty, Greg grooved on it. He didn't talk much and when he did it was about Heidegger and nirvana and what he called "the Oriental no-mind concept of life." Cathy London, another philosophy student, explained, "It was the idea that you flow with the movement rather than consciously exert yourself." What made no sense to Mary Collins, an anthropology student, and to most of his other friends, was the *gun*. Three guns, actually—a pistol, a rifle, and a shotgun, all loaded. "Why did he have the gun?" Mary Collins asked. "Without the gun none of this would have happened." Dr. Richard Leggett, who had talked on the telephone to Greg just minutes before the cops arrived, was also puzzled. "Everything he believed in was essentially nonviolent," the professor of philosophy said, shaking his head.

Something had happened a year or so before, something traumatic and senseless. No one seemed certain of the details, but three men with shotguns had forced their way into Ott's house, tied up Ott and a girl friend, and stolen some goods, including all his leatherworking equipment. "He said it was the most fearful moment of his life," Cathy London recalled. "He had never experienced such a feeling of total hopelessness. That's when he got the guns." Maybe the experience changed him, or maybe it just brought him back to a place he had been before. "You know how dope dealers like to play big shot," another girl friend said. "They talk about blowing away pigs and stuff. They don't mean any of it. It's the old macho thing."

Nobody who knows him likes to talk about it, but ten years ago Greg Ott spent fifteen months in psychiatric detention at Timberlawn in Dallas. He was seventeen at the time. The son of a career Army officer, Greg had stabbed another teenager at Fort Sam Houston in San Antonio. This wasn't the first time he had demonstrated tendencies toward aggression. He had once tried to stab his mother and, on another occasion, his older brother. Faced with the choice of being prosecuted for assault or submitting to psychiatric care, Ott bent to his family's wishes and entered Timberlawn. The diagnosis was paranoid personality.

In a hearing last March, Dr. Doyle Carson, who had treated Ott, pointed out that a person with a personality disorder shouldn't be confused with a psychotic. "A personality disorder is more in the area of someone having immature features about his personality." One trait of a paranoid personality is hypersensitivity, which causes him to think frequently that people are mistreating him. Ott's pattern of response to insults had been, in the doctor's words, "to defend his self-esteem by striking back physically." Carson thought that Ott felt his masculinity was being threatened. "He had a lot of doubts about whether or not he was strong and manly and would interpret critical comments directed toward him as meaning he was weak." Carson also explained that personality disorders are not unusual in late adolescence, but it is not unusual for a person to outgrow the problems.

Greg Ott was not discharged from Timberlawn. After fifteen months there he just ran away. Dr. Carson recalled that he refused a staff recommendation to have Ott readmitted. "He simply wasn't heading in the same direction we were," the doctor said. By this time Ott's parents had moved out of the state and he was on his own. You might say he became a man at Timberlawn. About that time Ott met Ron Mickey, who for the next ten years would be his closest friend. "They were like brothers," Shirley Smith told me.

Nothing had ever shaken the scholarly community of Denton like the slaying of the Texas Ranger. There was hatred and sorrow and great confusion as people tried to sort out the details. The case was less a murder than a political hot potato. If the victim had been someone else—one of the deputies, for example—the case would have attracted very little attention, and District Attorney Jerry Cobb might have been inclined to file a lesser charge than capital murder. Cobb had never had a capital murder case; to memory, there had never been a capital murder tried to conclusion in Denton. Cobb was only thirty-four years old; it was a type of political pressure he could do without.

"Hell, yes, I'm on the spot," Cobb admitted weeks before the trial. "It's not a capital offense unless you can show that the officers were acting in the lawful discharge of their duty *and* Ott knew they were police officers. You always have trouble proving it when the officers are not in uniform." There were times when Cobb must have thought the case hopelessly circumstantial. No one actually *saw* Ott pull the trigger. The bullet that killed Bob Doherty had been so badly fragmented it was impossible to say it came from Ott's .38. Witnesses told conflicting stories. Captain Dwight Crawford claimed that he shouted "Police officers!" twice before a shot was fired, but agent Ben Neel, who was inside the house with Ott and Jimmy Baker, didn't hear him. Deputies Gilliland and Douglas had sworn that as they were climbing out of the truck they heard voices inside shouting "Drop that gun or I'll kill you!" and "He's got a gun!" but agent Don Jones, who was much closer to the house than the deputies, didn't hear either shout. Neel claimed that he shouted "Police officer! Freeze!" just before he fired at Ott. Could this have been what Gilliland heard? Not likely, because by the time Neel shouted this, Deputy Gilliland had already made his way to the northwest corner of the house where Doherty was about to kick in the door. Remember, Neel had just spent considerable time and effort convincing Ott he *wasn't* a cop. The whole fiasco took place in a matter of seconds. Wasn't it reasonable to believe that Greg Ott didn't recognize this as a police raid until *after* the Ranger was killed? Some of the officers agreed that the first thing Ott said after he surrendered was "Why didn't you tell me you were police officers?" So this was Jerry Cobb's case and he had no choice but to pursue it with a vengeance.

There was a lot of backstage maneuvering in the days just after the killing. Jimmy Baker, who helped set up the raid, had also been charged with capital murder, but that charge was quietly dropped, and after some days of freedom Baker went to federal prison for violating probation. Kenneth Ray Bunyard, who had started the whole chain of events, *now* volunteered the information that while trying to take a nap in his cell he overheard a conversation between Ott and one of Ott's attorneys. According to Bunyard, Ott admitted he saw someone at the door just before he fired. A day after the killing, Bunyard and Mary Nosser were married in jail. By the time the trial started in May, Bunyard was again walking the streets of Denton. Jimmy Baker, the only eyewitness who was not a cop, first confirmed the police version of what happened at Ott's house, but two months later, in a taped interview with his lawyer, Baker changed his story, claiming the only reason he lied in the first place was that two Rangers threatened to kill him in his cell. Baker *now* claimed that Ben Neel fired not one but two shots, and that Ott fired back at Neel rather than at the door, which would have been in the opposite direction. If Baker was telling the truth, the bullet that killed Bob Doherty must have come from Neel's .45. Certainly there was plenty of time that night for a cover-up, and without an identifiable bullet, who could say?

It would be up to Jerry Cobb to convince the jury that Greg Ott wantonly and deliberately killed a Texas Ranger, his motives being to save himself and protect his stash of marijuana. The jury would have to believe that Greg Ott was a violent and dangerous man who had killed once and if set free would likely do so again. It would be a tall order, but by the time the trial had ended Cobb had not only convinced the jury, he had also convinced himself. What is more, he had convinced Alan Levy, one of the two lawyers hired to defend Greg Ott.

Retired Colonel Bruce Ott had spent more than twenty years in the military and been around the world a time or two, but until he watched his son tried for capital murder he had never been inside a courtroom. He was a stiff, curt, red-faced man with silver hair and bifocals, good Pennsylvania Dutch stock. He was a self-made man. Against his family's wishes he had worked his way through veterinary school and now held a top position as head of research for a New Jersey pharmaceutical company. Marion Ott came from a well-placed family on Long Island and could still laugh about the time long ago when Bruce's family thought filet mignon was the name of her French poodle. Greg was the second of their six children. Their oldest son lived in New York and was an airline pilot. Mary Ott Joyce, their only daughter and the apple of her daddy's eye, was married and lived in Michigan. The next brother was

studying medicine in California, and the two youngest boys still lived at home in New Jersey. "It's
brought us all together," Bruce Ott kept telling people. But it went without saying that this was the worst
experience of their lives.

It came as no shock to Marion Ott to learn that her
son was fooling around with marijuana, but the old
colonel was dumbfounded. The connection of his son
with two crimes, marijuana and murder, was almost
incomprehensible. Bruce Ott sat in the courtroom
next to his wife and daughter, trying very hard to sort
it out. Marion Ott knew as a certainty that her son
did not deliberately kill a Texas Ranger, and the colonel had sworn to spend his last dime if that's what
it took to get an acquittal in the murder case. "I guess
I'm the redneck's redneck," he said at one point, "but
why did he have to be messing around with marijuana?" His daughter, Mary, reminded him that he
was exceptionally fond of martinis. He reminded her
that martinis were not illegal. The second or third day
of the trial Mary amazed herself by blurting out,
"Daddy, would it shock you to know that I've been
smoking marijuana for five years?" Only a lifetime of
military bearing prevented him from crying. All he
could say was, "I'm very disappointed in you."

The Otts had retained the two lawyers originally
appointed by the court. Hal Jackson and Al Levy
were respected courtroom lawyers with good connec-
tions. They were known as the Odd Couple. Jackson
was the fifty-eight-year-old silver fox of Denton
criminal law, a lifelong native and a highly decorated
war hero; Levy was a twenty-eight-year-old boy
wonder in town who had immediately tested the
waters by running for district attorney. Levy had run
against Jerry Cobb and Cobb's top assistant, Fred
Marsh. The three of them remained good friends.
Marsh and Cobb frequently kidded Levy that his one

225

mistake was running as a Republican. Jackson was the odd part of the couple. He regarded prosecutors as worthy quarry, but damned if he would go for the throat and damned if he would let the other fellow go for his. Whatever their differences in age and style, Jackson and Levy worked well together. Levy was glib and funny and self-effacing, while Jackson played counterpoint as the stumbling old fool, leading juries up alleys of his choice and then pouncing on them.

Once the town had recovered from its initial hysteria, Levy and Jackson put their plan into action. The first order of business was to prevent future outbreaks of hysteria—the emergence of another unexpected jailhouse informant, for example, or loose talk about their client's days at Timberlawn. Several of Greg's old friends were urged to take long vacations, including Ron Mickey, who, according to a report, was threatening to bring a Dallas motorcycle gang to town and lead a jailbreak. Their defense rested on the well-founded theory that an intelligent, independent-minded jury would see the incident of February 20 as a massive police foul-up.

There was *reasonable doubt* that Greg Ott even fired a pistol, much less at a man he knew to be a cop. There was hardly any physical evidence, and part of what the prosecution had was mutilated by the bunglings of the Denton sheriff's office. The state might have proved the bullet hole in the door was made by a .38, except some deputy had rammed his pencil through the hole so it would look neater. The test that could have proved that Greg Ott indeed fired a pistol that night was inconclusive because the deputies had first insisted on fingerprinting their man. Jackson had calculated that the state's weakest witness would be agent Neel, who fired the first shot. Neel's own record was not lily-white. He had been involved in other dope shootouts and had killed a suspect in an abor-

tive dope raid in Houston. The most recent example
of Neel's proclivity toward the wrong move came less
than a month before the killing of Ranger Doherty.
Neel awoke one morning to find not only his prize informant but also $9500 in state buy money missing
from his home. The informant's whereabouts and
how he managed to get the money out of the locked
trunk of Neel's car were mysteries that still bothered
the DPS. The department had suspended Neel for five
days, which indicated it was not entirely happy with
his performance.

Unfortunately for the defense, Jackson was not able
to get much of Neel's biography to the jury, but he
still had a use for him. During direct examination, the
prosecution had asked Neel to step over to the schematic near the jury box and draw the trajectory of the
shot he fired at the fleeing Greg Ott. When it was the
defense's turn to cross-examine, Jackson asked Neel to
return to the schematic and *continue* his line of trajectory. Cobb quickly objected, and Judge Bob Scofield,
who several times seemed on the verge of having
Jackson clamped in irons, just as quickly sustained
the objection. But it didn't matter. Suddenly everyone
in the courtroom was drawing a mental trajectory.
*The bullet would have gone right through the door
where Ranger Doherty was killed.*

When it came time for the defense to present its
case, Levy and Jackson had to answer one quick and
momentous question: had the state proved its case?
Although the jury had been permitted to examine
a photograph of Ott taken on the night of February 20—the one in which he looked like Charles
Manson—the defendant they had seen in the courtroom was scrubbed, groomed, and attractively at-
tired in a three-piece suit borrowed from Jackson's
closet. This was the impression they hoped the jury
would take with them. Levy took a straw vote among

members of the press, who mostly agreed that the worst they could get was involuntary manslaughter and long probation. The lawyers weighed whether to call Jimmy Baker as a witness and decided it was a poor risk. They would have to vouch for Baker's reputation, which was hardly what their client needed at the moment, and they couldn't really be sure what Baker would say under oath. "Anybody who tells two different stories has obviously lied once," Hal Jackson reasoned. The only other nonpolice witness was Ott himself, and they would call him only as a last resort—in the punishment phase after a verdict of capital murder. They couldn't afford to open up Ott's psychiatric record, however dated and oblique. The jury already knew that Ott was a dope dealer; if they also had to wrestle with expert testimony that he had once been diagnosed as having a paranoid personality with aggressive tendencies, then, sir, it would be time to make a fist and wait for the last needle.

Levy and Jackson decided to call only three witnesses, all of them law officers who would testify that the mysterious Jimmy Baker had *also* been charged with capital murder. This was done merely to make the jury wonder where the hell was *Baker* and why didn't the state call him as a witness? Only an hour or so after the defense began, it rested its case. Things looked pretty good. Bruce Ott was so happy that he offered to buy martinis all around. Marion Ott protested that it would be bad luck to celebrate prematurely and led the colonel off by the arm. In retrospect, it was a wise move.

Al Levy's closing statement was predictably incisive, except for one very unfortunate slip. Pointing to the door with the hole, which sat in the middle of the courtroom, Levy told the jury, "When Greg Ott fired that shot . . ." Say what? This was the first and only evidence the jury had that Ott did fire a shot. When someone asked Jerry Cobb later why he didn't pounce on Levy's slip in his own closing statement, the young district attorney said sheepishly, "I was thinking so hard what I was going to say I didn't even hear him." Cobb's final statement was short and explosive. He described Greg Ott as a "man ready to kill for his stash," and demanded that Ott be convicted of capital murder and pay for his crime with his life. Later, outside the courtroom, Cobb would fight back his own tears and describe it as the hardest thing he had ever done.

It took the jury about four hours to find Ott guilty of the lesser crime of murder.

When Judge Scofield read the verdict, the only one at the defense table who didn't look slightly relieved was Greg Ott. There were tears in his eyes as he was led off in handcuffs. The jury would still have to come back in the morning and deliberate the sentence, which could range anywhere from five years to life. But the threat of the death penalty had ended. "It feels like a tie," Al Levy told reporters. Levy seemed as relieved in defeat as Jerry Cobb did in victory, and Bruce Ott watched in wonderment as the two lawyers shook hands.

"I can't understand lawyers," the colonel said, shaking his head. "They laugh and joke with each other while my son's life is at stake."

That night as Levy, Cobb, and Fred Marsh were cooling their emotions and indulging in some serious drinking, Levy called it "probably the best verdict I've ever seen."

"Ott's a violent and dangerous person," Jerry Cobb said. "His whole personality proves it."

"If he hadn't killed the Ranger he would have probably ended up killing someone else," Levy agreed.

"Where's your evidence?" I asked the lawyers. I hadn't seen it. The psychiatric report was ten years old and vague to the point of being irrelevant. True, Ott didn't conform to some people's standards of behavior, but not a single witness had testified to an act of aggressive behavior since that time long ago in San Antonio. "I got some pictures to prove he was into S&M and bondage and all kinds of kinky sex," Cobb said. The following morning, with a couple of Texas Rangers looking over my shoulder, I examined the material seized from Ott's home. There were photographs of whips, body harnesses, dildos, and spiked collars, the sort of stuff you'd see in any pornography shop. There were also some lesbian magazines and a book titled *Sex With Dogs*. "What do you think the jury would have thought if they'd seen this stuff?" one of Cobb's investigators asked.

The only witness called by the defense in the punishment stage of the trial was Greg's mother. She was not called as a character witness—that would have opened up those doors Levy and Jackson wanted to shut—but rather to testify that her son had never been convicted of a felony. But, on the grounds that she hadn't really kept up with her son for ten years, Judge Scofield refused to allow her testimony. Greg Ott kissed his mother's hand as she walked down from the witness stand. She didn't have it in her to smile again. A few hours later, when the jury returned and sentenced Greg Ott to life in prison, Marion Ott fainted.

I don't know what went through the minds of the jurors, but I think they felt obliged to pinpoint the blame for the tragedy of February 20. Obviously the jurors believed that Ott did not know he was shooting at a cop, otherwise they would have found him guilty of capital murder. But if Ott didn't know the man on the other side of the door was a cop, who did he think it was? The prosecution argued that he shot to protect his marijuana, but I don't think this is a reasonable assumption. In the few seconds of action, all Ott really had time to know was that his house was being broken into from all directions and that he was being shot at. In that situation my guess is that he did what any other Texan inside his home with a gun in his hand would do. He fired back. Because of fate, a member of one of the legendary police agencies of the world was killed. I believe that in their honest attempt to attach blame, the jurors reduced the tragedy to a single notion: *dope dealer kills Texas Ranger.* No matter how they weighed the evidence, that was the crime.

What lingers is not so much the crime as the tragedy. Caught up in the scent of the chase, five heavily armed law enforcement officers, none in uniform, surrounded an isolated house in the middle of the night, hoping to trap and arrest a man with twenty pounds of marijuana. That is their duty, but why were they pursuing it as though they had just cornered the whole French Connection? Ott was a dealer of illegal chicken feed, not an all-points-bulletin fugitive. He wasn't going anywhere, except to class the next day. The crime of selling twenty pounds of marijuana to an undercover agent would probably have been worth no more than a long probation in Denton County. It wasn't the crime that obsessed the officers; it was the chase, the irresistible urge, against common sense, to play cops and robbers. Because of this, a Texas Ranger was killed and a twenty-seven-year-old graduate student will spend at least the next twenty years of his life in prison. Bob Doherty should be taking his long-overdue vacation right now, just as Greg Ott should be working on his master's thesis and living according to the terms of his probation. Instead, two lives are destroyed. This is the tragedy for which no blame has yet been fixed.

August 1978

Postscript

The tragedy of the events described in this story never fails to move me.

Greg Ott won't be eligible for parole until 1998. He's doing time for a crime he may never have committed. The government never directly proved he fired the gun. A lot of people still believe that the bullet that killed the Texas Ranger — poor soul — came from the gun of the narcotics agent, Ben Neel. Certainly there was a reasonable doubt.

I'm sure of one thing: Greg Ott never *intended* to kill a cop.

I learned recently that Bruce Ott and his wife had exhausted their savings in a futile effort to win an appeal. Nobody who knew Greg Ott believed he was a "violent and dangerous person," not then, not now. I don't understand why that doesn't matter in the eyes of the law.

10

Tom Landry
Melting the Plastic Man

What was the old world coming to? I asked Tom Landry. Landry was at his desk, his back to an autographed picture of Billy Graham, facing the Super Bowl VI trophy, impassive as a museum director, fielding questions with technical, theological, thermoregular certainty, impervious to the demons that my senses told me were present in staggering numbers.

I mean *where is it leading us?* This obsession with being first, being best, being Number One. Tampered transcripts at Ball High in Galveston, rigged Soap Box Derbies in Akron, highly subsidized eleven-year-old Chinamen making a shambles of the Little League World Series, bribes, kickbacks, burglary, perjury, Watergate. Had the monster of our pioneering escaped in the rose garden? It seemed to me that this preoccupation with being Number One was rushing us toward the Temple of False Idols, and from there to the paranoiacs' ward.

"I don't mean football or even sports in particular," I said. "I'm talking about this country, across the board. This thing, this passion . . . this *belief* that in the search for success the means justify the end. . . ."

Yeah, Landry knew what I meant. He had been challenged before, and I had heard him expound his beliefs many times—in interviews, press conferences, damp locker rooms, and Fellowship of Christian Athletes banquets. "Take away winning," he had said, "and you take away everything that is strong about America." But I wanted to hear him say it again.

"You're talking now about the negative side of winning," he began, and I fancied that there was a hitch in the toneless economy of his voice. "Generally, achieving goals . . . which in many cases means winning . . . is really the ultimate in this life we live in. Being the best at whatever talent you have, that's what stimulates life. I don't mean cheating or doing things that are bad. That's the negative side. But here's the thing: what are the alternatives? If you don't believe in winning, you don't believe in free enterprise, capitalism, our way of life. If you eliminate our way of life, what is the effect . . . what are the alternatives?"

I said that I couldn't name them all, but humility was probably one. Peace. Joy. Freedom from the stigma of failure. If this country had the same appetite for peace and brotherly love as it had for war and puritanical vengeance . . . if free enterprise was more than a code word for greed . . . we might become the beacon of the world that we imagine ourselves to be.

Tom smiled his Ice Age smile: I had known him for fourteen years and we had had this discussion many times. Tom did not see a contradiction between the terms *pride* and *humility*, any more than some politicians and military men see a rift in slogans like "Bombs for Peace."

"Achievement builds character," he told me. "People striving, being knocked down and coming back
. . . this is what builds character in a man. The Bible talks about it at length in Paul, in Romans. Paul says that adversity brings on endurance, endurance brings on character, and character brings on hope."

"Then hope . . . not joy, peace, or love . . . hope is the ultimate goal?"

"That's right," he said. "Character is the ability of a person to see a positive end of things. This is the hope that a man of character has. It's an old cliché in football that losing seasons build character, but there is a great truth in it. I've seen very little character in players who have never had to face adversity. This is part of the problem we see in this country today
. . . young people who have never really had to struggle in life, when they do eventually face problems where they need to turn to character, it's not there. They turn to the alternatives: drugs, alcohol, or something."

Drugs, alcohol, or something. Hmmm. I wondered what that *something* could be. Al Ward, the Cowboys' assistant general manager, who had known Landry since 1945, recalled that Landry's own life was a progression of goals . . . to make his high school team at Mission, Texas, to make it at the University of Texas, to make it with the New York Giants. "But each time he reached his goal," Ward said, "the kick wasn't there. Then he found religion. Now he is satisfied with life." Though he had been a Methodist since boyhood, Landry claims he didn't become a Christian until 1958, two years before he became the Cowboys' first and only head coach. "I was invited to join a Bible-study breakfast group at the Melrose Hotel in Dallas, and I realized I had never really accepted Christ into my heart. Now I have turned my will over to Jesus Christ," he explained. There is nothing unusual in getting off on Jesus, or even using Holy Scripture to justify any act or event, but in coming to grips with the alternatives—that is, *eliminating* them—Landry seemed to have refined the narcotic qualities of Paul's definition of character.

Landry was relaxed, more so than I had ever seen him, strangely relaxed considering that it was less than three hours before game time, perversely relaxed for a man who detests small talk and was now being bombarded with it: thirty minutes, my allotted time, had elapsed and I hadn't yet mentioned football to the man who is supposed to be the finest brain in the business. Landry's cobalt eyes studied me, waiting for a question, and I tried to remember what had happened in the year since I saw him last. He appeared warmer, less regimented, even vulnerable. Why?

Well, two things were obvious. The Cowboys had not repeated as Super Bowl champions, thus laying waste all that talk about a Cowboy dynasty. And fifteen of the forty players who did win the Super Bowl had been traded or forced into early retirement. Unlike previous champions—the Giants, the Packers, the Colts—the Cowboys weren't waiting for the skids, they were rebuilding while they were still near the top.

But there was something else, something Cowboys president Tex Schramm mentioned earlier. We were talking about the criticism that Landry treats his players like so many cards in a computer file.

Schramm said: "You have to remember, Tom is a very honest, straightforward person. He is not a con artist. He treats his players like adults. Some coaches sell their players a bill of goods . . . you've seen it, they stop just short of holding hands when they cross the street . . . and these coaches get away with it because their consciences don't bother them. Tom can't do that.

"I think one thing that happened last year was that Tom tried to adapt . . . he tried to have a double standard. Even though it was against his nature. This year there is one standard and everyone conforms. Tom has gone back to his original concept of gathering about him the type of players he likes."

It *is* staggering, the roster of nonconformers who had gone down the drain. Duane Thomas, Tody Smith, Billy Parks, Ron Sellers, Dave Manders, and in years gone by talents like Don Meredith, John Wilbur, Lance Rentzel, and Pete Gent, to name very few. Landry lifted his eyes and they vanished. Thomas was a landmark in Landry's experiment with the double standard. Thomas got away with things that in Meredith's time would have called for thumbscrews. There were those in the Dallas organization (players, especially) who resented Thomas' leading them to two consecutive Super Bowls almost as much as they resented not getting there without him last season. The official theory is that the Cowboys paid last year for the sin of putting up with Thomas in two previous campaigns.

Take the case of Billy Parks, heretofore a good white boy with a sterling reputation as a pass receiver. In the aftermath of Duane Thomas, Parks insisted on wearing white football shoes and speaking out against the war. Once he refused to play because his black friend Tody Smith was hurt, and another time he took himself out of a game because his presence on the field was keeping a black receiver on the bench.

Now they were gone, the nonconformers as well as the nonachievers, and Landry looked more relaxed than I'd ever seen him. You know the illegal smile, the one John Prine sings about? Landry wore what you might call a *legal* smile.

He told me: "I've come to the conclusion that play-

237

ers want to be treated alike. They may talk about individualism, but I believe they want a single standard. Yes, that belief is behind many of the trades we made. If a player is contributing and performing the way he ought to, he will usually conform. Now if he isn't performing well and not conforming to team standards either, he ought not be around. We can put up with someone who is getting the job done as long as he'll conform. But we just can't get along with a player who doesn't conform or perform. No way."

There is a common misunderstanding among football experts that the best team—the team with the most talent—wins. It is true that you don't win without talent, but in the National Football League there are five or six teams of more or less equal ability. In those delirious hours after Super Bowl VI when the Cowboys were drunk with victory and talk of the new dynasty rained down, Landry permitted himself a Virginia reel around the dressing room, then he struck a note of caution. The question, Landry said, is will the Cowboys perform at the same level next year.

"At the championship level," he said, "there is a very narrow edge between winning and losing. You don't have to take much away from a team to keep them out of the Super Bowl. The hunger that makes a player work hard enough to win is inherent in some, but in others it has to be built in. The edge comes from trying to achieve a goal. Once you've achieved it, it is very difficult to look back at the price you've paid and then make yourself do it again."

At the bottom of the sweet cup of Super Bowl VI, Landry read the future. Though they were essentially the same team that won the Super Bowl, the 1972 Cowboys were found lacking. There is only one Super Bowl, and it's no disgrace not to get there: in recent years, only Vince Lombardi's Green Bay Packers have been able to repeat as champions.

That is what hurt, the fact that Lombardi had done it. There had been no double standard at Green Bay. All-pro guard Jerry Kramer once remarked, "Coach Lombardi treats us all the same—like dogs." Even before his death a few years ago Lombardi was a football legend, a vain, volatile, uncompromising dictator, a living metaphor for Number One. Could Tom Landry afford to be something less? Not if he had character.

It wasn't Jesus or Paul that Tom Landry had in mind when he did corrective surgery on the 1973 Cowboys team, it was Vince Lombardi.

Lombardi and Landry were guiding forces behind the great New York Giants teams of the fifties, and when pro football climbed out of the coal yards into the affluent living rooms of America in the early sixties, they were major influences. Jim Lee Howell was the head coach of the Giants, but it was Lombardi's offense and Landry's defense that gave the Giants character. After Lombardi moved on to the head job at Green Bay and Landry took on the new franchise in Dallas, Howell resigned, explaining, "Ten victories don't make up for two defeats."

"Lombardi was a much warmer person than Landry," says Wellington Mara, the Giants owner. "He went from warm to red-hot. You could hear him laughing or shouting for five blocks. You couldn't hear Landry from the next chair. Lombardi was more of a teacher. It was as though Landry lectured the top forty percent of the class and Lombardi taught the lower ten percent."

Landry was still a player-coach when he designed the modern 4–3 defense, pro football's equivalent of the doomsday machine. Later, at Dallas, Landry pioneered a method of combating that defense—the multiple offense.

"Landry was a born student of the game," says Em Tunnell, the great defensive back who played with (and later for) Landry. "But he was kind of weird. After a game the rest of us would go out for a beer; Tom would disappear. He was always with his family. You never knew what was going through his mind. He never said nothing, but he always knew what was going on. We didn't have words like *keying* [i.e., reacting to prearranged schemes] in those days, so Tom made up his own keys and taught them to the rest of us."

By training, Landry was an industrial engineer: he had a need to know what was going on. "I couldn't be satisfied trusting my instincts the way Tunnell did," Landry explained. "I didn't have the speed or the quickness. I had to train myself and everyone around me to key various opponents and recognize tendencies."

"Most of us just played the game," Frank Gifford recalls. "Landry studied it. He was cool and calculating. Emotion had no place in his makeup."

Another former Giant, Dick Nolan, who went on to become head coach of the San Francisco Forty-niners, says, "I remember one time Tom was at the blackboard, showing me that if their flanker came out on the strong side on a third-down play and the fullback flared to the weak side, I was to follow the fullback out a few steps and then race back quickly because they would be bringing the wingback inside me to take a pass. 'But Tom,' I said, 'what if I commit myself that completely and the wingback isn't there?' Tom just looked at me without any change of expression and said, 'He will be.' "

Landry's reputation was constantly exposed to ridicule in the mid-1960's, not only because his Cowboys twice lost championship games to Lombardi's Packers, but because Landry himself came across as such a cerebral paradox: a rigid, humorless figure stalking the sidelines of the Cotton Bowl in his felt snap-brim and burial-policy dark suit. Like the team he coached, Lombardi was purely physical: seething, kicking, pushing, openly humiliating those around him, and getting results. If the Packers were the bludgeons of pro football, the Cowboys were the slide rules. Paul Hornung once observed, "Lombardi would be kicking you in the rump one minute and putting his arm around you the next."

Landry would react to a great play or a poor play in the same dispassionate manner, as though it were ancient history. When a player was down writhing in agony, the contrast was most apparent: Lombardi would be racing like an Italian fishwife, cursing and imploring the gods to get the lad back on his feet for at least one more play; Landry would be giving instructions to the unfortunate player's substitute.

Landry once explained: "The reason I take on the appearance of being unemotional is I don't believe you can be emotional and concentrate the way you must to be effective. When I see a great play from the sidelines, I can't cheer it. I'm a couple of plays ahead, thinking.

"Lombardi's style of play was very different from ours. The Green Bay system of offense—we call it the basic system—was that you were going to run the power sweep regardless of what the other team put up against you. Run that play over and over until you could execute it in your sleep. It was all execution. So Lombardi had to develop the players to an emotional pitch, keep them doing their best all the time against a defense that knew what was coming. The Packers had to stay very high emotionally to win.

"Our system is different. We run a multiple offense and must take advantage of situations as they present themselves. Everything we do from every formation doesn't work against every defense, so we have to concentrate, we have to think. Our defense is also quite complicated. It depends on reading movements and formations and knowing where to go. Therefore the nature of response from the sidelines must be very different. The players don't want to see me rushing around and screaming. They want to believe I know what I'm doing."

Lee Roy Jordan, Dallas' middle linebacker, explains: "Landry isn't a praising coach, he's a corrective coach. If you do something right, that's what you oughta do. He only talks when you do something wrong. If Tom says 'damn it,' you know something severe has happened."

There were traces of empathy when the Packers referred to Vince Lombardi as *Il Duce*. Landry has been called Old Computer Face, a description that has all but vanished with the nonconformers and nonachievers. Pete Gent used to say he could tell when Landry was mad; the muscles beneath Landry's ears would pop out and his eyes would sort of glaze. "His normal method of discipline is to treat you like a number," Gent said. "He seems to be concentrating on talking to you mainly to keep you from vanishing."

Gent, author of the bitterly critical pro-football novel *North Dallas Forty* (read: Dallas Cowboys), agrees with another ex-Cowboy, Duane Thomas: "Landry *is* a plastic man. And yet, there is this paradox—in Landry's presence you do not feel the cool platitudes of plastic and computers. You feel something more visceral. You feel fear." Meredith and other ex-Cowboys have said the same thing. It is the fear that no matter how hard you try or how much you care you will be found inadequate.

Landry hadn't read Gent's novel and didn't plan to, but he was aware of the general criticism: big-time football is dehumanizing, brutal, and unfairly stacked on the side of management.

In rebuttal Landry said: "It's an amazing thing, this whole area of criticism . . . the one thing a player respects in a coach is that the coach makes him do what he doesn't want to do in order to win. Lombardi had great respect from his players, not because they liked him personally but because he made winners of them. That is what all coaches are attempting to do, make players do things they don't want to do in order to achieve success. The people who usually level this sort of criticism [read: Gent] are the people who don't achieve."

By Landry's code, you could stick Gent's ration of character on the back of a postage stamp. Gent was not a great player, but he hung around for five years. Landry never understood why Gent, Meredith, and others sat at the rear of team meetings, laughing hysterically. Gent explains why in his novel: they were cracking and passing snappers of amyl nitrate. Gent once observed of Landry's playbook, "It's a good book, but everyone gets killed in the end." Gent's own book has already earned him more than $500,000. Nonachiever indeed.

Meredith, the honky-tonk hero, was a special case. From the beginning he was the Cowboys' future. Coming off a brilliant career as an All-American quarterback at SMU, Meredith approached pro football as though he were Popeye saving Olive Oyl from the cannibals. Meredith's quality was leadership, an ability to strike a spark of hope in the most hopeless situation. That is why he was called Dandy Don, a name Landry never appreciated. Meredith could rally a team from certain defeat, or splinter the sobriety of a practice session by jerking off his helmet and threatening Cornell Green with bodily harm. He played it for laughs: the notion of Meredith threatening a head-hunter like Cornell Green was beautifully absurd, and everyone appreciated it—everyone except Landry, who reminded the Cowboys in the meeting that night: "Gentlemen, nothing funny ever happens on a football field."

I don't know if Landry ever saw it, but beneath all that tomfoolery and searching Meredith was essentially the person he joked about—a good ol' East Texas boy, eaten up with talent and the Protestant vision of material success, fairly begging to excel and be recognized. Meredith endured against his own better judgment. He played many games when he could have rightly been in the hospital.

Meredith's unhappy decision to slide into premature retirement came after Landry supplied an obstacle Meredith wasn't prepared to endure. Landry pulled Meredith from the 1968 play-off game with Cleveland and replaced him with Craig Morton. Ironically, Landry pulled Meredith for throwing an interception that should have been credited against Landry's disciplined system of play. According to Landry's gospel, the Cleveland defensive back who intercepted Meredith's final pass should have been on the other side of the field. Unfortunately, the Cleveland defensive back was in the wrong place. It wasn't that Landry was wrong; Cleveland just wasn't right. Meredith couldn't endure the consequences—the humiliation that after all these years of enduring he could be benched for nonachievement.

When Meredith went to Landry, his pride crushed and personal problems weighing around him like a ninety-thousand-ton infection, thinking that at last he had made the right choice, a choice that would please Landry, the choice to quit football—then Landry would stay in character and say straighten up, don't do it, forget it ever happened and smile tomorrow. Instead, Landry looked at him coolly and said, "Don, I think you are making the right decision."

Landry contends that he was "treating Don Meredith as an adult," respecting Meredith's right and ability to decide for himself. But given their relationship, a relationship Landry controlled, that was no way to treat Don Meredith.

When I was a sportswriter in Dallas, Meredith and I had this unspoken arrangement whereby he would tell me what I needed to know and I would change his quotes to make both of us appear literate. Meredith had only one reservation to this arrangement. "Watch out for my image," he would caution me after every interview. Meredith saw himself as a thirteenth-century troubadour persecuted for his good intentions. He saw Landry as the Black Monk, a creature who could swallow himself without changing form. If Landry understood the depth of Meredith's paranoia, he never let on.

Sitting now across the desk from Landry, looking through the man and seeing my own reflection, I wondered: what image does Landry have of himself? I have been in many coaches' offices and observed that the decor is narcissistic — for example, the walls of Bear Bryant's office are papered with pictures of the Coach and His Team, the Coach and His Family, the Coach and Phil Harris, the Coach and His Buick. But there are only two small pictures in Landry's office — a small, gold-framed portrait of his family, and the large autographed picture of Billy Graham looking down from infinity. Is it possible that Landry sees himself as a rock?

I asked Landry if he thinks he has changed in the last four years and he took a long time to answer. "I've tried to," he said. "I think I've become more aware of people as individuals. I know the criticism — that I look at my players as numbers — and I guess there's something to it. People my age . . . we grew up with the Depression, the War . . . a time of ICBMs and pin-striped suits and rampant materialism. But the times are changing. I see that and I make an effort to change, too."

Has Landry changed? I asked Clint Murchison, Jr., the Cowboys' owner. "His hair has gotten shorter," Murchison said. Anything else? "Not that I know of," Murchison said.

They are subtle, befitting their instigator, but the changes are there. There are fewer rules, veteran players tell me. Veteran players (though not rookies) can wear their hair any way they please, and with a few exceptions, like Bob Lilly and Roger Staubach, most of them look like candidates for a drug raid. Landry personally sees to it that the word *optional* is printed on the schedule announcing the time and place of the weekly Sunday devotional. And the double standard, while officially refuted, exists as a practical matter.

"Just before training camp," Al Ward tells me, "Walt Garrison asked Landry for permission to ride in a rodeo. Landry has strictly forbidden Garrison to rodeo, but of course Garrison does it anyway. But this time, when he asked permission, Landry just said, 'I don't want to know about it.' "

In the preseason game against Kansas City Landry did something that no one in the press box could remember seeing him do before — he walked over to an injured player and inquired about his health.

What was it that Paul said again . . . about adversity and endurance and character and hope? Hope for what? More adversity? I look at Tom Landry again and now I know his self-image. Landry sees himself as a circle. So be it.

November 1973

Postscript

In the opinion of one washed-up sportswriter, Tom Landry is the best coach who ever lived. I didn't believe that when I wrote this story. I can barely remember writing it, and I can't remember what I was trying to prove. In the early days Landry did seem cold and distant, but that image disappeared long ago. When pressed, even Meredith and Gent will now admit a fondness, maybe even a love, for the man.

Without question, the Cowboys were the team of the decade in the 1970's. They won two Super Bowls (1972 and 1977) and lost a third (1978) partly because an official blew a pass interference call that enabled the Steelers to win by four points. Only two coaches in NFL history (George Halas and Curly Lambeau) have won more games, and Landry shows no signs of letting up. The 1982 season is his twenty-third as head coach of the Cowboys.

The last time I saw Landry was after the Cowboys beat Philadelphia and clinched their division in December 1981. I thought he wouldn't remember me, but he interrupted a press conference, walked over, and shook my hand. He'd stopped wearing those "burial-policy dark suits" and looked like something out of *Gentleman's Quarterly*. I asked if he remembered that time on Murchison's private island when he mixed me a martini, using the classic Landry recipe — two parts vermouth to one part gin. "Yes," he said, a trace of a smile on his face. He's still a man of few words.

11

The Middle-aged Man and the Sea

Chuenque Bay, California, Monday, April 4
First Day

A solitary autobus no larger than a sand flea jams
gears and belches smoke as it crawls up the mountain
and disappears on the single road to civilization.
That's *my* bus I am watching vanish. There won't be
another bus for twenty-four hours, if at all. When in-
stinct and years of conditioning tell me to cry out—
cry, "Stop! Wait! I'm coming with you!"—why do I
hesitate? I look around me at the strangers upon
whom my survival now depends and I realize I am
not the only one having second thoughts. Why don't
they cry out? The only thing worse than being a fool
is knowing that you have fallen into the hands of
other fools.

Two days of hard traveling have delivered me to

this remote, uninhabited, abruptly beautiful bay south of the small fishing village of Loreto and 150 miles north of La Paz. Chuenque Bay is the jumping-off place for the Southwest Outward Bound School's thirteen-day sea kayaking course. In the morning we will load our kayaks and paddle south along the western shore of the Baja peninsula. We will camp on barren volcanic islands and sea-locked clear-water coves, wherever there is shelter or a place to land along this jagged coastline where the mountains of the great Sonora Desert plunge into the Sea of Cortez. Except for a few tiny fishing villages accessible only by boat, nothing human has ever dented this fortress of nature. Having prepared for this trip by taking up jogging and cold-turkeying alcohol and other drugs to which my hedonistic system has formed an alliance of two decades, I have wallowed now for several days in sanctimonious glory. Suddenly I feel apprehensive; I came here seeking a simple vehicle for escape, but as I behold the uneasy specter of my new companions and speculate on their motives, I experience a sinking sensation of an actor who has stumbled onto the wrong stage.

Our chief instructor, Ernest Tapley (always called Tap), calls our attention to a phenomenon in the sky: a blinding sun that has been absolute monarch slips behind towering peaks, simultaneously illuminating a full moon that appears as dramatically as the titles of a movie screen. "Many of you may never have seen this before," Tap says, in a singsong voice. I study the faces of my eight fellow Outward Bound (OB) students as they bustle around the campfire, a little too ready to go.

Until today, none of us had ever met. A big part of the trip is supposed to be learning to work with strangers against a hostile environment. The students come from Washington, California, New Mexico,

Texas, Illinois, Ohio, Virginia, Connecticut, New York. There are two college students, a teacher, an architect, a bank-computer expert, a nurse, a man between jobs and wives, a rich girl on the bum, and me. All have paid $450 tuition plus transportation for the opportunity of experiencing thirteen days of hardship, deprivation, and danger. The youngest is eighteen and, at forty-two, I am the oldest. Also, according to one theory, the best. Kurt Hahn, the crusty old headmaster who founded Outward Bound in Wales in 1941, did so after observing this apparent contradiction: studies of British merchant seamen shipwrecked and cast adrift demonstrated that, contrary to popular belief, it was the *older* seamen who survived. Hahn concluded that the younger ones lacked a feel for wind and weather and, more than that, a faith in their own inner resources. Hahn's first OB course offered seamen thirty days of small-craft training, athletics, hard traveling by compass and chart, rescue training, and practical lessons in why you'd better trust your fellow man.

That curriculum is not too different from the one we're offered. There are dozens of other OB courses we might have selected—mountaineering in Colorado, sailing off the coast of Maine, backpacking in the Big Bend or Gila Wilderness, white-watering in Canada, cycling in Nova Scotia—but no doubt the reason each is here goes somewhere beyond logic. There is something in this confluence of sea and desert that transcends the visceral imperative of mere adventure. In contrast to the land, the sea is a shimmering, live storehouse, a silent world of plenty, a place to be loved and feared and finally to be dealt with. The sea is the reason we are all here.

Mark, a small Japanese-American who works for a large Midwestern bank, tells me: "I could have gone to Europe for what this is costing. But what could I do in Europe? Hang around a bunch of old museums? I'm not interested in seeing something someone else did." This is Mark's second OB course. Mark's teeth chatter as he speaks; he zips his windbreaker to the neck and burns his fingers attempting to pour coffee into his tin OB-issue cup. "Maybe we're all crazy," says Frank, a tall, wire-haired young man who has L.A. written all over him and snaps his fingers when he talks. "Hey, man, you're from Austin! All *right!* Where it's *at!*" Four of the nine students are female and Frank has already connected with the prettiest, a student from Connecticut named Carla. Carla says she wants to prove something to the people back home. Barbi, a tall, thin nurse from Cleveland, replies that the only person she has to prove anything to is herself. Linda, a chubby twenty-year-old rich girl from Virginia, says she is here because it's *real*, because she's sick of people *copping out*. Ann, a large-boned blonde schoolteacher, believes that by exposing herself to the external pressures of this environment, an inner self will emerge, some being she has lived with but never met.

Frank, Barbi, and Linda supervise the preparation of a thin, underseasoned, meatless stew (Linda doesn't eat meat, and anyway, there's not any), then we gather in a circle and listen as Tap outlines the course. Tap is a taciturn, superbly conditioned, remarkably capable man of fifty-two, a sort of wilderness philosopher with a weathered face, gentle eyes, and an easy rapport with nature. A good look at Tap's face suggests he probably hasn't slept under a roof in four decades. He explains that for the next thirteen days we will move down the coast, learning various skills and gaining confidence in our abilities. After the first week we'll each do a forty-eight-hour solo without food or equipment, and shortly after that the instructors will abandon the group to find its own way back

to civilization. As each day seems harder, Tap is telling us, it's really getting easier. "You'll do things you
never believed you could do," Tap says, lighting his
Popeye corncob pipe. "You'll learn your own capa-
bilities, and you'll learn to work with others, and
maybe the best of yourselves will come out. What we
want you to take back is not a feeling of the ocean or
the mountains, but a feeling about yourselves and
others. It's my experience that as the stress increases,
so does compassion."

Well, it's late. Tap will have us up at first light, running down the beach. I find my sleeping bag and turn
it around to shade my eyes from the brilliance of the
moon, accidentally discovering that this position
offers more protection from the wind and blowing
sand. I lie on my back, thinking of a better me and
listening to the waves against the rocks. From somewhere on the other side of the grove I can hear Barbi,
the nurse, talking to Linda, the rich girl. Barbi has
decided to quit her job in Cleveland and move to Salt
Lake City. Linda says she can hardly wait to go running down the beach at first light and asks that Barbi
please call her Meriwether in recognition of the fact
that explorer Meriwether Lewis was her fourth great
uncle.

Dear God, what am I in for!

Second Day

History may record this as the sorriest day of my
life. I hope so. I'd settle for that in a second, knowing
that it was all downhill from here.

Was it only eight miles that we paddled today? All
I know is that translates into seven back-breaking
hours—fighting currents and three-foot swells and
imminent danger of capsizing, which, miraculously,
no one did. There is a hot well of pain where my
shoulders once connected to my neck, and my lower

back feels pulverized. I can't turn my head without turning my entire body. My arms and face are sunburned, my lips cracked. In my haste to load the kayak this morning I failed to adjust the rudder peddle properly: for seven hours the only way I kept from capsizing was to hyperextend my left leg, which is now totally paralyzed. When our team of four singles and one double kayak beaches for the night in a sheltered cove below the cliffs of Candeleros Point, I have to be helped out of the cockpit. When I try to put weight on my left foot, nothing is there. Tap says I probably pinched a nerve. He assures me the feeling should return in a few days.

The nine students have been divided into two groups of what the instructors feel to be equal strength and ability. Except for one chance encounter, we won't see the other group again until the last day. Our instructors, Tap and his associate, Liz Nichols, make the kayak assignments. Since I am the largest and therefore presumably the strongest, I have been assigned to the rear cockpit of the double, behind Barbi, who was presumed falsely to be the weakest in our group of four. This was a mistake in judgment: Barbi could hold her own in a Marine platoon. It was Mark, the flyweight Japanese-American banker, who fell behind today. The fourth student in our group, Meriwether, is surprisingly strong for a chubby rich girl. Meriwether has the lungs of a drill instructor. I couldn't hear what she kept yelling back at poor Mark, but judging from his pained expression it had something to do with Pearl Harbor. I'm not particularly enchanted with Barbi, either. All I saw all day was the back of her life jacket and down-turned sailor's cap, but as I implored my aching, numbing leg to execute one more *hard left rudder*, her whiny, nursey voice kept repeating: "You're over*compensating* again."

But now the day has ended: despite the loss of one leg, I feel refreshingly whole. We hug the fire, finishing the pan-fried *cabrilla* (a sort of rock bass) that Tap caught while the rest of us were locating firewood. We study the constellations and listen to Tap's stories about serving with the famous 10th Mountain Division in World War II. Barbi finds it necessary to bring up The Bomb. "That seems so far away," Mark observes. Maybe so, Barbi answers, but if they *do* drop it, she'd just as soon be right under it. I fall asleep thinking of The Bomb hurtling down on Cleveland.

Third Day

Gulls squawk like teenagers showing off a new stereo. The only sounds are the gulls and the scraping of tennis shoes as we jog along the rocky beach at first light. There is that surreal sky again, only now it's reversed: the sun is an overture in orange as it scales the backside of Monserrate Island across the way, and the moon hangs like a melting wafer above the protective cliffs of our cove. Formations of rock, some as large as office buildings, squat in the clear green water. Along the beach are bleached bones, a large shark, a manta ray, a dead burro.

Before breakfast, we undergo another test by swimming out beyond the rocks to Liz' waiting kayak, then returning to shore. There is a magic moment as we observe three dolphins leaping in unison, three bodies completely clearing the water in a spontaneous ballet.

After breakfast, without being told, I adjust my kayak rudder in preparation for a lesson in sea-rescue techniques. Later, we carry our diving bags to a rocky point, wiggle into our wet suits, and enter another world. We glide effortlessly on the surface, breathing through snorkels, observing incredible varieties and numbers of fish that take no notice of our intrusion as they feed among the undersea caves and boulders. Tap and Liz demonstrate how to dive for scallops, which appear like great crusted biscuits on the rocks below. While we tread water, Tap pries open a shell and offers me a raw scallop the size of a hockey puck. It tastes salty, clean, and good. I choke on it as a wave washes over my face. When we are able to go deeper, we locate giant lobsters lurking below shelves of rock. Even inside our wet suits, the water is soon uncomfortably cold—sixty-three degrees, Tap informs us. Tap sends us back to warm up on the shore while he spears three large fish for dinner.

Late in the afternoon Harry and Libby Frishman and some other people from the OB base camp arrive in the Zodiac, a motorized rubber raft. They have brought along a fresh pineapple and have caught a bonito to augment the feast tonight. The bottom of an overturned kayak serves as our banquet table as we dine on fresh lobster with lime butter, raw and broiled scallops, rock crabs, fish cakes, smoked bonito, and Tap's indescribable skillet biscuits with honey. "These are the moments you'll remember," Liz says. Liz is one of those rare young women who find it very awkward to think of themselves as beautiful. She might think of herself as strong, or capable, or even graceful, but beautiful is something with a lot of teeth and hair on the cover of *Glamour*. A new Buick is beautiful. Forming a mental picture of Liz in a dress, or a bra, or carrying a parasol, or shaving under her arms is as incongruous as imagining a frisky colt pulling a Budweiser wagon. Like all the Outward Bound women I have met (the instructors, not the students), Liz seems fresh and natural, at peace with herself and her surroundings.

Fourth Day

Tap wakes us as soon as the moon clears Monserrate Island. He wants to get away early, while the sea is warm and calm. By 3 A.M. we have loaded our kayaks and are paddling south. It seemed cold when we climbed out of our sleeping bags, but now we discover a curious temperature reversal as a slight tail wind fans the trapped solar heat of the sea and pushes us along. This temperature reversal is especially apparent each time we pass along a cove or inlet and smell the sweet, fresh, cold air pressing down from the desert canyons. When mariners spoke of *smelling* the land long before they saw it, it must have been this smell.

Mark is riding with me now, in the front of the double, and we move along easily, listening to the clean sounds of our paddles and the nocturnal barking of sea lions from the direction of the island well off to our left. The moon is bright enough to read by. We land on a boulder-strewn beach with hardly a place smooth or level enough to lay out a sleeping bag, but we are too tired to care. When Tap wakes us again, the sun is already high. We can see Monserrate clearly now. It appears on the horizon as a slumbering dragon, but Tap points to a ribbon of deep blue water four or five miles offshore and tells us that we might expect wind. Using the island as a reference point, we plot our position on the chart: we are about halfway between Candeleros and San Cosme Point, on line with the southern tip of Monserrate. Eleven or twelve miles of open sea lie between us and the northern end of the island that is our next campsite. Tap leaves it to the group to decide how long we will stay here. We vote to cross tonight as soon as the moon is high.

In the afternoon Tap and Liz send us out alone to locate a stash of fresh water buried on a cove a few miles away. This is the first time the group has been on its own and there is a general feeling of exhilara-

tant, so have our minds. Viewed from your living room in Austin, Dallas, or Houston, crossing a twelve-mile patch of the Sea of Cortez in a kayak in the middle of the night sober might seem grounds for being committed. Here it is just a trip. Like the sunburn, or the unaccountable cuts and scratches or the stiff left leg, the trip has become a part of me, another experience barely perceptible in the rush of new things. I can *feel* the sea; not just on my face, but in my arms, working on my shoulders and back, running up my nose to my brain. By dawn we have covered three fourths of the distance: already the sun is burning off the thermal haze that belts the four-mile-long hunk of volcanic fusion named Monserrate. We sit dead in the water for a few minutes, resting, passing around hard-candy fruit drops, painting our noses with zinc oxide. Barbi wants to rest a while longer, but the others vote to push on and that's my command. A cruel mistress, leadership. Unexpectedly, a finback whale rises, blows, and sinks comfortably beneath the sea. A *whale!* This has barely registered before a second whale, this one about the size of an eighteen-wheeler, surfaces a few hundred feet off our bows. Paddle, m'hardies: *break your blooming backs!*

The long, white, smoothly curved beach where we put in has all the markings of paradise. The water appears so clear and pure I have to remind myself not to drink it. Outcroppings of rock protect the cove at both ends, and there are ledges of smooth rock that seem custom-made for a campsite. Tap and Liz make their own camp well down the beach from us. As leader, I volunteer to dig the latrine while the others rig a nylon fly to protect our food and equipment from the sun. Later, we bathe and scrub the caked salt from our clothes. Gnat-size flies called *bobos* swarm in the stillness of the afternoon, but soon the breeze

tion as we race our three kayaks to a promontory peaked by a tall, solitary cactus. I can hear Mark giggling as the bow of our boat noses out the two women. When we reach the cove we discover the second group of kayaks, their occupants lounging in the shade under a nylon fly, looking frayed and out of sorts. We gather from the conversation that they are not all that enchanted with nature. We fill our eight one-gallon water jugs, borrow some sugar and cheese, and paddle off, feeling very capable and superior. Back at camp, we watch as Liz — assisted by Barbi, the nurse — demonstrates mouth-to-mouth resuscitation and other lifesaving techniques. You can't mistake the feeling of camaraderie as we practice mouth-to-mouth. Is that a flash of alarm I see in Barbi's eyes as our lips connect? A trifle compared to the look on Mark's face as I bend my mouth slowly in the direction of his.

Meriwether wants to trade kayaks with me. Having devoted four days to the precision adjustment of the double, I resist. "That's just another cop-out," Meriwether snaps. Okay, okay. Long after dark I am on my hands and knees, holding my flashlight in my teeth and adjusting the rudder on my new craft.

Fifth Day

As part of the weaning process, Tap and Liz have retired as leaders and will be mere observers from this point. Our first responsibility was to select a leader, which proved almost impossible. Nobody wanted to go first. After a lot of bickering and hedging on everyone's part, I volunteered for today. Tomorrow will be someone else's kettle of snakes.

The moon is nearing its last quarter, so for safety we maintain a tight formation as we cross toward the dim outline of the island. It's hard going, but our bodies have adjusted to hard going, and more impor-

will come and blow them away.

Sixth Day

Something is rotten in paradise. At first I thought it was the *bobos*. There hasn't been a trace of wind, and the tiny pests pepper any exposed skin and ring in your ears. They don't bite, but they drive you mad. There is something else, though, something more insidious. Except for an occasional chilled criticism — "I wouldn't do that"—neither woman has spoken to me. I speculate that Barbi is subconsciously punishing me for leadership qualities I obviously lack. The others rigged the fly backwards so that instead of sheltering us from the sun it cut us off from any possibility of a breeze. Maybe I shouldn't have jerked it down and stomped on it. Meriwether didn't like the way I baked potatoes. Mark, who has this mania for cleanliness and propriety (he even goes to the latrine to brush his teeth), returned from the latrine picking thorns from his hands and complaining that I dug it too near a thornbush. Nobody has been able to locate much suitable firewood or even kindling, and that is becoming a problem. When I suggested this morning that it was someone else's turn to be leader, no one appeared to hear.

After we've dived in shallow water to gather lobsters and shellfish, Harry Frishman and the crew of the Zodiac arrive for supper. Seeing as how it's easier to cook than supervise, I do most of the cooking and cleaning up tonight. Long after dark, while the others are still drinking coffee and talking around the fire, I stumble out in the dark to find my gearbag. My assorted sunburns, fire burns, aches, and abrasions are nothing compared to my despair and resentment. Right now I would trade a lifetime of this fresh air, picture-postcard, personality-expanding exploration for ten minutes inside a loud Austin bar. It is so dark

I am forced to crawl on hands and knees. I finally locate my flashlight, which is full of *seawater*. If I had suddenly been dropped on the dark side of the moon, my despair could be no more complete. I am afraid to move, afraid of what might be out there! I wait until the others have gone to their places, then I haul my sleeping bag near the light of the campfire where at least I can see how many snakes and scorpions are inside the liner. I unscrew the head of the flashlight and pour out the red gunk that used to be batteries: I have brought spare batteries but there is no way I can find them tonight. I try disappearing inside my sleeping bag, but someone has dumped lobster shells on the fire and the stench is overpowering. I locate a ten-gallon cooking pot, fill it with water from the sea, and pour it over the precious coals of the campfire. "What are you *doing!*" three voices sing out from the dark. I lie back and attempt to concentrate on the barking of sea lions, but all I can hear is Barbi asking Mark how come he never married. I wake at first light to discover that the strings of my tennis shoes have been cut or *eaten*. Tap speculates that mice did it. Tell me one more time about how stress breeds compassion? The final agony is realizing I *can't* quit. There is no place here to resign.

Seventh Day

It's good to be back at sea, or so I tell myself as we paddle at an easy pace four miles to the opposite end of the island. By watching the frenzy of the gulls we locate a school of yellowtails feeding near the surface. In a few minutes we have all the fish we can handle. They must go twenty, twenty-five pounds each. We are moving to the southern tip of Monserrate to escape the flies, but when we arrive about noon Tap is concerned about the cloud buildup over the mainland. Our choices are to camp here and hope the weather holds or use our remaining six hours of light to cross over. Barbi, today's leader, calls for a vote. We're unanimous for heading back to the mainland.

Now begins the most arduous journey of all. For a back-breaking, mind-gutting seven hours we paddle against a current so strong we dare not miss a stroke. It's open water and high swells all the way to Agua Verde Bay. After about five hours we can barely detect the tall lighthouse-shaped spiral of rock that guards the mouth of the bay. Like a good leader, Barbi passes out pieces of candy.

The trick is to occupy your mind. If you watch the mainland you suffer the illusion of going nowhere. I devise a game: I pretend that I have been shipwrecked for six weeks and now there are *only a few more hours to go*. What's a few more hours? Watch the yellow blades of the paddle. They throw water in your face, laughing and saying *don't you think I know that trick?* Think of cold glasses of beer. Think how much fun all this will be to write. Think of The Bomb. Another hour passes. The lighthouse-shaped rock looms much larger. Sun almost gone. "We're getting there!" Meriwether shouts. By God, so we are! With a strange detachment, I watch my paddle dig deeper and faster, reaching out with a mind of its own. As I plow into the calm waters of Agua Verde Bay, I hear Tap shouting for me to slow down. I sit dead in the water, allowing the current to turn me about, realizing for the first time that I'm easily fifty yards in front of the group. Tap is sucking on his Popeye pipe, dog tired just like the rest of us, but grinning like Mother Victory herself.

Harry Frishman and the people from the Zodiac are waiting for us on the beach. Tap calculates that we did twenty miles today. Harry thinks that's a record. We shake hands all around, then work together to pull the loaded kayaks to a high spot on the beach.

Barbi is already organizing dinner. I know it's against the rules to drink from the water bottles, but my tin cup is buried at the bottom of my gearbag: I lift a half-full bottle to my lips and drain it. Barbi, bless her heart, pretends not to notice this transgression. I believe today is Easter, but I'm not sure.

Tomorrow we begin our forty-eight-hour solos. Duck soup, I'd call it.

Eighth and Ninth Days

Years from now, when I want to recreate the meaning of the word *peace*, I will think of this experience. A phrase from a song, I believe by Cole Porter, keeps passing through my mind: *alone together.* Make it two words. Alone. Together. After all these years, it makes sense.

We were each permitted to pick our own solo site. Mark selected the mountains; Meriwether, Barbi, and I chose the sea. We discussed what was proper to take with us—a gallon jug of water, of course; a book of matches; a sweater; the cotton liners of our sleeping bags, which could be used as shelter from the sun. Barbi wanted to take her notebook, but Meriwether said this was a cop-out and the rest of us agreed. Meriwether wanted to do her solo naked, but Tap suggested that this might be misunderstood by passing boats of fishermen. Carrying along any type of food would be considered a serious violation of the spirit of the solo. The solo is for fasting and meditation.

My place is a small inlet of volcanic boulders, tidal pools, and steep cliffs pocked with caves. I select the largest cave as my headquarters and hang a dried starfish over the entrance to give it personality. The Starfish Hilton. The cave opens to a sort of ledge or porch several feet above the high-tide mark. From here I can see the lighthouse-shaped rock we used as a guide to Agua Verde Bay, and beyond that streaks of deceptively calm water darkening around the base of Monserrate Island. Storm brewing, mates! The second group is probably camped on Monserrate: I'm glad I'm not with them. A large school of dolphins passes close to shore; a gull hovers, looks, and dives like a torpedo bomber, then reappears from the sea with a yellowtail struggling from its bill; a frigatebird, its crooked wings a holdover from the time of dinosaurs, intercepts the gull in flight, robs its supper, and soars straight up with hardly a movement of its wings.

Jumping from boulder to boulder, I explore the beach. When you look closely, there are many traces of man — a badly tangled section of nylon fishing line, a hand-carved club used no doubt to beat in the heads of sharks, even a can of American-brand charcoal lighter fluid with enough fuel remaining to start tonight's fire. God helps those who help themselves. I gather what I judge to be plenty of firewood, then scoop out a place in the rocks and sit writing in my notebook. Certainly I agreed that Barbi's notebook was a crutch. But I wasn't about to put *my* notebook on any referendum.

I pass the first night feeding the fire, watching the movement of the constellations, and dozing on my bed of rocks. I underestimated my need for firewood, and by the time Gemini, Auriga, and Orion have revolved beyond my horizon, and Scorpius has fully spread over the southern sky, the wood has been reduced to a heap of coals and I am too cold to sleep. I wrap my cotton liner around my shoulders, move closer to the coals, and wait for dawn.

Twenty-four hours into my solo . . . feeling spacy but good. Plenty of water remains. Who cares about food? A small boat passes close to shore; some fishermen wave, I wave back. The sun is high and hot. I sit by a tidal pool, a tiny private aquarium where little sea creatures abide for my benefit. Using a sharp rock for a blade, I pry loose a spiny sea urchin and cut it open. I remember eating a sea urchin once in a Japanese restaurant on Sunset Boulevard. I remember eating in a lot of places. I remember in great detail. I remember a great deal. How long, I ask myself, since I've gone without a drink? It must have been the ten days before my first one. I've already cinched up my belt to the last notch and still my jeans hang loose around my hips. I cool off in a sheltered pool, then return to my cave for a nap.

By late afternoon a cold wind from the north is whipping up the sea. I move my camp around the point, where there is better shelter and more firewood. After gathering an enormous pile of wood, I pass the night watching it disappear. I wonder about the two women down the coast, and about Mark, somewhere up in the mountains. I remember Tap telling us that the temperature can drop thirty degrees in a thousand feet, and wonder if Mark remembers. The bright orange star in Scorpius is Antares, one of our brightest neighbors—just 391 light-years away, sharing our loneliness. Now it seems clear why man has always thought he was the center of the universe. What else can a poor soul *believe*?

An hour after the sun has cleared the mountains, I can see the Zodiac coming for me. They're going to ask how it was, and I'm going to try not to act too smug when I tell them I've done time alone before. I once did three weeks alone on a shell bank in the Gulf of Mexico. It damn near drove me crazy. I was finishing a novel and for several days after my return I called my family and friends by the names of characters I had invented. But forty-eight hours is not enough time to contract a decent hallucination. With a stick I write in the sand *PASO AQUI*.

Middle-aged Man

Tenth Day

Meriwether and Barbi don't look too hot, and Mark looks like he's spent a week in a haunted house. Pots of soup and coffee bubble on the grill. Tap and Liz pass around cans of *jugo de albaricoques* (apricot juice) as the debriefing begins. Mark says he almost froze to death the first night: for reasons he hasn't quite understood himself, it didn't occur to him to build a fire. Meriwether says that her longing for food overcame her fear of being alone. Barbi has experienced grave misgivings about moving to Salt Lake City. She doesn't *know* anyone there. She describes her solo as "lonely," something like her apartment in Cleveland. "The trouble with living alone," she says, "is there's no pattern—no reason to get up in the morning." Liz solicits my impressions of the solo. I tell her that I decided to worship the sun, except of course at night, when I will worship the fire. Barbi gives me the kind of look she might give Charles Manson.

This will be Tap and Liz' last day with us. In a couple of hours they will load their kayaks and head back toward Chuenque Bay, twenty-three miles up the coast. This is the beginning of what they call *finals*: from here on, it's just the four of us. We divide up the food and water, then wave as Tap and Liz disappear, literally paddling off into the fading sun. In what daylight remains, we ready our equipment and dive for clams in the clear, sandy shallows of Agua Verde. Mark squeals with delight as he captures his very first clam in waist-deep water. We open some clams with our knives and eat them raw with a little lime juice.

Meriwether and Barbi decide that we will celebrate the beginning of finals with a feast of beans, clam chowder, caramel-flavored pudding, hot chocolate, and coffee. Mark, who has been elected to lead us back to Chuenque Bay, quickly acquiesces. I calculate that this meal will require about twenty percent of our remaining supply of eight gallons of water. Nobody is impressed with these statistics until I hoist a water jug and drink down a couple of quarts. "What are you *doing!*" everyone chants in unison. So I tell them: I am having a drink. It may be my last for a couple days, but I'm having a drink and, by God, *enjoying* it.

I drag my sleeping bag far down the beach. Long after dark, I can hear my companions muttering. When Mark wakes me at dawn, he apologizes for "that little misunderstanding last night." I shake his hand and tell him to lead on.

Eleventh Day

Strange how in moments of crisis the brain reveals its storehouse. We'd been fighting the sea for a couple of hours when, without even realizing it, I called for the mutiny.

When we paddled out of Agua Verde Bay this morning, Mark and me in the singles, Meriwether and Barbi in the double, we were met by a chilling wind from no discernible direction. The others had bundled up in their orange-hooded windbreakers issued by OB, and as we swung wide around Point San Pasquel and the wind rode straight into our teeth, their billowing windbreakers made them look like three tiny floats in Macy's Thanksgiving Day Parade. Our plan was to rendezvous with the other group six or seven miles up the coast at a place not on the map—a place called Verne's Cove. But as we ventured into the open sea it became obvious we'd see more than we bargained for before we saw Verne's Cove. It was my craven opinion that we better hug the shoreline, even though this contradicted the generally accepted principle of a straight line being the shortest distance between two points. Meriwether was for paddling straight across, guiding on the tip of what she took to be an island. My old eyes took the island to be a peninsula. Since neither an island nor a peninsula showed on the map, Mark decided we would split the difference. Not that Mark's decision carried much weight: in another ten minutes it was apparent that we were being swept out to sea. By now the wind was blowing so hard we could barely hear each other shout. If I had brought my paddle up more than chest high, the wind would have snatched it out of my hands.

Mark had fallen far behind, which made it difficult to follow his lead; but we didn't dare tread water now. Yet Tap had drummed it into us that good survival technique depended on appointing one leader and following his decisions. There had been a splendid example of this wisdom one afternoon when Liz' kayak suddenly capsized in calm water off Monserrate. Liz did it on purpose ("I needed to pee," she told me later), but we didn't know this at the time. We all turned immediately toward the craft in distress — exactly as we had been trained to do — but became confused when Barbi and Meriwether started barking conflicting orders. Tap had also said something else. He had said *in times of crisis a new leader may emerge.* In a medical emergency, for example, it would be only natural to listen to Barbi. Banking problems, consult Mark right off. Without bothering to analyze the appropriate calling for this emergency, I shouted for everyone to paddle like hell for the nearest point of land: by now, this was a slice of beach a mile or more in the opposite direction. I knew they couldn't hear me, but they couldn't mistake what I was doing. *I* was paddling like hell for land. For what seemed like two hours (it was probably closer to one) we hit that paddle like we never knew we could.

Waves taller than our heads came straight over the bow, lashing against our sunshades. I couldn't see Mark at all, and all I could see of the double was occasional orange flashes as the women dipped between waves. When we had battled close enough to shore to feel some protection from the cliffs, I slowed my stroke to allow Mark to catch up. Gradually, I could feel the wind at my back: when I feathered my paddle out of the water, I could feel it *pushing* me. It was like having a sail. Our position to the wind and the land changed every several minutes, but a pattern had emerged. When we rounded a point and faced another open body of water, we paddled straight for land. And when we had fought to about the center of the cove, we relaxed and allowed the wind to carry us around the next point.

An hour later we beach and I verify our position with three passing fishermen who are wisely hugging the coast. They've never heard of Verne's Cove, of course (that's the OB name; the place isn't indicated on any map), but judging from the other landmarks it has to be just around the corner. We all veto Mark's plan to carry the kayaks partway overland, and twenty minutes later we see Libby Frishman waving to us from a deep-set white cove. Libby has rigged her fly like a giant flag to catch our attention. Our instincts have already turned us toward a grove of palms—they're the first we have seen in days—and when we see the fly and then see Libby waving, we know another battle is won. This time there are no congratulations as we beach our canoes and go through the ritual of lunch. Libby tells us that the other group is stranded on the island. The Zodiac has gone to the rescue, but they probably won't make it across today.

I spend the remainder of the afternoon talking with Libby, who helped found the Southwest Outward

Bound School in Dallas in 1971. It used to be called Texas Outward Bound, but the staff changed the name and moved the headquarters to Santa Fe two years ago. The school still has strong ties in Dallas: many members of the board of governors, including the chairman, live there. Since OB is a nonprofit organization, it depends on donations and the goodwill of the business and educational communities. A few OB students, especially in summer, are young people with personality problems. There are cases where judges have *sentenced* kids to OB. Many of the instructors are wilderness nomads whose only mailing address is the OB headquarters. Some are graduates of OB or of the National Outdoor Leadership School in Wyoming (which Tap helped found), and most have worked as ski instructors, professional mountaineers, or members of rescue patrols. Harry Frishman, who grew up with the Sierra Club in California, was a climbing guide and avalanche forecaster before joining OB seven years ago. Climbing a tall mountain is Harry's idea of a day off. Harry's father was a doctor in Long Beach before he gave up his practice a few years ago to teach skiing in Colorado. Libby tells me: "I guess if you were trying to define an Outward Bound instructor, you'd say it was someone who would think nothing of hitchhiking from Asia to Europe with twenty-eight dollars."

Twelfth Day

We decided not to wait for the other group. We did fourteen miles, following the coast, then crossed over to Danzante Island and located a small secluded cove exactly where Tap described it. Beautiful! Clear water and a beach so white it stings your eyes. A green cabin cruiser flying an American flag has also anchored here for the night: an abrupt callback to civilization. How I wanted to hoist our martini flag and see if her captain abides by the international code of civility! From the cliffs above the cove we can see the entrance to Chuenque Bay, no more than two miles away.

Barbi tells me I'm putting too much water in the beans, and I invite her to go to hell. My Outward Bound spirit is wearing thin. Meriwether is sitting on a rock, reading *One Hundred Years of Solitude*, but I can see her smile. Meriwether and I talk about literature and about good restaurants in San Francisco, where she's going to meet her boyfriend. She can hardly wait to tell him about this trip. Mark, dead game to the end, is trying to break a stick to put on the fire. The stick is too thick to snap across his knee, so he places it on the ground and jumps on it. I suggest to Mark that he employ the services of a large rock — meaning use the rock for leverage — then watch in awe as he lifts a rock that weighs nearly as much as he does. He staggers over and *drops* it on the stick, which sinks into the damp sand. For the first time in days I laugh. It's a laugh of appreciation, of compassion, even of love. How can anyone not love Mark? Kurt Hahn, the OB founder, used to describe his own pleasure at watching the daily improvement of his wilderness novices, of observing, as he put it, a student "shed the misery of unimportance." Mark looks at me through his thick glasses, slowly comprehending that I'm not laughing at him, but at *all* of us. I am about to demonstrate when Barbi freezes me with a surgical look. She stoops beside the rock and directs Mark to do the same. "One, two, *three!*" Barbi says, and together they lift the rock shoulder high and drop it again on the stick. The stick disappears in wet sand.

Thirteenth Day

It must be the excess of clean living: I'm high on *something!* I can hardly contain the feeling of conquest and accomplishment as I paddle the final two miles into Chuenque Bay. We *did it!* Whoever could have doubted otherwise? Tap and Liz are waiting to greet us as we beach our kayaks. They are openly pleased and proud. We clean the mud from our boats and haul them to a secure place on the rocks, then clean our equipment in tubs of fresh water. Tap has caught a giant sea turtle for tonight's final feast. I regret that I cannot stay, but then I really don't want to stay. Whatever it was I came here to do is done, and stretching it out now will only weaken it. I shake hands with each member of my team (the other group won't arrive for several more hours), then ask Harry Frishman to give me a ride to the bus station in Loreto. I just have time to catch the daily bus to La Paz. I am loading my gear in the pickup when Barbi calls me aside.

"I don't want you to leave without telling you something," she says, struggling to maintain that hard nurse register. Okay, I'm listening. "You remember that day you . . . French-kissed me . . . when we were doing mouth-to-mouth?" I nod that I recall, though not very well. "I just want you to know . . . on that day I lost every bit of respect for you."

"A joke in bad taste," I apologize. I open the pickup door and climb in, but Barbi hasn't finished.

"Bad *taste!*" she says. "It wasn't just the sexual thing. It was . . . it was a very serious situation. You were joking about something you knew nothing about. Your joke could have cost someone's life."

Well, it didn't. We're all alive. I don't know about the others, but I've never felt better. My arms are blistered, my leg is still numb, my hair feels like seaweed, and my skin would take the paint off a battleship, but that's all cosmetic. There's only one me, and while he may win no prizes, I can live with him. When you think about it, that's not such a bad feeling. Six hours later I am sitting at a sidewalk cafe in La Paz, a trifle dizzy from two beers. It's truly a difficult decision, but I think I'll order another.

July 1977

Postscript

This story was supposed to be my reward for doing the very long and difficult welfare piece on Patrick Henry Polk. I remember *Texas Monthly*'s editor, Bill Broyles, saying, "Pick something easy. A travel story, for instance." I didn't realize until it was too late that I would be traveling in the Sea of Cortez, by kayak.

Some months after I completed the course, I heard that three Outward Bound students attempting the same seven-hour crossing from Monserrate to Aqua Verde Bay were caught in a storm and drowned. The sea kayaking course was canceled. Not long ago I read that the Southwest Outward Bound School had closed for good. I'm sorry to hear that. It was one of the great experiences of my life.

12

The Ultimate Game

My first image of Super Bowl X was a traffic jam around an airplane painted by either Captain America or the fourth-grade class at Eanes School. Someone told me to sit back with the niggers—two hundred years into the great experiment, *nigger* is a euphemism for *player*.

My second image was an overfed man with a television camera backing down the aisle of the Cowboys' inbound flight taking film of Too Tall Jones. It was a tight fit for both men. Too Tall wore a maroon leather suit patched with yellows and browns, and a black cowboy hat. He was compelled to stoop as he moved from cabin to cabin. If this airship were too full of Too Tall Joneses, as it will be someday, it would not fly.

The airplane that flew the Cowboys to Miami turned out to be one of two Braniff Bicentennial ships painted by Alexander Calder, "the father of kinetic art": the other Calder plane would return the team to Dallas a week later, richer and wiser. The name Braniff does not appear on the ship — only the giant signature CALDER. Streaks of red and blue on white suggested that we were ascending to the galaxy of Super Week aboard God's own comet.

At the Fort Lauderdale airport were more TV cameras, a band, fans cheering and waving banners, and a police motorcycle escort waiting to convoy the Cowboys to the Galt Ocean Mile Hotel, where they would camp during the final week of preparation for Super Bowl X. Champagne, steak, and lobster salad had been served in flight, and now more champagne was waiting as the team fought its way into the lobby, paling in the glare of lights. The owner of the hotel welcomed the Cowboys and invited them for a cruise aboard his ninety-six-foot yacht. He wore a blue cowboy hat with the white block-letter D, as did room clerks, bellhops, waitresses, lifeguards, chambermaids, and everyone else. A woman seated at a table sold copies of Roger Staubach's life story.

Staubach himself maneuvered among the hand-held microphones and poised note pads, saying yes he was glad to be here, and no he didn't think his Pittsburgh counterpart, Terry Bradshaw, was all that dumb. In this most overcovered of all sporting events, Staubach would be the most overcovered Dallas Cowboy, a task he accepted with grace and skill.

Lugging a computer printout thick as the Pittsburgh telephone book, Tom Landry signed two autographs for every one yard of lobby captured. Alicia Landry, his wife for twenty-six years, clung fearfully to a backgammon set. "I brought it along so that Tom can get his mind off the game for a few minutes," Alicia told a woman gossip columnist in a mink-trimmed cowboy hat. "He always beats me." This was Alicia's birthday — she didn't know it yet, but her husband had wired ahead and ordered a dozen long-stemmed roses for their ninety-five-dollar-a-day suite at the Galt.

Texas E. Schramm, the Cowboys' president and the man who put together much of what was to happen this week, shook hands with a couple from New Jersey who told him they had been faithful Dallas Cowboys followers since 1966. Schramm was pleased but not surprised. Even before they became the Cinderella team of Super Bowl X, the Cowboys were probably the most popular team in the National Football League—at least among the masses, those who believe that a football field is twenty-four inches across and sells cars. A onetime Los Angeles *Times* copy boy and the Austin *American-Statesman* sportswriter, Schramm still oversees the Cowboys' weekly newspaper—circulation twenty thousand, including fifteen thousand from outside the Metroplex, of whom five thousand are from out of state.

The Cowboy chairman, Clint Murchison, Jr., hadn't arrived from Spanish Cay, his private island in the Bahamas, but he was represented by Bedford Wynne, one of the club's original board members. Bedford stalked into the lobby in his new blue cowboy boots, waved to the crowd, and shattered a full quart of J&B on the floor. "The only full one you've ever seen me drop," he reminded me. Bedford might be thought of as the Bicentennial Man—affluent, undeterred, a pioneer who knows his time will come. Over the years Bedford has invested in such enterprises as microwave ovens, a water-distilling plant, and a record album commemorating Freddy Steinmark, the UT football player killed by cancer. They say he lost a bundle in an enterprise that sold non-nicotine cigarettes. Bravos, they were called. Bravos smelled and tasted like burning lettuce leaves, which in fact they were. Toots Shor once threw two sportsmen out of his saloon for lighting up a Bravo. Lately, Bedford has been making mysterious trips to Egypt and frequently drops names like Sadat and Husein. Egypt, so I read, is preparing to market lettuce cigarettes, though this could be a coincidence.

With the precision of a well-drilled two-minute offense, the Cowboys staff had set up headquarters and opened the hospitality room, which would remain open around the clock and serve as a watering station and hangout place for coaches, media, family, and friends. Before the week ended, Dallas' entire forty-four-member administrative staff would be on the scene, everyone from Kay Lang, the former Ice Follies chorus girl who started out with Tex Schramm and the Rams and has been the Cowboy ticket manager since the club was organized, on down to Radar, an impish black man with a goatee who is Dallas' "electronics coach"—a euphemism for he who keeps the movie projectors working. The hospitality room would also become a collecting place for the usual number of walk-ons—Boots Garland, onetime Cowboy "speed coach," a free-lance adventurer who teaches athletes how to run and who once won four thousand dollars hanging for two hours off a bridge in Mississippi; Jungle Jamey, pro football's best-known gate crasher, who once showed up at the Cowboy camp carrying a white rabbit and a ten-pound smoked buffalo shank; and finally, Willie Nelson, Jerry Jeff Walker, and assorted Austin musicians and crazies.

"Don't you think Super Bowl X is the quintessence of the Bicentennial celebration?" the woman gossip columnist with the mink-trimmed cowboy hat asked me. "I haven't met you. I'm Pat Byrd . . . B-Y-R-D . . . as in Senator Byrd, my ex-husband. Yes, he just threw his hat into the ring. That same Senator Byrd."

I told Pat Byrd that I wouldn't be surprised, then

slipped out the back door of the hospitality room and walked down to the ocean. It had been seven years since I had traveled with the Cowboys, and I was trying to sort out my feelings. I remembered the first time the Cowboys had come to Miami, the 1965 Runner-up Bowl. There had been a lot of bellyaching about curfews and the players' wives not being allowed to fly with the team. Except for the night before Super X, there would be no curfew this week for the Cowboys. Wives came and went as they pleased.

The Cowboys were young then, in '65. The Runner-up Bowl was the team's first taste of anything resembling success, and though the opposing Baltimore Colts cursed their fate and referred to the event acidly as the "Left-over Bowl," it was that once-in-a-lifetime for Dallas, the coming of age. The Colts did most of their hard work in the night spots of the Gold Coast, but Landry whipped his team every step. Predictably, the Colts humiliated the Cowboys. Ah, '65 — Perkins, Meredith, Clarke, Lilly, Andrie, Jordan, Edwards, Neely, Pugh, Green, Renfro. And the first really class crop of rookies, players like Craig Morton, Bob Hayes, Danny Reeves, Pete Gent. I'd never seen a rookie get beat around worse than Gent, or hang in tougher. Hayes got tough when Red Hickey threatened to send him home to mama. On the team plane flying back from New York — the game in which Dallas staked its claim to the much-despised Runner-up Bowl — Hayes had his first glass of champagne. Also his second, and his fifth and sixth. No one in the organization — certainly not Landry — had ever heard a player break into "Darktown Strutters Ball" over the intercom of a team charter.

The heroes of '65 are mostly gone now, gone to other teams, gone to TV, gone to literature, gone to fat business arrangements with concerns owned by Murchison or men of his class, gone into that peaceful oblivion of small-town America where every kid knows that the tall guy with the big shoulders once played for the Dallas Cowboys. There are still a few who carry on—Jordan, Edwards, Neely, Pugh, Renfro. Reeves and Cornell Green now work in the organization. That is what remains constant—the organization: Murchison, Schramm, Landry, Gil Brandt, Kay Lang. *They* are the Dallas Cowboys. The rest of it comes from Rent-a-Jock. It hasn't changed. *Spread your seeds thick, lads, the harvest is short.* Nothing has changed at all.

From the niggers' wing of the Galt came the sounds of laughter and the smell of funny cigarettes. Definitely not lettuce.

Quintessence or not, nobody ever said Super Bowl X was egalitarian. "The sports spectacular of the century," as Tex Schramm liked to call it, was a great gathering of the elite—bankers, brokers, publishers, corporate executives, politicians, network moguls, celebrities, something like two thousand media people, and your accidental gadfly, like the New York cab driver who had been saving ten years for this trip and would blow it all by Sunday without ever seeing the game.

One evening in the Cowboys' hospitality room—as we were listening to Clint Murchison, Jr., and Senator John Tower harmonizing on "Beautiful, Beautiful Texas"—Tex Schramm remarked: "This is the prestige event, the place to be if you're anybody." Raquel Welch might as not pop up at the NFL press room. Juice and Broadway Joe and Hornung, Phyllis and Irv and Brent, Jurgy and Jenke, Jimmy the Greek, Smashie, all the Main Men were there.

The face value of a ticket was twenty dollars, but one didn't just walk in off the street and purchase a ticket. What it came down to was who you knew: this was it, the payoff. In Dallas and Pittsburgh, where the largest allocations of tickets went (thirteen thousand each), you had to be a season-ticket holder even to be considered for admission to Super Bowl X. More than a thousand Dallas season-ticket holders camped all night in SMU's Moody Coliseum, hoping to be among the elite. The Cowboys could have sold out two or maybe three times their allotted tickets. One Dallas corporate executive advertised that he would fly any four people to Miami in exchange for four tickets. Hundreds and maybe thousands of counterfeit tickets were sold. Jimmy the Greek complained that he could secure only eighty-nine tickets, and CBS executive Bill Brendle, a specialist in these matters, was forced to trade eight on the fifty-yard line for twenty-four in the end zone—otherwise CBS would have been entertaining sixteen most unhappy guests. Something like five thousand innocents signed on for a travel agency package deal, complete with air fare and hotel but without, they discovered too late, tickets to the game.

On the other hand, Willie Nelson and his band arrived unannounced six hours before the game and were able to secure eleven seats, through the good offices of Bedford Wynne. Willie sat on the fifty, a few seats down from Clint.

Ten years ago when the "First AFL-NFL World Championship Game" (the name Super Bowl was coined later) was played in the Los Angeles Coliseum, more than twenty thousand tickets went begging. The value of Super Bowl I was incalculable to pro football, however—it signaled the end of a costly eight-year war between the NFL and the upstart American Football League, sealed the terms of the two leagues' merger, pried open the purses of the sports-hungry TV networks, and, if you will, put the niggers in their place. No longer could they use one league to bid for their service against the other. Inevitably this led to the labor movement. According to Schramm, player salaries have about quadrupled, while ticket prices, TV contracts, and other sources of revenue funneled through an ingenious arm called NFL Properties have merely tripled. All in all, niggering ain't a bad life. Figure that O. J. Simpson makes $350,000 — the O. J. Simpson of thirty years ago, Steve Van Buren, made $15,000, or $1,000 less than the play-offs' bonus paid to every member of the losing team of Super Bowl X.

It's staggering to realize that seventy-five million Americans, and another fifty-five million in foreign countries, watched live TV coverage of this Super Bowl. Who would have believed it? Pete Rozelle and Tex Schramm, that's who. When the NFL defied tradition and moved west with the first major league franchises in 1946, Schramm was a pioneer of the new wave. As general manager of the Los Angeles Rams, Schramm was the papa-dad of the modern scouting system. Schramm gave Pete Rozelle his first job in pro football, and when Schramm moved on to CBS and then to the newly formed Dallas Cowboys, he was influential in persuading some of the NFL mossbacks to accept Fast Pete as a compromise commissioner.

"For years," Schramm reminded me, "the league had been controlled by Bert Bell and his friends. It was basically a struggle between the haves [i.e., New York, Chicago, Baltimore, Philadelphia] and the have-nots [Los Angeles and San Francisco]. TV revenue was very small and very selective in those days, but you didn't have to be a genius to see that the boom was coming. Pete was young, energetic, he understood merchandising, he understood TV, he stayed on top of things. Most important, he wasn't a threat to either side."

Having harnessed the monster tube, the task now is to control it. It is the nature of TV to want more.

Like some faded flower trying on her old wedding dress, Super Bowl X bulged at every seam, leaving the observer to wonder what they would do next — shoot the players out of cannons?

The oracle of television has completely taken over. The Landrys and Don Shulas still draw the X's and O's, but TV calls the time-outs, changes the rules, educates the public to what it needs and what it needs to understand, blueprints the season, primes the pump, and brings the Too Tall Joneses out of ancestral swamps. If the Players Association ever decided to boycott the Super Bowl, television would show it anyway, starring Tony Orlando and Joe Garagiola.

After a week of debauchery, watching the Super Bowl is almost as tough as playing it. Anybody with any sense wanted to be home with the old TV. It was uncomfortably cold in Miami, and watching Super Bowl X from an upper deck in the Orange Bowl was like curling up with a good postage stamp. There were a lot of things going on, but without the end zone camera, stop action, and instant replay, no one could say just what they were. We didn't see the fashion show. Or watch Phyllis, Irv, and Brent, the stars of the game, chitchat at the Palm Bay Club with Namath, Hornung, and Hugh O'Brian, or watch them board their yacht for the trip down Biscayne Bay to the stadium, or see how they conquered the last ten blocks by helicopter. As Phyllis, Irv, and Brent were escorted from their landing spot on the fifty-yard line, the best of us were caught in a traffic jam on IH 95. A friend watched as dozens of vehicles were abandoned on the shoulder of IH 95. Liberated occupants tumbled down the grassy slope toward the stadium, binoculars beating wildly and thermos jugs sloshing. Only it was the wrong stadium: the Orange Bowl was still three miles down the pike. After many hours of suffering and deprivation, a privileged few retreated to the CBS hospitality room in Miami Beach, where they sipped medicinal remedies and watched a video-tape of the day on a seven-foot TV screen.

"That's when I felt like I'd seen the Super Bowl," my friend told me.

In his curious, perceptive way, Duane Thomas said it best. When they asked him back at Super Bowl V how it felt to play in the ultimate game, Thomas posed his own question: "If it's the ultimate game, why are they playing it again next year?"

'Cause CBS says so.

I knew it was Press Day at the Galt when I stepped out on my balcony to sniff some sea breeze and a woman two balconies down took my picture. A day before, when the media had inundated the Pittsburgh headquarters, defensive tackle Ernie Holmes had finally complained to Dallas sports editor Blackie Sherrod, "You guys in the press make us sound like them iguala bears always up in the top of trees eating juicy leaves." As defending champions, the Steelers and their followers had been through it and were understandably blasé. Neither Holmes nor defensive end Dwight White blinked an eye when a midget in a yellow Pittsburgh hard hat with a blinking black light asked for a favor: would Holmes and White each kindly lift him by a leg and shake him in the air? They did.

By some unexplained, arbitrary choice made at NFL headquarters, the Steelers were quartered much nearer the Everglades than the ocean and Gold Coast — in a landlocked resort called Miami Lakes Inn, where the only bar in the hotel was off limits and there was a curfew every night. Linebacker Jack Lambert expressed the sentiments of the team when he said they all prayed that a shark would take off both of Roger Staubach's legs.

But now it was the Cowboys' turn, and the Galt swarmed with writers and TV and radio men eager to hear firsthand about the shotgun offense or the flex defense or how Dallas liked to banjo the ends and loop the gaps and frigate the quibits, and why Cliff Harris wore a fireman's helmet with a flashing red light, and how Randy White ate the heads off toads, and how a team with twelve rookies could make it to the Super Bowl, and how was the pressure?

Fine, thank you. The pressure was just fine. While a crew from Channel 8 in Dallas set up equipment on the beach, Harvey (Too Mean) Martin lolled under an umbrella with his arms around two Oriental nifties in bikinis. Too Mean wore a golf cap, aviator shades, and a T-shirt with the message GOOD & PLENTY across the chest. Bob Lilly was gone, but the dooms-day defense flourished, in excellent hands. Too Tall and Too Mean were the perfect pair of ends.

When the camera was ready, Channel 8 sports director Verne Lundquist called Too Mean away from his idling. Too Tall was already in position with a hand mike. All year Too Tall had played the straight man, but today the roles reversed. While Lundquist stood back, Too Tall interviewed Too Mean on the application of the flex defense, then he socked him with the big one.

"I came up a year behind you and watched you grow into your position of defensive *right* end," Too Tall said eloquently. "Tell our audience, how does it feel playing defensive right end knowing there's a legend at defensive left end?"

Stretched out on a sun chair, rookie linebacker Thomas Henderson was finding it difficult to stay awake and answer questions at the same time. Henderson, less than a year out of tiny Langston College, had been out most of the night with one of the Pointer

Sisters and therefore slept through Landry's morning meeting. Henderson, one gathers, will eventually join the forty-five or fifty other ex-Cowboys who populate more tolerant rosters around the league.

A reporter asked Clint Longley, Dallas' young backup quarterback, if he was one of the three NFL quarterbacks rumored to be homosexual. "No," Clint said with a twinkle, "but I'm sure Roger is."

Landry shaded his eyes from the poolside reflection and spoke into a battery of microphones, explaining just one more time why, if Staubach is so smart, Landry calls all the plays. "If Roger calls the plays, he can do it about as well as I can," Landry said in his flat, Sunday school manner. "He obviously knows what we're going to do. But the coaches don't. When we call the plays from the sidelines, we know exactly what is going to be run and we can look at the point of attack against the kind of defense that is being used and know exactly whether this play is a good one and whether we should continue using it. A quarterback can waste three or four calls that way." The interviewers tossed knowing glances at their sound men, pleased and begging for Landry's approval. Even after sixteen years and three Super Bowls, the misconception of Landry as a stoic who lives in a white box and pulls the wings off pretty insects persists. You wouldn't want to engage Tom in a long cocktail conversation, but as Dan Jenkins pointed out, Steeler coach Chuck Noll makes Landry sound like Don Rickles. Landry's impenetrable Gandhi image—like Lombardi's volatile impersonations of Hitler—has certain voodooistic advantages that the Cowboy staff makes no attempt to dispel. On the contrary, their inside joke is that the Tom Landry you see agonizing on the sidelines is, in fact, a professional actor named Rocky Romance. The real Tom Landry lurks under a hood, scribbling messages in Sanskrit.

A New York–based writer wants to know if Landry enjoyed Pete Gent's 1973 best-selling novel, *North Dallas Forty*, portraying the Cowboys as a seething mutation of dope fiends, paranoiacs, fruits, cretins, and homicidal maniacs—managed by direct descendants of Daddy Warbucks and Genghis C. Khan. Landry replies mildly that he doesn't read that sort of book but is halfway through *The Rise and Fall of Richard Nixon*.

"Jee-*sus*," wails a voice behind a palm tree. It is Peter Gent, alive and well and covering it for *Sport* magazine. Gent made a half-million dollars and a lasting place in the mythology of football with his novel, but he didn't always handle fame and fortune as well as friends wished. Last time I saw Gent, about one year ago, he carried several loaded guns and believed that the CIA and the Mafia were neck and neck in the race to bring about his end. Today, Peter looks trim, confident, and as comfortable as could be expected under the circumstances.

Gent has driven thirty-five miles from Miami to interview his ex-teammates, but now he can't think of a single question worth asking. I tell him I feel the same way. "The next time someone comes up to me and says '*Well, whataya think?*' I'm moving to Canada," I tell Peter.

"Both quarterbacks [Staubach and Bradshaw] claim to be in solid with the Almighty," Gent says. "I'm not sure how that works in the rule book. Maybe God changes sides at halftime."

Press Day is getting out of hand. In their panic to determine just what's going on here, the ladies and gentlemen of the media are stepping over each other. In the lobby, several dozen drunk fans are staging an impromptu pep rally.

"Just how dumb is Bradshaw?"

"What did he say?"

"Watch out. You're stepping over my cable."

". . . against your basic odd defense . . ."

"Up yours, turkey."

"What did he say? He looks older than his picture."

After a while veteran linebackers Dave Edwards and D. D. Lewis slip discreetly through the kitchen door and out a side entrance of the hotel. They've had it. The ears can't take any more, and the tongue is going fast. Fuzzy Edwards' hair is a lot longer than I remembered, and he's losing it in front. Fuzzy has been a fixture at strong-side linebacker since 1965, Dallas' first winning season. He is the silent, lethal type, seldom spectacular, but absolutely professional. He has slowed a half-step, but so what? For something more than two hundred consecutive games Fuzzy has stomped and been stomped on, and he still enjoys football. Cowboy followers are certain that the club is phasing him out—this may be his last game—but they were saying the same thing last year when the Cowboys didn't even make it to the play-offs. In camp last summer Landry acknowledged that this was the best group of rookie linebackers he'd coached, then he said, "It's going to take a pretty good effort by someone to beat Dave out. The challengers come and go, and when the dust clears there's Edwards, doing his job."

A biplane towing a streamer advertising jock-itch powder circles low over the Atlantic and I think of a question.

"Are you surprised to be at the Super Bowl?" I ask.

"Naw," Fuzzy laughed. "Not any more than I'm surprised to be anywhere. When I first came here in 1962 [as a free agent] I wasn't supposed to make the team."

"How can they keep writing that we didn't expect to be here?" D. D. Lewis asked. "There are twenty-five teams who didn't expect to be here. Pittsburgh is the only team that really thought they'd be here."

Both Lewis and Edwards thought this was the most enjoyable year they'd spent with the Cowboys. The energizing influence of twelve rookies had a lot to do with it. Landry had always bent, however slowly, with the times—it was the secret of his success—but this year he was bending faster, and good, strange things were happening.

"But don't believe that bull about Landry being relaxed at the Super Bowl," D.D. warned. "He wasn't very relaxed chewing ass this morning, and he ran us nearly to death yesterday afternoon and will probably do it again today."

"It's like Renfro said this morning," Fuzzy added. "We didn't come down here to throw in our jocks."

How else can you say it? The National Football League's Tenth Annual Gala was obscene. Roman Number X. Obscene. Not vulgar, understand, not wicked, and especially not offensive to the spirit of the Bicentennial, which it may in fact have been; it was obscene in the sense of self-glorification.

More than half of the invited guests to the Friday night party were media people, some top echelon. Three thousand invitations were issued, and nobody knows how many got in with counterfeit tickets. They picked the perfect spot—Hialeah, the spot Gatsby would have picked. Old-time elegance. Well-guarded gates and long driveways through towering palms, uniformly spaced and all precisely the same height and girth. Gaily striped tents that dispensed an astonishing variety of beverages and roving waiters with silver trays of pretty things on toast. A clubhouse buffet featuring several tons of sand crab and wide columns of prime tenderloin. A choice of domestic wines. A swinging forties band inside, and outside—rising like an apparition in front of the storied Hialeah clubhouse—the three-hundred-member ensemble of Up With People (you'll recall them from the Coke commercial) singing about how we are "Two Hundred Years and Just a Baby."

And, yes, a full moon hung over Miami. God, how the heart ached to see Red Grange's mud-splattered ghost plowing through the flamingos. Just once.

Landry blushed and posed with his arm almost around Phyllis George. Alicia gabbed with old friends, including Father Dudley, the priest who has been sitting on the Giants' bench praying for the lads since back when they still folded helmets in their hip pockets. Rozelle talked to Lamar Hunt, whom he once considered a fly-by-night multimillionaire, and to Paul Hornung, whom he once suspended for gambling on his own team, and to politicians who expressed continuing self-interest in the NFL. Dick Fincher, who owns one of the biggest Olds agencies in Miami or anywhere else and was once married to Gloria DeHaven was there, and George Owen, who was once married to Mo Dean. Gil Brandt, the Dallas super-scout (his ex-wife is now Mrs. Clint Murchison, Jr.), gave me a fountain pen with a retractable window pumping the virtues of being a Cowboy.

I asked Gil a tough question. I asked him to think back over all the players he had scouted and signed for the Cowboys—what was his most satisfying accomplishment? Gil thought for a long time, then gave me one-two: (1) turning up the fact that Staubach had attended the New Mexico Military Institute and was therefore eligible for the draft a year sooner than anyone else realized and (2) maintaining relationships with an assistant basketball coach at Michigan State who put him on to Pete Gent.

Phyllis George was telling the Jenkinses how her daddy used to try on her Miss America crown, and how when they'd go to a restaurant in Denton he'd run in first and shout, "Here she comes!" Dan and

June Jenkins were joining Phyllis and her parents later at the Raquel Welch show. The guy in the dark glasses who looked like a witless Al Pacino, the one who had been around all week, was chatting with a couple of high rollers from Dallas who should have recognized that he was what they call a "ten percenter"—a bounty hunter for the IRS. Irene, the first known sportswriters' groupie, was there, drinking strawberry daiquiris. An Atlanta sportswriter I hadn't seen in years reminded me of the time I got into a so-called fight with Norm Van Brocklin in Birmingham. I reminded Lamar Hunt of the time his older brother tried to bribe me to write nice things about Lamar's first football team, and Lamar recalled one of Jenkins' great lines: *The man of a thousand tackles*—E. J. Holub—Dallas *Times Herald*—December 11, 1962." Cornell Green, the ex-Cowboy headhunter who now scouts for the team and is therefore privy to these functions of the flesh, spotted Gent and swung him around like a broom; and though it was a gesture of goodwill, the flash of cold terror in Peter's eyes told me he wasn't altogether comfortable in his new profession.

And there was old Doc Bailey, bless his heart. He remembered the time we caught salmon off the coast of Astoria, and I remembered the time he got me a Dexedrine prescription in Portland. Joe Bailey was one of Washington, D.C.'s best-known heart specialists and a longtime running mate of Clint Murchison, Jr.—Doc's son Jody is now business manager of the Cowboys. Doc Bailey, Bob Thompson, and Irv Davidson, the lobbyist who worked for Caribbean dictators, were the backbone of the Chicken Club: a loose collection of ne'er-do-wells that is mostly dormant now, having experienced the ravages of age and too many slugs of scotch down the old pipe, but back in the early sixties they were the nemeses of the

Rozelles and Schramms. Their most infamous stunt was helping former Redskin owner George Preston Marshall celebrate High School Band Day at D.C. Stadium. They helped by seeding the field with chicken feed and providing five thousand live and hungry chickens that would be set free just as the assembled bands were forming WELCOME. The plot was foiled by a guard someone forgot to bribe. George Preston Marshall is long gone—but so is the Chicken Club. The Rozelles and Schramms have football now, and it's so sanitary you can eat off it.

"God, we used to give Pete Rozelle fits," Doc Bailey chuckled.

"I think I'll go ask Pete whatever happened to our application for a franchise in Santa Fe," I said. "Remember? Bob Thompson had a government contract to build an underground nuclear stadium if he could land an NFL franchise. We were going to call ourselves the Santa Fe Nuclear Holocausts."

"That's right. Our colors were ash and yellow. Whatever happened to that application?"

Fast Pete. He stood there like a ramrod in a Ken Doll suit, smiling through ice, saying the right thing and moving on, doing his job. Pete was a salesman who believed in his product: Pete would have sold tickets to the French Revolution—but only if he believed in it.

Sure his parties were obscene. So are mine. I love obscene parties.

I don't know if they showed it on TV, but the Coral Gables High School Band did a fine pregame enactment of Kent State. Berserk gunmen wasted fat tuba players and drummers who toppled and lay like wooden soldiers as the gunmen continued to rampage. Splendid theater.

My other indelible recollection of Super Bowl X

happened during the actual playing of the football game. It was that split second before Bradshaw released the bomb that blew the Cinderella team back to the pumpkin patch: D. D. Lewis, blitzing from Bradshaw's blind side, got one hand on the Pittsburgh quarterback, and a split second after that, when it no longer mattered, Cliff Harris made Bradshaw disappear for good. Game of inches, right?

Afterwards, I dropped by the Dallas dressing room. I wanted to get D. D. Lewis' game jersey to take home as a souvenir, but he had already given it to Willie Nelson's sister. I read the next morning there was a lot of weeping and tearing of hair in the Dallas dressing room, but I saw none. The Cowboys accepted their defeat as one of those twin possibilities when two good teams play.

"I don't know what happened on the blitz," D. D. Lewis was telling reporters. "I got my left hand on him [Bradshaw], but he didn't budge. Cliff got tripped or he would have been there sooner. I was sure we would force a fumble. Instead, it was a touchdown."

A Pittsburgh reporter in search of praise asked D.D. what he thought of the Steelers, and D.D. said they were a pack of hot dogs. "Especially Lambert," D.D. said. "All that Mickey Mouse shit . . . intimidating. If he's all-pro, Lee Roy Jordan is all-world. But don't make me sound bitter. As the black knight said, my business is my pleasure."

"And what is your pleasure?" the reporter asked.

"None of your business," D.D. smiled.

In the training room Golden Richards was being treated for several broken ribs. Richards is a frail, gentle, soft-spoken Mormon kid from Salt Lake City, and also the fastest man on the team. The Steelers elected to defend him by punching him in the ribs every time he came across the line of scrimmage. Golden pointed this out to the officials, but they never called a penalty. Golden said he had no complaints. Neither did Tom Landry. "What they were doing to Richards was a judgment call," Landry said. "They just elected not to call it."

A long season had ended; in maybe a few cases, long careers had ended. Cliff Harris still had the Pro Bowl to endure, but the main thing on his mind just then was the team's postgame party that night. He asked if it was true that Willie and Jerry Jeff and those guys would be there. I said I didn't know. Jerry Jeff Walker had stayed up all night, picking and singing in the NFL hospitality room; his wife, Susan, observed the occasion by giving Jerry Jeff's Super Bowl ticket to a bus driver. Willie Nelson and his troop arrived after an all-night flight from Jerkwater, Tennessee, looking like they'd crawled out of a Goodwill box.

Outside the dressing room door, Willie leaned up against a steel girder, his Dallas Cowboy stocking cap pulled down over his ears and his eyes painted by Alexander Calder. Willie was a longtime Cowboy fan: he went back to Don Meredith, who was a longtime Willie Nelson fan and used to mystify even the best of them by trotting into the huddle and singing, "Hello, Walls."

Willie, Jerry Jeff, Jimmy Buffet, Billy C., and some other excellent musicians arrived as the party was starting to run down. To the great delight of the players and the bewilderment of the Cowboy establishment — who must have thought the Bolsheviks had landed in Fort Lauderdale — this group of gypsy outlaws replaced the standard hotel band. "The day is saved," publicity man Doug Todd grinned. Not to mention the night. Even some of the assistant coaches were on the dance floors. It was the first time I'd seen a losing team at a victory party. Tom Landry, Jr., a young Dallas attorney, told Willie Nelson how much he admired his work.

Willie thanked young Tom and inquired about his father.

"He's gone up to his room," Tommy said. "He's looking at the game film."

Slumping into his seat on the team bus headed back for the airport, Ralph Neely couldn't stop thinking about inflation. The six-foot-six Cowboy tackle had closed out his eleventh season with a sixteen-thousand-dollar bonus check, but now it didn't seem like so much money, not when you considered that his chassis had all that mileage and no warranty.

"I'll tell you what causes inflation," he told Dr. Marvin Knight, who sat with his wife in the seat just in front. "Credit cards. Get rid of credit cards, inflation goes with it."

"That's probably the fact of it," Doc Knight agreed. Doc Knight, who had plastered and patched and wired together the Cowboys for sixteen years, recalled that when he interned at Walter Reed those many years ago, he established his credit by (1) borrowing money and (2) paying it back with interest. "That's the way it works in this country," Mrs. Knight said. "The only way to establish credit is borrow money."

"Another thing that keeps prices up," Dr. Knight told Neely, "pilfering . . . shoplifting. Ten percent of the stock on the shelves is pilfered. The cost is passed on to you-know-who."

Neely was silent for a time, watching the winter erosion of the beaches and yachts frozen by foreclosures, condominiums that went unrented at the height of the tourist season, and old ladies in torn stockings waiting on concrete benches. Neely had thought about taking a short vacation, but changed his mind. Tomorrow or the next day he'd be back at his winter job, selling computer service for one of

Clint Murchison's companies. Amazing, the amount of data you could put on a little piece of tape. All of a sudden it made him feel small. And old. And expendable. He tapped Doc Knight's shoulder: "In a couple of weeks I think I'll come in for a complete checkup. Just to see how the old body's holding up."

I looked at my official Super Bowl X watch, opened my Super Bowl briefcase, and took out my Super Bowl program. I wanted to read the winning essay in the NFL Charities' $25,000 scholarship contest. The subject was the NFL's role in American history, and though it had been argued by good authority that the league had no role in American history, Anna Leider, the contest winner, thought otherwise. "Football," she wrote, "is the mirror of America."

Anna pointed out that the people of this nation (like the NFL) overcame enormous odds in their expansion west, forming an orderly, law-abiding society, freeing themselves of prejudice, and representing many distant regions. She did not mention drugs, labor disputes, rampant commercialism, or media hype. She did not mention that it took the NFL a quarter of a century (from 1921 to 1946) to move west of Chicago; or that even then it went kicking and screaming; or that as recently as ten years ago black players were subject to quotas and in some cities (Dallas, for example) found it almost impossible to locate good housing near their place of business; or how the cardinal rule is still *don't get caught.* But Anna's main point seemed well taken: whatever Super Bowl X was, it was us. There was no pretense, no attempt to gloss it over. What other league in what other nation would open itself to such scrutiny, and say—proudly, no less—this is how we are. This is America, two hundred years down the road.

March 1976

Postscript

This story should have been called "The Ultimate *Trip.*" Six years later it reads like something from the pad of the demented Dr. Duke. I almost forgot to mention the game.

Now I remember. This was the week I spent with Jerry Jeff Walker and friends. I averaged about two hours of sleep a night, which was two more than Jerry Jeff and some others averaged. There is a drug scandal currently brewing in the NFL (and in other sports), but I promise you the trend is no more apparent than it was at Super Bowl X. Only no one talked about it, 1976 being the Bicentennial and all, and certainly no one wrote about it. I'm certain it didn't affect who won or lost the game. Thomas Henderson, who was a rookie that year, later blamed cocaine for ruining his career, but Henderson played superbly that day. I mention this not to defend the use of drugs but to point out that drugs in professional sports merely reflect society in general. Drugs have been prominent in sports for a long time, at least as far back as the late 1960's. Tear out the front page, chief, we've got a prizewinner. I can handle it . . . I can *handle* it!

13

Delbert McClinton
Twenty-five Years of One-Night Stands

You had to know Fort Worth in the 1950's to understand Delbert McClinton's unquestioning obedience to his obsession. It was a unique city experiencing a unique age—an adolescent, slightly schizophrenic, bawdy, brawling cow town looking for a quick ride and celebrating its rites of passage. The official image was manifested in some rich old anachronism of a wildcatter astride his prancing palomino, leading Comanche Chief Quanah Parker and thirty-eight domesticated Indians down Main Street in the Fat Stock Show parade. But just below the surface of the white fundamentalist illusion was an enormous multiracial underbelly of outlaws, scammers, and downtrodden survivors. Gamblers, small-time hoods, hookers, quick-change artists, spiritualists, mystics, and black musicians thrived in the shadows: if you didn't already know the blues, there was no way to explain. Hardly a week passed when the body of some local gangster wasn't dredged out of a shallow grave near Lake Worth. Just about every hotel on the south end of downtown Fort Worth was a whorehouse. Would-be Fort Worth musicians like John Denver (he was known as Henry John Deutchendorf when he played with Delbert McClinton) may have listened to Patti Page, but McClinton himself was inexorably drawn to the Negro rhythm and blues bands that played mightily in the roadhouses out on the Jacksboro Highway. Many years later, the term *outlaw* would connote a type of musician who had turned his back on the prissy, showy, overarranged sounds of Nashville, but in those days the meaning was quite literal. The men in the smoky light who wrote, played, and sang of society's dark side were frequently car thieves or drug pushers or door-to-door Bible salesmen — men who had been to prison or were ready to jump a freight to keep from going.

By the late 1950's, Delbert McClinton and the Straightjackets were the house band at Jack's, a joint just beyond the city limits patronized by gangsters, gamblers, and students without IDs. You could always tell the nights a raid was planned: the jackass on the neon sign stopped kicking. B. B. King, Lightnin' Hopkins, T-Bone Walker, and Big Joe Turner were weekend regulars at Jack's. The Straightjackets played backup for the stars and supplemented the entertainment throughout the week. They were just about the only white band anyone ever heard at Jack's. They didn't sound white. Delbert's first record, a cover of Sonny Boy Williamson's "Wake Up, Baby" released in 1960, had so much soul that it was the first white single to be played on KNOK, Fort Worth's black radio station.

At the time, racial mixing wasn't enough of a threat to attract attention. Any white who listened to *that kind* of music wasn't likely to disturb the well-scrubbed youngster reciting lines from a high school play or studying a three-iron shot on the club fairways. Anyone who *played* it was probably a Communist and bound for hell. The Straightjackets weren't the kind of guys who got invited to Rainbow dances. They were so far on the other side of the tracks, it wasn't even the same railroad.

Delbert picked up an occasional gig playing Blue Monday, which is what they called the one night of the week that black folks were permitted inside the Skyliner Club, a sort of honky version of Jack's. It was one of those places designed to squeeze tears out of rocks—a seedy ballroom with revolving lights and a forty-acre dance floor and a policy of charging another buck every time a customer took a deep breath. They charged a cover, charged again for a table, then for a tablecloth and each ice cube and glass of water. About the nicest thing the fat little man who ran the joint ever said to anyone was, "Remember, the Skyliner didn't come looking for you."

One night at the Skyliner, Delbert heard a sound that spun him around: Jimmy Reed playing blues harmonica. "It's hard to explain to anyone now, but it was a totally different sound," Delbert says. The harp replaced the guitar as Delbert's instrument of preference. It's still his trademark. Jimmy Reed taught Delbert a few licks, and several years later, while touring England with Bruce Channel, Delbert taught them to John Lennon, a then-unknown musician with an unknown group called the Beatles.

Delbert McClinton opened his first beer in a week and sat on the couch with his feet plopped on one of the packing crates. It was all happening fast. The comfortable place in Fort Worth that he'd worked so long and hard to acquire wasn't his place anymore. He was leaving. He couldn't say he was sorry. He was ready to try L.A. again. This time he was in control.

This time would be different, he was saying. A house on a cliff overlooking Malibu and the ocean instead of a hippie pad in Venice with black walls and blacker ceilings and busted pipes. A woman who wouldn't run out at ten minutes before midnight, leaving him with a fractured ego, a guitar, and two bottles of cheap wine. A five-year-old son, a cockatoo, and a cat named Wild Kingdom. A hit album, *The Jealous Kind.* A record company with a better than even chance of being in business this time next year. Although he is hardly the overnight success some critics have reported, Delbert McClinton has arrived.

People on the street recognize him now. Not only in Fort Worth, where his special blend of rock and blues has been a staple for almost three decades, but walking down State Street or waiting for a light at Fifty-fourth and Madison or inching along the Hollywood Freeway in his pickup truck. *Hey, you know who you are?* He does. Forty years teaches a man that. Success is something you measure in scar tissue. Fame and fortune are products of luck, but success is something personal and uncompromised, something torn from its socket. If Delbert had been successful ten years ago, when he first tried to make it in L.A., he would probably be dead now. Another legendary burnout. They would probably be making a movie about him, about the ultimate one-night stand where he lurches onstage with nothing but a can of gasoline and a kitchen match.

A man has to grow roots before he can remember them, before he can translate them into meaning and write about them. Delbert grew a passel of them ten years ago. It was that *fed-up* time a lot of people feel when they're approaching thirty and nothing is happening in their lives; he was fed up with his marriage, fed up working beer joints, fed up with the humiliation of Monday morning trips to the unemployment office. "When my unemployment ran out," he recalls, "I ran out." He headed for the West Coast with a beautiful divorcée who had just come into a pile of cash and a new Chrysler. He remembers that they were crazy in love; then, with about ten minutes' notice, she split for good. Nothing in Delbert's misspent youth prepared him for that kind of shock. That was the night he picked up his guitar and wrote his first really good song: "Two More Bottles of Wine."

> *I'm 1600 miles from the people I know*
> *Been doing all I can but opportunity*
> *   sure comes slow*
> *Thought I'd be a star by today*
> *But I'm sweeping out a warehouse*
> *   in West L.A.*
> *But it's all right*
> *   cause it's midnight*
> *And I got two more bottles of wine.*

He felt a little better when the song was finished. He felt bigger. Something had been torn away, yet the man had grown. "I'd hate to think I'd have to suffer like that every time I wrote a song," Delbert said as he watched Donna Sue, his wife for the last seven years, moving among the packing crates. The cockatoo fluttered from an empty shelf and perched on Delbert's head. The kid, Clay, was in the backyard watching Wild Kingdom dismember a sparrow. "I don't ever want to be that depressed again," he continued. "I want to be thought of as an interpreter of those feelings . . . a teller of stories of the things I've *done*, not the things I do. I'm not that unhappy now. I don't need to get down to get profound."

The L.A. experience wasn't all agony and depression. It was during this time in his life that he teamed up with an old hometown buddy, Glen Clark, and did some serious composing. A lot of the songs that he and Clark wrote in the early 1970's are still part of Delbert's repertoire. Delbert was looking forward to a lengthy reunion with Glen Clark in California. "He lives in the Valley," Delbert said. "That's only a six-pack away from Malibu."

He looked at the crates, shaking his head. After more than half a dozen albums for companies that were doomed, after nearly twenty-five years of one-night stands and a stream of honky-tonks, there wasn't a hell of a lot to show for it. Taking stock was no big deal: the inventory wasn't heavy, but it was paid for in full. Someone told him a long time ago that a musician had to love what he did, not merely enjoy it or take satisfaction from it. He had to *love* it the way he had never loved anything else: it was a love that sustained the soul and got the body up for one more round. He knew it was true.

His mama had once used the word *obsession. The boy just got obsessed.* Delbert remembers the exact moment: He was about fifteen. He'd been hunting squirrels in the grove below the railroad hump where his daddy worked as a switchman. He was heading back in the direction of a tumbled-down black barbecue joint when he heard the sound from the outside speakers. Someone was singing "Honey Hush." Delbert felt a flush that started in his ears and ran through his body like a current of electricity. He cradled his shotgun and started running toward the music. "It wasn't like anything I'd ever heard before," he recalls. "It *definitely* wasn't Patti Page. Ever since that moment, I've looked for something that would make me feel that way again. It was like falling in love. There is nothing like that first night." A few days later, Delbert and his brother pooled their money, bought a three-dollar guitar and started their own band, the Mellow Fellows. Delbert learned to play "Folsom Prison Blues" by watching where other players put their fingers.

That was the end of Delbert's schooling but the beginning of his education. His band played the beer joints and the black dives and the small clubs and roadhouses on the edge of town, anywhere, anytime, for any amount, or for nothing. Once they played the Big D Jamboree on the same bill with Jerry Lee Lewis. The band changed names a couple of times. Musicians came and went. But the obsession became a way of life.

Over the next few years, Delbert formed several different bands and recorded on several different labels, traveling constantly and staying just a bus ride ahead of the bill collectors. None of his records rattled the charts, but a couple of his songs were recorded by Waylon Jennings and Doug Sahm. One of them, "If You Really Want Me to I'll Go," got a lot of play. Until he paired his talents with Glen Clark in California, Delbert thought of himself as a performer, not a writer. "Two More Bottles of Wine," which Emmylou Harris made into a Number One country hit in 1978, was the genesis of a new, more cerebral approach to music. Delbert and Glen were among the first to prove that country music didn't have to be played in two/four time or rhyme *kiss*, *miss*, and *bliss*. There was a sophisticated, rock-hard intelligence to the rhythm and a lyrical flow of poetry in the words. It was the kind of fresh new sound that such writers as Willie Nelson, Kris Kristofferson, Jerry Jeff Walker, and Billy Joe Shaver were advancing. The genre came to be called progressive country, though Delbert's version transcended labels. It was blues, ballads, hard rock, kicker, whatever came out. Delbert never gave much credence to musical divisions: there was Patti Page and there was Big Joe

Turner, and the eons of space in between was where those with talent did their best work.

After a couple of albums with Clark, Delbert returned to Fort Worth, married Donna Sue, and began modifying the pressure-cooker approach that had once been his basic method. He rounded up two members of the old band—lead guitarist Billy Sanders, who was selling used cars, and sax player Robert Harwell. In 1975 Delbert resurfaced under the ABC label and recorded what is probably his best work. The album was called *Victim of Life's Circumstances* and spoke of the highlights in Delbert's own life—an endless procession of honky-tonk nights, broken dreams, county jails, biscuits and gravy, bone-handled knives, lonely lustful women on the make and the displeasure of looking down the barrel of some irate husband's Saturday-night special. He wrote and sang every song on the album.

> *I'm a victim of life's circumstances*
> *I was raised around barrooms and . . .*
> *Friday night dances*
> *Singing them old country songs*
> *Half the time . . . ending up . . .*
> *Some place I don't belong.*

With a little push, *Victim* might have taken Delbert to the top. But that's ancient history. A pattern had emerged. One year translated into three hundred one-night stands, one good album, a deep breath, and *el foldo pronto*. You could set your calendar by it. All his albums won critical praise, but none of them sold. One critic called Delbert "the avatar of Southern rock." More than one writer was inspired to label him "the best white R&B rock & roller in the world." After cover stories in *Time* and *Newsweek* celebrated Bruce Springsteen as the musical wave of the future, Nick Tosches wrote a blistering piece in *Penthouse* describing Springsteen as "a fake, a poseur, a culture thief" and extolling the honest, genuine talents of McClinton. *Victim* was the best LP of 1975, Tosches wrote.

Delbert gathered a small but incredibly fanatical following in hundreds of towns across the country. People who had never heard him on record stood in line for hours to hear him in person. Audiences sensed that his music was pure and uncompromised. Bumper stickers that read HONK IF YOU LUV DELBERT appeared in Fort Worth, Raleigh, Denver, and Oakland. You had to *see* Delbert to know. You had to see the eternally boyish face, the gotcha eyes, the half-guilty smile; you had to take in that power and presence with your own eyes; and then the easy rock-candy voice made sense and the rapport of souls was constant if not comprehensible. There were better musicians with better voices and better poetry, but it was hard to imagine anyone with more soul. Delbert was the musician that musicians came to see. Jerry Jeff Walker, Kris Kristofferson, Willie Nelson, Doug Sahm, Emmylou Harris, Crystal Gayle, Jimmy Buffett, Leon Redbone, whoever happened to be in whatever town Delbert was playing managed to catch his last set. John Belushi, who became a movie star by mimicking a soul singer, was so impressed that he got Delbert booked on *Saturday Night Live*. Later, Delbert wrote "B Movie Boxcar Blues," the best song on *The Blues Brothers* sound track. The Lone Star Cafe, the downtown Fifth Avenue joint that was becoming the Carnegie Hall of the Texas chic and transient kicker set, was another stop on the road that never ended.

After so many years, the road feels like home. It has its own rhythm and language, its own style of mutual reassurance. After four or five shows, you can't remember what it is like to be anywhere else except on a bus or on a stage or in some strangely familiar room near the ice machine and fire exit. Delbert finds it easier to write on the road. No telephones, no drop-ins—only a medley of pavement, hamburger joints, junkyards, and upturned faces. He remembers one time doing six months straight with only a single two-week break. A schedule like that would have destroyed most musicians, but it somehow sustained Delbert. "I never found any place I wanted to stay in more than a couple of weeks," he says. Last year he cut back. He did only 250 one-night stands. Once a year, the bus would stop long enough for Delbert to make an album. Once a year, they totaled it and found they had broken even. Until Delbert and Donna Sue's son was born five years ago, they had no permanent address. They camped wherever they were welcome. During one stint, they lived in the Cullen Davis mansion, which later was the scene of the most sensational murder in the history of Fort Worth.

In 1978 Delbert recorded for Capricorn. The Muscle Shoals Rhythm Section, probably the best backup group in the business, worked with Delbert on the album, and a year after Capricorn declared bankruptcy in 1979, Muscle Shoals Sound Records signed him. In turn, the Muscle Shoals label is distributed by Capitol, a company as solid as any in this tenuous business.

Last summer, Delbert and his entourage traveled to the remote Muscle Shoals studio in the hills near Sheffield, Alabama. Recording *The Jealous Kind* was a sobering experience, literally and figuratively. Delbert had just turned forty and was feeling it. "For years I'd been throwing down a pint of tequila during a set," he recalls. "You're up there on the stage and the adrenaline is pumping. Hell, you know you're wonderful! But I'd listen to the tapes later and think,

'Jesus, is *that* how I sounded? I wouldn't pay to hear that!' " Uppers, downers, sunshine, multidimensional herbs, it took a heap of madness to get by. Donna Sue sent notes to the stage, warning "Sing, don't talk!" A psychiatrist friend spoke of his great envy for Delbert—how he by God *lived* his fantasies. "People like me need people like you," he told Delbert. There were times when Delbert was moderately sober, times when he looked through the lights and smoke and read the disappointment on the faces. "They felt cheated 'cause I *wasn't* drunk and disgusting," he says. It wasn't enough to hear him sing of the agony of life's circumstances, they wanted to bear witness. When Delbert went crazy, so did the people, but the people had finished work. The booze and the drugs and the music were their ways of relaxing. With Delbert, the opposite was true. He started wondering what he'd been missing all those years.

"I decided I was going to do this album sober," he says. "I was going to *remember* doing it. At my age, I wanted to be responsible for myself. If they were happy times, I wanted them to be happy for real. If it was a bummer, I wanted to handle it like a grown-up. You can only fool yourself for so long."

Everyone involved with the album worked a little harder than usual. The nearest saloon was fifty miles away, and the narrow, twisting roads made it seem like a hundred. Listening to the mating of crickets was the vortex of high times. There was some beer in the studio, of course, but nobody got lost for long. "Everyone was bustin' ass," Delbert says. When the album was completed, producer Barry Beckett told Delbert: "It's a real pleasure to work with professionals." Delbert liked that. He felt that way, too. You may not be able to detect it on *The Jealous Kind*, but there is a polish and fullness missing on earlier albums. It sounds almost, perish the thought, *com-*

mercial, a word Delbert finds revolting. "I just went in and tried to make a good-sounding album without feeling like a whore," he says.

The album is not a rampant hit, but six months after its release, *The Jealous Kind* is still on the charts, and the label is still in business. The company wants Delbert to tour Europe, but he doesn't have time. "I got to make it while I'm hot," he says. The new bookings will be out any day. He'd like to relax the grind of one-night stands, do something like two weeks on the road and a week off. Instead of 250 appearances, maybe he can get by with 225. Instead of beer joints, he'll be playing large auditoriums and college concert halls. When you've got a record in the Top Ten, the difference is thousands of dollars a night. In a few months, he'll return to Muscle Shoals to cut a new album.

"I still don't have a penny," he said, while watching the movers wrestle his furniture into the truck. "Trying to keep a ten-piece band and a bus and a road crew alive, it's taken everything. I've been too busy making a living to make any money. Maybe this year."

On the day that Donna Sue, Clay, Wild Kingdom, and the cockatoo moved into the house on the cliff overlooking Malibu, Delbert and the band were in Baton Rouge, Louisiana. After twenty-five years on the road, he hardly noticed.

May 1981

Postscript

I didn't realize it until I actually interviewed Delbert McClinton, but I remember seeing Delbert and the Straightjackets when I was in junior college at Arlington State. Jack's was everyone's hangout. You could usually catch Big Joe Turner or B. B. King, and there was always a little letdown when Delbert's band played because they were *white*. Hip college kids didn't listen to whites, even when they sounded black. I saw my very first marijuana cigarette in the parking lot at Jack's. I remember it well, because the cops were *inside* raiding the joint.

14

The Crude Feud

Texas and Oklahoma are neighbors only by a quirk of geography. They are separated by the Red River, which used to separate New France from New Spain. What really separates them is a century and a half of history, the Alamo as opposed to the Dust Bowl. When you hear a Texan or an Oklahoman call the other *neighbor*, it just means they share ownership in an oil well. They are like tribes connected by a common hatred, two peoples who look on one another with the special loathing usually reserved for cannibalism. Oil and football prescribe the characters of the two universities, and to a degree the states. Longhorns see themselves as big, fast, wealthy, wily, capable, cultured, and anointed by the Almighty. The good guys. They see Okies as poor, ignorant, Bible-thumping outlaws. Okies see Texans as loud, arrogant, smart-ass bullies. They see themselves as big, fast, wealthy, wily, Bible-thumping outlaws. Jesus and football are one-two, but the order depends on the year and which side of the Red River you occupy.

There is something else in this rivalry, something harder to define but something that has to do with the times in which we live. Just as Army-Navy symbolized all that was glorious and traditional during World War II, Texas and Oklahoma are two states of the here and now. Strange to say, *trendy*. Witness Texas chic, a disease in which people wear cowboy boots, ride mechanical bulls, and talk about the last time they saw Willie Nelson at the Lone Star Cafe. Witness the popularity of such shows as *Dallas* or *The Best Little Whorehouse in Texas.* Somehow, *The Best Little Whorehouse in New Jersey* just doesn't sound right. There are many who would contend that the words *Okie* and *chic* are mutually exclusive, but there is no denying the popularity of Oral Roberts and his message to the Masses of Unhealed.

It will pass. As trends change and populations shift, as priorities are reordered and California drops off the map, things will change in ways we cannot imagine. The next great college rivalry could even be Long Beach of Nevada versus College of Pacific at Provo.

It really started with the postwar boom. Texas and Oklahoma had been knocking heads since 1900, but the game didn't take on the aspects of a Roman circus until 1946.

Americans had survived a depression and won a world war. People in Oklahoma, and certain parts of North and West Texas that identify more with Norman than with Austin, lived through the special humiliation and despair of the Dust Bowl, of hungry, crying children, uprooted families, brutal and demeaning labor and starvation wages of California migrant camps. A new dirty word shoved itself into the nation's vocabulary—*Okies*.

After the war many natives returned to Texas and Oklahoma to find bustling prosperity and full employment, most notably in the emerging oil industry. Oil was the future. There was a lot of it in both states and the men who controlled it would control the universities. There was a need for some chauvinistic yoohooing, for some new and viable heroes, for some unapologetic breast-beating and some restitution. The moguls of Oklahoma set out to make Okies a name that would be respected, even feared, coast to coast. There was no better way of doing that than by beating Texas in football.

"A good many people in the oil industry had gone to either the University of Texas or the University of Oklahoma," Darrell Royal observed. Royal participated in more Texas-Oklahoma games than anyone (four as a player, twenty as a coach) and is eminently qualified to speak on the subject. When asked why the rivalry is so bitter and so intense, he started talking about people in the oil industry. "There is a lot of coffee talk [by a lot of wealthy and powerful men] about the Texas-Oklahoma game," Royal said.

The results of this coffee talk—the cajoling and challenging and high-stakes wagering—are not always apparent to the public, but the university administrators get the message. OU president George Cross wasn't trying to be cute when he promised in 1951 to "build a university the football team can be proud of."

Many of the best coaches and top players were still in the service when OU hired Jim Tatum before the 1946 season. Tatum brought with him a young assistant from Minnesota, Bud Wilkinson, who had built a reputation coaching at such places as Syracuse and Iowa Preflight. This was before a crackdown by the NCAA and the resulting spate of recruiting restrictions. In those days an oilman could buy a dozen football players for the price of a Cadillac.

Tatum resigned after one season. In 1947 Wilkinson took charge of a program destined to be one of the most successful in college football. Wilkinson was immensely popular, a hero the likes of which Oklahoma had not known since Will Rogers. He had a smile that would curdle cobra's milk and an elitist air that made him appear wise and unapproachable. The prematurely gray fox.

When Wilkinson's first OU team was thrashed by Texas, 34–14, Sooner fans went berserk, pelting the field with bottles and stadium cushions. Referee Jack Sisco, who had allowed the Longhorns a controversial touchdown and called a couple of untimely clipping penalties against Oklahoma, needed a police escort to reach safety, but not before he'd coldcocked a Sooner fan. Thus did bitterness become high fashion.

Wilkinson's 1948 team lost its opener to Santa Clara, then won ten straight, including a much-celebrated 20–14 game with Texas (the first win since 1939) and a Sugar Bowl victory over North Carolina. In 1949, the Sooners rolled over eleven consecutive opponents, and in 1950 they won the school's first national championship. Wilkinson's teams were schooled in fundamentals and characterized by big, mobile linemen (Buddy Burris, Stan West, Wade Walker), breakaway backs (George Thomas, Leon Heath, Buck McPhail, Billy Vessels, Tommy McDonald), and a procession of All-American quarterbacks (Jack Mitchell, Darrell Royal, Eddie Crowder).

Wilkinson was without question a master recruiter. A bit *too* masterful in the judgment of some Texans who believed he staked his reputation by manipulating the best young players in Texas. The myth that still prevails in Texas is that Wilkinson offered the sun and the moon. True or not, it is a story with a *Hansel and Gretel* quality: good and evil are clearly marked. It goes a long way toward explaining the animosity. Texans still find it incomprehensible that one of their young athletes would go to Oklahoma to play football. Better to die a baby! Yet it happens all the time. Starting back in 1950 when tackle Jim Weatherall of White Deer became the first Texan to make All-American for Oklahoma, eighteen of OU's thirty-seven consensus All-Americans have been Texans, including such stars as Billy Sims, Joe Washington, and Greg Pruitt. Twenty members of the current OU squad are native Texans, including All-American guard Terry Crouch of Dallas. Only rarely does it work the other way (there were two Oklahomans on last year's UT roster), and in such cases Texans regard the phenomenon as something akin to rebirth.

The prototypical Oklahoma player, particularly in the Wilkinson era, was Royal, who grew up in the small, dusty town of Hollis in southwestern Oklahoma.

Darrell was an Okie's Okie. In the late 1930's his family loaded everything it owned into an old whippet and joined that long line on Highway 66. Half a lifetime later Royal recalls the bitterness of that experience. "You only had to open your mouth and they knew you were from Oklahoma," he says. "I remember feeling uncomfortable and unwanted. After three months I hitchhiked back to Hollis to live with my grandmother." Royal was one of the service veterans that Tatum and Wilkinson recruited, a sterling athlete in the versatile Doak Walker mold. (He still holds the school record for the longest punt return.) Wilkinson took credit for recruiting Royal, but in truth he couldn't have driven him off with a stick. "I grew up listening to Oklahoma football on the radio," Royal remembers. "We'd put the radio on my grandma's porch and play football in the yard and listen to 'Boomer Sooner.' " His high school coach took him to Norman to see Indian Jack Jacobs and Cactus Face Duggan and the other Oklahoma greats of the late thirties. Royal didn't need any selling from Wilkinson.

He was married and had a baby daughter when he went to talk to Wilkinson about a scholarship. Wilkinson told him he didn't *believe* in scholarships. Of course he offered one, but he professed to truly believe young men should play for the love of the game. *He* had, though of course he was being well paid now.

For a glorious decade Wilkinson kept the pump primed, winning three national championships. His magnificent 1956 team pulverized Texas 45–0. But the Texas-Oklahoma game history has a funny way of evening out, and of drastically affecting the lives and careers of those involved. Blair Cherry, a highly successful coach at UT (1947–50), was forced by alumni pressure to resign after his 1950 team lost to Oklahoma by one point. Oklahoma went on to win the national championship and Texas finished second. Cherry later became a successful oilman, but the bitterness outlived him. "Cherry never forgot or forgave," Dallas *Times Herald* sports columnist Blackie Sherrod wrote.

Wilkinson was at the peak of his career in 1957 when Texas unexpectedly hired his pupil, Royal, a late entry to a list of more than 125 candidates. Royal's assignment was axiomatic: beat Oklahoma. He lost his first OU game, then won eight in a row. Wilkinson must have seen the writing on the chalkboard. Before the 1960 game his publicity man, Harold Keith, told sportswriter Dan Jenkins: "Our great years are behind us. Circumstances won't permit us to continue [winning] as we have. I don't imagine they will allow any college team to approach our record [forty-seven straight victories, still unmatched]." In the fall of 1963, shortly after Texas blistered the Sooners 28–7, Wilkinson resigned. The prematurely gray fox ran for the Republican nomination for Senate, but the people of Oklahoma rejected him.

Royal's career was very much lackey to the ebb and flow of Texas-Oklahoma. The only way you could win a national championship was by beating Oklahoma and Royal won the national title three times. He didn't match Wilkinson's forty-seven-game winning streak, but he came closer than anyone.

In 1968 Royal revolutionized college football, introducing the wishbone and the triple option. The Longhorns scored in the final minutes to beat Oklahoma 26–20, then rolled to a thirty-game winning streak and back-to-back national championships. The wishbone caused radical alterations in defense and inspired hundreds of coaches to copy it. Two, Barry Switzer of Oklahoma and Bear Bryant of Alabama, have won championships with the wishbone and continue to use it. There is a suspicion that the wishbone greatly prolonged Bryant's career and eventually will enable him to become the winningest coach in college history.

Many believe Royal's career was shortened by events connected to the Oklahoma rivalry. Royal insists he decided to retire *before* the start of the 1976 season, but his five straight losses to Oklahoma must have weighed in that decision. Royal was convinced, and remains so to this day, that Barry Switzer and his staff recruited and kept athletes by violating NCAA regulations.

A few days before the 1976 game Royal accused two of Switzer's men of spying on UT workouts. Switzer laughed at the accusation and so did the state of Oklahoma. Royal called the OU coaches "sorry bastards" and offered to put up thirty thousand dollars of his own if Switzer could pass a lie detector test, an offer Switzer found himself able to refuse. The two spies later admitted their guilt. Five years later, Switzer still refuses to discuss the incident.

The 1976 game is best remembered by fans of trivia as the one in which President Gerald Ford flipped the coin, flanked in icy silence by Royal and Switzer. Royal remembers something else. He remembers that when he walked onto the Cotton Bowl field for the final time, thirty thousand Oklahoma fans stood, booed, and chanted, "Sorry bastards."

University of Texas coach Fred Akers calls it the Number One game in America. Oklahoma's Switzer agrees. "When you beat the University of Texas, I don't care what your won-lost record is, it's the biggest day of your life. We look at this game as though it were the national championship." Darrell Royal used to call it "a knucks-down gut check," a term that needs no explanation. The metaphor of war is trite and not particularly accurate. It conjures up missiles, computers, and space-age electronics. This is something out of another time, something primordial, something that has evolved *backwards* until it can be articulated with a few grunts and gurgles and some cracking of bone.

These are no-doubt-about-it football schools, two of a vanishing breed, schools that measure success in national championships (five for Oklahoma, three for Texas); in major bowl appearances (total thirty-seven), and in years among college football's Top Ten. (Since 1950, about the time this rivalry began to take on extraordinary dimensions, there have been only three seasons when neither finished in the Top Ten.)

The effects that this game has had on its participants cannot be reckoned on the sports pages. It has been a game of sudden heroes and instant victims, one in which split-second decisions altered careers and even lives.

In the 1947 game, Bobby Layne completed a touchdown play that probably was illegal, precipitating a near riot. Bill Bradley, one of the best athletes to play at Texas, lost his starting quarterback job just before the 1968 Oklahoma game; he was converted to defense and later became all-pro there.

My favorite memory involves one of the most gifted running backs in OU history, Joe Don Looney. I'd interviewed Looney in his dorm room a few days before the 1963 game. He'd had some sort of argument with one of the coaches and was cloistered in his trashed-out room with all the shades drawn, bucknaked on his bunk, reading a copy of *Playboy* and doing things that his mama never taught him. It wasn't a great interview, but it was memorable. Looney had a miserable game against Texas (four yards in six carries) and was kicked off the team a few days later. He was a Number One draft choice in the NFL, but he never came close to his enormous potential.

I heard a story later that he recruited three young beauties and moved to an island in Polynesia for the purpose of propagating his own super-race. Still later, I learned he was tending elephants for some guru in India. Blackie Sherrod heard that Looney was back in the United States trying to put together his own elephant act. "It's like the story of the guy who quit his job polishing the cannon in the city park," Sherrod said. "They asked what he was going to do now and he said he was going to buy a cannon and go in business for himself."

It's a game of cause and effect, one that has outgrown reason. Fans bet incredible sums months before the odds are posted. It's been said that people in both states have stipulations in their wills that their ashes be scattered over the floor of the Cotton Bowl or onto the superstructure of the Goodyear Blimp. One of the more bizarre sidelights to this year's game is a harangue by Robert Heard, an Associated Press reporter from Austin who took time to write a 544-page book about Texas-Oklahoma. "He managed to attack the whole *state* of Oklahoma," says OU publicist Mike Treps. "He wrote things like . . . 'Oklahoma doesn't even have an *amusement park.*' "

One of the enormous ironies of this rivalry was the role Oklahoma played in the integration of the University of Texas team. Texas was one of the last major football schools to recruit blacks. A lot of civil rights advocates blamed Darrell Royal, but Royal had no say in this matter. The policy was controlled by wealthy and politically powerful alumni known unofficially as the Orange Coats, mostly oilmen. They used to joke among themselves that the reason blacks were so fast was "the lions and tigers got all the slow ones." Texas' 1969 national championship team had not one black player. It was only in 1958 when a black OU fullback named Prentice Gautt voluntarily segregated himself from Texas tacklers that the Orange Coats began to reexamine their feelings. The first black recruited by Texas was Julius Whittier, in 1969, shortly followed by Roosevelt Leaks, who helped take the Longhorns to three straight Cotton Bowls and made All-American in 1973.

Young athletes have heard about it from the veterans who heard about it from the veterans before them. They've grown up hearing about it. But it's still an indescribably awesome feeling when they walk down the tunnel from the dressing room, half sick with fear but three feet off the ground, hearing the bands and cannons and seventy-five thousand hysterical fans who have talked about this game—and not much else—since last August. They can see the neon booms of the State Fair of Texas over the rim of the Cotton Bowl and hear the mad roar of the midway. Everything is in Technicolor. Half the Cotton Bowl is red, the other half orange. The turf is greener, the sky bluer, the images sharper. It is said that on this day the great ones reveal themselves and the lesser ones fade forever into mediocrity.

"It's unique," says Bud Wilkinson. "You got a large stadium and each school is responsible for half the tickets, so that on every play half the people are happy and the other half is disappointed. That's the reason spectators get so involved."

Wilkinson remembered one of the stranger plays of the series, in 1953. With less than two minutes to play and OU leading 19–7 but facing fourth down on its own one-yard line, Wilkinson sent word to quarterback Gene Calame to retreat into the end zone, to give Texas a deliberate safety. It was a play OU had practiced all week.

As the Sooners broke the huddle, one of the linemen told Calame, who was starting for the first time, "If you see daylight, don't be afraid to run out of there." Calame did. He got to the Oklahoma three. Two plays later Texas scored, narrowing the margin to five points with twenty-nine seconds to go. When Texas recovered an onside kick, the Oklahoma half of the Cotton Bowl could have passed for the county morgue. One can only imagine what was going through Calame's mind. Suddenly there was a thundering belch, followed by a death rattle from the orange half of the stadium; Texas had been offside on the kickoff. The Sooners won 19–14 and went on to win all their games, including a stirring Orange Bowl upset of Jim Tatum's Number One Maryland team.

Wilkinson refused to criticize Calame, who went on to become all-conference. Twenty-eight years later Calame, and many others, remember the play. So does Wilkinson. "We should have practiced that safety better," he said recently, his tone as distant and cold as the memory.

Almost everyone who has played in the game or directed it from the sidelines, recalls the sleepless torment of the previous week and the visceral fear of walking down the ramp.

Darrell Royal remembers: "It's strange how you can go down that ramp in perfect health, then a few minutes later actually be physically hurting just from making decisions on the sideline. Every play is so vital, every foot of AstroTurf. A fumble, an interception. One soft block and a yard less gained, that can be the difference."

Curiously, Royal's strongest memory is locked in a moment of despair. It came in that nightmarish 1976 game, a bitterly fought 6–6 tie that followed a week of highly publicized accusations that OU coaches had spied on Texas workouts.

Royal had his team so sharp it glowed. The Texas defense manhandled Oklahoma for three quarters, yielding only two first downs. Yet the Longhorns clung to a perilous 6–0 lead with 5:45 remaining. It was the moment for one of those decisions. Texas had the ball inside its own forty and Royal's stomach felt like Nadia Comaneci was inside doing triple backsprings. Royal considered a quick kick, which would jam Oklahoma deep in its own end of the field, but opted to play it safe with a routine dive into the line. The ballcarrier fumbled and ten plays later OU tied the game. A simple extra point could have won for Oklahoma, but there was a bad snap and everyone went home feeling rotten.

Five years later, Royal still has trouble with his

composure when he thinks of that fumble. "I never felt as sick as I felt about that one," he says. "I wanted that game more than any I competed in or coached."

Commerce is one of the three major east-west thoroughfares through downtown Dallas. In the late 1940's, when the Friday night parade of lunatics was inaugurated as a prelude to Texas-Oklahoma games, the street was a glittering passage of fine hotels, restaurants, bars, bookstores, and shops. Forty years later the street looks a bit down at the heels but nobody seems to care. In October, tens of thousands of Texas and OU fans will gather there for the annual riot. All Souse Eve, as it's been called.

Old-timers talk about memorable Texas-OU weekends, but they do not always recall touchdowns, fumbles, or tricky formations. They recall the riot of '67, also known as "The Night It Rained Furniture."

Indian Jim Frye and I parked across town and walked in the direction of the clamor. Ten blocks away you could hear band music and car horns and feel the psychotic buildup. Motorized traffic had been snarled since midafternoon and now it was completely paralyzed.

By the time the sun disappeared below the skyline, forty thousand to fifty thousand swaying fans milled around Commerce and Akard, a zigzag intersection that had become a rallying point because of the two big hotels, the Baker and the Adolphus. Police stood behind barricades to keep unwary motorists out and the revelers in. Dallas is basically a conservative cut-the-jokes-Jack city, but this particular pageant encourages myopia. *Let 'em eat football!*

Bars were jammed. People stood four-deep at the Akard Liquor Store. Students dangled from hotel windows, lowering six-packs to thirsty bypassers. A naked man in a bathtub rode in on the bed of a pickup truck, and another man hawked rolls of Boomer Sooner toilet paper. Somewhere in that bobbing, pulsating crush Cecil "Big Red" Samara, who was almost always pictured on the front page of one or both Dallas newspapers, did a sprightly jig around his idling red-and-white Model T. Four speakers fixed to the cab blared "Boomer Sooner" at about 130 decibels. Cecil wore the same red-and-white outfit he wears 365 days a year. There is a proviso in his will that he be buried in it. The first song at his funeral will be "Boomer Sooner," followed closely by "Oh, How I Love Jesus."

Several hours before it started raining furniture, Indian Jim and I ducked into the Baker hoping to find two cups of ice. This was before the open-saloon law passed in Texas. Two coeds wearing cutoffs and nothing else jiggled across our sight line, then vanished. A gang of high school toughs pushed through. Someone hit Indian Jim in the eye with a sign that said TUCK FEXAS! There was some sort of ruckus by the elevator. A guy in a silly red hat claimed that when the elevator door opened, someone flashed a Hook 'em Horns signal, shouted, "Take *that*, Okie!" and doused him with a bucket of what might or might not have been warm beer. "Smells like it was brewed through a horse," Indian Jim observed.

"You'd think a smarty-pants school like Texas could come up with something better than 'I've Been Working on the Railroad,' " Indian Jim said. The Indian was born in Durant, Oklahoma, and though he cared almost as much about the university as he cared about chicken pox, there was an odd note of chauvinism in his voice.

I felt it, too. I'd studied a couple of years at the University of Texas; though, like Frye, I'd graduated from TCU, where beating Texas in football was the only event more memorable than watching Bob Lilly eat Volkswagens. My heart reserved no warm spot for Texas. It merely hated Oklahoma! I couldn't help reminding the Indian that the very word *Sooner* connoted all that was foul and reprehensible in the race. Sooners not only stole the land from the Indians, they stole it from each other. Sooners was the name given to the avaricious, unpitiable greedheads who jumped the gun during the Oklahoma land rush.

"It has always amazed me," I said, "that the University of Oklahoma picked a metaphor that means liar, cheater, and thief."

"It has always amazed me," he said, "how people from Texas, who stole everything they have from Mexico, can be so sanctimonious and self-righteous."

We were interrupted by the sloshing of a fifty-pound block of ice floating in a plastic janitor's wastebasket full of Everclear and grape Kool-Aid. "Hairy buffalo," a girl said, passing two cups.

Sirens wailed like trapped animals. A paddy wagon was overturned. Another wagon inched along Main Street behind a phalanx of motorcycle police. The newspapers said there would be seven hundred police assigned to *control* traffic. That was obviously a euphemism. *Forget the fire hoses, boys, this is a job for the dogs!*

The bonfire on the street between the Baker and the Adolphus flickered as high as the second floor, illuminating the glazed faces that danced around it or hung from windows. We were standing near the fire, talking to a man in a chiffon dress, when something crashed and splintered on the street, barely missing some people.

"What the hell was that!"

"Looks like a desk chair," Indian Jim said.

"Where did it come from?"

"Up there."

"A *desk chair*?"

"Look out!" someone yelled, and the crowd began backing off as the front edge of some much larger piece of furniture appeared at a tenth-floor window. People cheered as the second piece of furniture tumbled and broke apart on the street. Whatever it was, its own mama wouldn't recognize it now. There was another shout, but this time what came showering down were a few sheets of hotel stationery and some envelopes. That's when I realized what the second piece of furniture had been in real life—a *desk*. In chaos there indeed was order.

By now the police were grabbing everyone in sight. There were 450 arrests, a modest number attributed to the modest number of gendarmes on duty.

After the Friday night bash of '67 they threatened to move the game out of Dallas. Someone is always threatening to do that, threatening or imploring or plotting. *Times Herald* columnist A. C. Greene, in a typical response, called the Friday night altercation "this annual disgrace" and "the worst thing that happens in Dallas," a chilling indictment considering some of the other events for which Dallas is known.

From time to time Dallas merchants complain, but then so do merchants in Austin and Norman, who could just as well go fishing that weekend. From time to time State Fair directors speak of bulldozing the venerable Cotton Bowl and using the land for a more profitable exhibit; after all, only two major games are played there each year. And from time to time you read that some unnamed official of one of the universities has proposed canceling the traditional trip to Dallas and playing the game home-and-home so more students can attend.

Fat chance.

The Dallas Chamber of Commerce estimates the weekend adds at least five million dollars to the city's economy. In fact, that five million dollars is probably on the low side.

As for the State Fair bulldozing the Cotton Bowl, remember those two major games generate millions of dollars that would otherwise go somewhere else, and, for the most part, the directors of the State Fair are businessmen, too. One of the more durable myths is that Dallas businessmen love to see Oklahoma win because Okies are more apt to extend the victory celebration an extra day. True or not, merchants reported heavy losses after the teams tied in 1976. "Everyone went home mad," said Wayne Gallagher, State Fair general manager. "It was almost frightening how low the activity was after that game."

Spokesmen for the universities admit that their athletic budgets are sustained by the proceeds of this game. Both schools have home stadiums as large as the Cotton Bowl, and the Texas-Oklahoma game probably would be a sellout if it were played in New Zealand. But it no longer is possible to pretend an event of this magnitude has anything to do with students. The *catch* is students. They are admitted to home games at half price. With Texas' enrollment at nearly 45,000 and Oklahoma's pushing 21,000, the philosophy of the neutral site is obvious. Each university reserves fewer than 10,000 student tickets for the game; the remaining 55,000 are sold to the public at fifteen dollars each. Only a small part of each student body can afford the two-hundred-mile trip or the weekend in Dallas.

The game itself has become a small excuse for a big weekend. The game could be canceled and thousands would never notice.

At work here are several psychological and sociological phenomena. There's the Fort Lauderdale Factor, in which students from all over create an event merely by showing up. Of the 450 arrested in

Dallas in 1967, only 45 were students at Oklahoma or Texas. They came in from New York, Pennsylvania, Missouri, Delaware, Illinois, Louisiana, Kansas, Arizona, even from the Dominican Republic. Then there is what sociologists term "legitimatized controlled deviance," which is two words too many to describe this scene. I like to call it the Werewolf Factor. A lot of God-fearing citizens, who for fifty-one weekends a year walk the streets of their hometowns worrying about the communist menace and the Antichrist, harbor secret drives to get juiced and kick the windows out of Neiman-Marcus.

The '67 riot still holds the distinction of being the most destructive, if not the most interesting. After that Dallas police initiated a plan, still followed, that is supposed to keep everyone headed in the same direction — east on Commerce. Okies on one side of the street, Texans on the other. Anyone who looks hard at a display window will soon be looking through bars. Newspapers still run front-page boxes tabulating the visitors who sleep as guests of the police, but the dynamics of the weekend are no longer measured by the number jailed. In 1970, when the police arrested 650 (believed to be the record), assistant chief of police Don Byrd called it "the lightest turnout for this rally I've ever seen." For the last few years arrests have been in the 300 to 500 range.

For those who plan to visit Dallas the second weekend in October, I have some advice. Take a sleeping bag. Every hotel room for twenty miles has been booked since last summer. The parade of lunatics no doubt will gather as usual around the Adolphus, but don't look for the Baker. It's nothing but a monster hole full of hard hats and heavy equipment. Someday the telephone company's regional office and computer center will occupy the spot where it rained furniture.

The game will be a sellout, as it has been since

1946. No problem. Go down to the jail Saturday morning and wait for the police to turn out the drunks. Mingled with the bail bondsmen and irate daddies will be several hundred ticket-holders with swollen heads, thick tongues, and no appetites for a hot afternoon in the Cotton Bowl.

As for the game, there is always a chance it will be a bummer. Both teams have a tough early game so they could meet with blotched records.

There's a feeling among some that the game is not what it used to be, that the wanton savagery and primitive lust have been run through the computer once too often, that like almost everything else in mass-market football it has become a social event for dilettantes. Part of the reason, I suspect, is that Texas coach Freddie Akers is rather bland, especially compared to Darrell Royal. You never hear Akers say, "They didn't come in on a load of wood" or "There's a lot of snot knocking between the okra." You have to remember, though, that Texas-Oklahoma can't be judged by a single season, or even a single era. Akers may yet learn to use the language.

Finally, keep in mind that this is the opening day of the State Fair of Texas, so start early. If you get bored, there's a good spot on the midway between the Chinese House of Fangs and the Ravenous Weasel where you can drink beer and watch the girls' dresses blowing over their heads. I think it's called the Fun House. You can hear the game from there.

October 1981

Postscript

I see Darrell now and then. He's still on the UT

payroll as an assistant to the president. I asked him once if he ever offered the president advice, and he laughed and said, "Oh, hell no. I don't want to remind him of anything." Darrell is still relatively young, but he takes retirement gracefully. He quit coaching because he couldn't stand the hot dogs and greedheads who were taking over, and now he spends most of his time with his family, or playing golf, or listening to Austin music. A few years ago Darrell's daughter was killed in a car wreck, and this year his son died in a motorcycle accident.

Not long ago Darrell, Bud Shrake, and Willie Nelson were playing golf when the subject of kids came up. There wasn't a man among them who didn't have problems with kids — in some cases, permanent sorrows. Darrell got to remembering some advice his own daddy gave him years ago in Oklahoma: "Don't ever get in debt, and don't ever be late for an appointment." Darrell has always followed those two rules, and he's had more success than almost anyone I know.

15

Stop the Press!

Thirty-nine years, two months, and fourteen days before the fact a journalism teacher in Denton advised Mary Crutcher that the Fort Worth *Press* was doomed. Mary remembered the prophecy on Black Friday, May 30, 1975, the day nobody believed would be so long in coming.

FAREWELL, FORT WORTH mourned the seventy-two-point Gothic headline written by editor Delbert Willis and hand-set in secrecy by shop foreman Bill Stringer. Willis had lived with the dreadful secret for two months, a long time to suppress even the most commonplace news. He had been up most of the night composing the farewell story. It was still dark when he took the piece to the Fort Worth Hilton and submitted it for approval to the faceless Scripps-Howard lawyers and executives who had tiptoed into town to preside over the death rites.

There had been talk, of course, but there had been

talk for years. Old-timers were inured to rumors. They assumed the change would be a matter of approach, of timing. They believed that Scripps-Howard would buy the morning *Star-Telegram* and combine operations, as it had done in El Paso and other cities. The morning *Star-Telegram* was a pitiful display of what can pass for journalism, one of those thin sheets that won't last through your first cup of coffee, but at least it had a monopoly. People woke up to the *Star-Telegram*, or thought they did.

But Capital Cities Communications, the New York–based corporation that had bought the *Star-Telegram* from Amon Carter, Jr., saw no reason to unload a good thing, and the deal never came off. So now it was time for the coup de grace. Delbert called Mary Crutcher and Jack Gordon and Marvin Garrett and a few other old-timers into his meager air-conditioned office that morning, talking to them one at a time, sparing them the ignominy of hearing the news in the general staff meeting that would be held as the presses began their final run. Or worse still, sparing them the humiliation of reading it first in the *Press*.

"I'd been living with it for two months, waiting for the other shoe to drop," Willis said a few weeks later. "If word had got out beforehand, the entire staff would have walked out and I wouldn't have blamed them."

Crutcher, Gordon, Garrett, Willis, Stringer—all of them had literally grown up at the *Press*, forty and even fifty years each, taking it one morning at a time and kissing the rumor good night. *Everyone* knew the *Press* would fold; the joke was, when? Black Friday. They couldn't believe it.

Those who were old enough to retire were encouraged to do so. Severance pay was one week's salary for each six months of service—up to a maximum of one year. Most of the young reporters would be absorbed into the Scripps-Howard chain. Good-bye, Fort Worth. Hello, Cleveland, Evansville, Memphis, Denver, Albuquerque, Fullerton. The real squeeze was on that age group that was too young to retire but too old to start over.

"Who wants a sixty-four-year-old woman?" Mary Crutcher asked rhetorically. Mary was the city editor, one of the best I've ever known. She taught some fine journalists how and how not. Just two who come to mind were Bud Shrake, who went on to become a novelist, screenwriter, and associate editor at *Sports Illustrated*, and Dick Growald, who graduated to UPI bureau chief in Europe, the Mideast, and Africa, and who had lately returned to Washington to cover the White House or Kissinger or anything else that caught his fancy. "When you phoned in a story to Mary," Shrake said, "you'd better have it straight down to the last hair and survivor." Growald has interviewed Kissinger, Sadat, Franco, Khrushchev, and Mao Tse-tung, but his strongest memory was dogging new clues until he was able to identify a young girl whose nude and trussed body had been pulled out of Lake Worth years ago.

Mary was still chewing ass and rewriting leads when Delbert called her into his office. She just sat there nodding, like what else is new. Then she slipped back to the newspaper morgue and began burning confidential memos, some of them dating back thirty years or more. "Some of this stuff could still be incriminating," she said.

Sports editor Andy Anderson, the "old luckless fisherman," was badly shaken. He sat at his desk under the "coal chute"—a storied ventilation duct that had rained black soot on generations of newspaper men—and he tried without success to recover his sense of humor. "Scripps-Howard claims the *Press* has been losing money for twenty-five years," he said glumly. "Well, they're ahead of me. I've been here twenty-six years."

Jack Gordon, the amusements columnist since 1935, walked around in a trance for days. Not the most talented man, Gordon was nevertheless an embodiment of what the *Press* stood for, a chronicler of good tidings, a matinee idol who loved to emcee the newspaper's annual Golden Wedding Anniversary Party at the Crystal Ballroom and chaperone tittering widows who signed up for the annual Jack Gordon Theater Party in New York. Gordon started as a cub feature writer fifty years ago, when the *Press* was just one year old and was located down the alley from the old Majestic theater. Once, years ago, he wrote something critical about an actress. That night she telephoned, heartbroken and sobbing that his review had ruined her career and she didn't know where she could go from here. Jack never got over those tears, and he never criticized anyone again, except to deplore X-rated movies and peddlers of dirty words.

He had known some of the greats. He opened a letter from his old friend Mary Martin, and remembered the time she came over from Weatherford to audition for Billy Rose, dressed all in black and singing a song about suicide called "Gloomy Sunday." Billy Rose advised her to go home, marry a service station attendant, and have babies. And Sally Rand's indignation when one of the chorus girls' babies stretched out and suckled on one of those legendary breasts right there in the wings of the old Casa Mañana. And Pat Boone, standing frightened and gawky, right in front of his very desk, weaving slightly as Gordon drafted a letter of introduction to Ted Mack.

"This has been my home away from home," he said, looking off at the ancient ruins of the pint-size city room, at the coal chute and the noisy fans that substituted for air conditioning, at yellowing files and vintage typewriters and permanent coats of dust. "I feel permanently dislocated. I feel very sad. It's like being evicted from a grand old mansion."

Marvin Garrett, a kindly old man with an apprentice nun's smile, returned to his desk by the stair door and started shuffling stacks of press releases and letters to the action desk as though nothing had happened, as though there would be another day and another deadline. He clucked his tongue as he read the news that would never get printed.

In the back shop, foreman Bill Stringer walked along rows of black dwarf Linotype machines, the old hot-type machines that had been obsolete for years, along strands of heavy metal tables, by the panel of fading pinup pictures—"something for the boys in the back shop"—photographs of Mitzi Gaynor, of Dagmar, of Jayne Mansfield, of Ann Blyth. Twenty-five of Stringer's men had been at the *Press* for fifteen years or more, and the new technology of the printing trade had passed them by.

Several of the young reporters who hadn't been hearing the rumors long enough to disbelieve went out and got traditionally drunk and talked of the legendary times of Growald, Shrake, Jerre Todd, Blackie Sherrod, Dan Jenkins—and of Mary Crutcher and how, after all this time, they would surely miss her.

The final edition of the *Press* sold out thirty minutes after a record press run. A week later it was a collector's item. Somebody finally did something right. If only Scripps-Howard had trusted them to say farewell. At least they could have written over-the-wall columns. At least they could have told their versions. Instead, Delbert Willis told it for them in a streamer across the bottom of page one. It said:

FW's TOMORROWS
BRIGHTER THAN EVER

The Fort Worth *Press* was a place to grow up, but you grow up only when you're young. It had an anti-institutional, sub-establishment, combat-residual quality, like a favorite uncle or a creek bank where processions of young minds study processions of cloud formations.

It had started in a one-room building in 1921, when Fort Worth was the huckster capital of the West Texas oil boom. Fortunes were made and lost in the lobby of the old Westbrook Hotel, which sits vacant now, like the *Press* building, and like the streets of downtown Fort Worth. The city supported three newspapers in those days, the *Record* and the *Press*, both owned by syndicates, and Amon Carter, Sr.'s home-owned and sanctimonious *Star-Telegram*.

Now Fort Worth has the morning and the evening *Star-Telegram*, both owned by a New York corporation. What happened to the *Press* is what has happened to competing newspapers all over the country. What with production costs and wages and unions and television and apathy and bad journalism, one newspaper after another has gone under. With the demise of the *Press*, there are only three cities in the country — Philadelphia, Baltimore, and San Antonio — that support competing afternoon papers.

A few weeks after Black Friday, Dean Singleton, a young publisher from the Fort Worth suburb of Azle, bought the *Press* name and subscription list and announced plans to publish a morning paper, starting August 10. Given the quality of its competition, Singleton's newspaper should do okay, but it will bear no resemblance to the place I'm talking about.

I had already put in two years on the police beat at the *Star-Telegram*, and I knew about air conditioners and elevators and freshly sharpened pencils, so my first morning at the *Press* in 1958 was like descending into hell. Correct that, it was like *ascending* into hell, since up is the only direction you can go from the *Star-Telegram*.

It was a little after 6 A.M. and I was late as usual. Taking the stairs three at a time, I bolted across the waking city room and through the swinging gate that separated sports from the other departments. That's when I realized that the only other person in the department was Puss Ervin, a retired postman who wrote our bowling column, frogged our arms when we looked too smug, and dished out advice like "take two and hit to right."

Puss had removed his shirt and was sitting in some BVDs that looked as though they'd been washed either two or three times since the New Deal. It was January, but it was hot as hell in there; black flakes snowed down from the coal chute. Puss sat hunched over his typewriter, a bent and frayed old sandlotter, sipping Bellows bourbon from a paper cup and trying to direct his gnarled, arthritic fingers to the typewriter. He didn't seem at all disturbed that nobody was making a move to put out a newspaper. Finally, Puss stood up, tugged at his baggy pants, then looked me over and said: "You'll never make it, son."

Half an hour before deadline our slot man, Sick Charley Modesette, arrived. Charley had been out all night, looking for his car. "You must be the new man," he said. "All the other bastards slept in, huh?" Charley started plugging the first edition with old pictures of sailfish and badly dated syndicated columns by Joe Williams and Harry Grayson. Charley never sweated it. Years before, when he was working on a paper in Douglas, Arizona, Charley learned that he was dying of Hodgkin's disease. His newspaper gave him a one-way ticket to New York, where he could undergo treatment if he could afford it. Miraculously, the swollen lymphoid tissue began to shrink. Charley had beat Hodgkin's disease and pickled liver and a bum heart and Douglas, Arizona. He wasn't about to let the *Press* take him under.

Every two or three weeks Shrake, Todd, Dan Jenkins, and I would be drinking beer at the Oui Lounge and we'd remember that tomorrow was Charley's day off, which meant he'd be working late, putting out the next day's edition. Todd, who could do great imitations, would call the sports desk and say, "Mr. Modesette, this is Dutch Meyer. I enjoy reading the *Press* and I admire your work. I'm going to resign as TCU's football coach and I want you to have the story first."

Charley would labor over the story—he was one of those writers who didn't believe in using the same word twice, so "game" would come out "tussle" and "putters" would be referred to in second reference as "green sticks"—then he would head for the Champagne Room, where he'd lose his car again. We'd come down the following morning and kill the story, and Charley would forget the entire episode on his day off.

Then a couple of weeks later, Todd would call again and say, "Hello, Mr. Modesette, this is Dr. Sadler, chancellor of Texas Christian University. Our board of regents has just voted to drop football and we want . . ."

There was an overlapping period in the mid-fifties when the *Press* must have had the best sports staff anywhere. Blackie Sherrod would eventually move to the Dallas *Times Herald*, where his column still wins every prize ever thought of. Shrake and Jenkins would become stars at *Sports Illustrated*. Jenkins would publish two best-selling novels, and Shrake would write a number of novels better than bestsellers. Todd would open one of Fort Worth's most successful advertising agencies.

We didn't have the budget or space or manpower

to compete with the *Star-Telegram*, not on a traditional level, which wouldn't have been worth our
while anyway. So we wrote free and wild. We respected nothing. The term *New Journalism* hadn't
been coined then, but that is essentially what we practiced. Every story tried to answer the question *why*.

No one took the *Press* seriously, except Walter
Humphrey, the editor, who walked around with a
pipe in his belt, advising everyone to let sleeping dogs
lie. Humphrey was so preoccupied with cutting production costs and promoting golden wedding anni-
versaries and spelling bees that he seldom bothered to
check what we were doing.

"I'd get called into Humphrey's office every week or
so," Jenkins recalls. "It wasn't so bad because it was
the only air-conditioned office in the building. He
usually wanted to know what *Himalayas* was doing
in a story about Birdville basketball."

Every day was a new war: there wasn't a man jack
among us who didn't feel infinitely superior to the
best man on the *Star-Telegram*. We could out-drink
them and out-fight them and out-write them. If we
didn't have a good story we'd make up one, if necessary we would *live* one, and it would be closer to the
truth than anything published by the *Star-Telegram*.

We were all young, restless, fiercely competitive,
frequently bored. We invented a sportswriter named
Crew Slammer and damn near got him elected Sportswriter of the Year in a national contest. Blackie promoted chinning and broad jump contests on the way
to breakfast at the White Way Cafe, and punished us
summarily for coming in late. His favorite punishment was ordering you to telephone Houston and
wake up that old grouch Jess Neely and ask him how
the hell his Rice football team was getting along.

We started a bulletin board of pretentious literary
leads clipped from other newspapers, and we cele-

brated great events in songs that we wrote. The genealogy of "You Never Went to That School, Buddy" says a lot about the pride we took in our profession.

There was once a TCU journalism student named Jim Hendrix who was a friend of mine and later became editor of a national aviation magazine, but on this particular day Hendrix couldn't rise to the occasion, as was absolutely required in the peer group. It was the 1956 TCU-Texas A&M football game. The Aggies won it, 7-6, in the final quarter. It had to rank as one of the most bitter defeats in TCU history, but when Blackie ordered Hendrix to the dressing room to gather some postgame quotes, Jim refused.

"I can't do it," he said. "I can't face those guys after what happened."

"That's not a very professional attitude," Blackie told him.

Hendrix gave him a hard, hurt look and said, "That's easy for you to say . . . but you never went to that school, buddy."

To which Todd and Jenkins quickly penned these words:

> You never went to that school, buddy.
> You never lived in Tom Brown Hall.
> You ain't had no dealings with M. E. Sadler
> You never attended a Howdy Week Ball.

I'm not certain, but I would guess that song had something to do with the fact that Jim Hendrix soon left Fort Worth and never returned.

Todd drove a delivery boy nutty squirting him in the back of the neck with a water pistol. The kid never figured out who was tormenting him. He once complained to the managing editor, "You've got a leak in here and it keeps following me around."

Jenkins recalled the day Todd came to apply for a

job at the *Press*. "He came racing through the gate and did a hook slide at Blackie's feet," Dan says. "Blackie loved him on sight."

Even though we were constantly broke and knew better, we gambled heavily on football and basketball games. Great songs such as "Duke Over Miami (Why Did I Pick Duke?)" were born on Saturday nights in front of the UPI sports wire. Our only distinguished visitors were Big Circus Face, Puny the Stroller, and Jawbreaker King, who made faithful trips to collect their winnings.

On one such Saturday night, the phone rang, and it was two juiceheads drinking at the New Gem Hotel across the alley. They demanded to know who won the Charles-Walcott fight in 1949. Todd told them Charles. "Hey, what did I tell you!" the voice at the New Gem shouted over the sound of saxophones. "Hey, would you tell this man here what you just told me?" There was silence while the phone changed hands, then Todd told the other sportsman *Walcott*. Then we collected a pot and sat back and waited for the first sound of an ambulance.

One of the side benefits of working at the *Press* was hanging out the composing room window, watching through the shadeless windows of the New Gem as the black hookers worked their trade on soiled mattresses under naked light bulbs. The hookers would be waiting around our car when we got off early Sunday morning. "One of them offered to screw me for a peanut patty," Shrake told me. "I took a look at her and decided to keep my peanut patty."

But mostly what we did was learn how to newspaper. Everyone learned to do it all. Get the stories, write them, edit them, fix them with headlines, dummy them on the layout page, and fight for them on the composing room floor. We learned to type on ratty, triangular-shaped copy paper with machines that must have come from Thomas Edison's attic, and compose great leads in the back of a bus returning from a wonderful weekend in College Station. The pay was rotten and there were no benefits like Christmas bonuses and retirement funds. When Shrake first started, he worked on a space rate. "One week I made thirty-two dollars and they put me on full-time — for twenty dollars," he recalled. "When I got married Humphrey gave me a whopping raise to thirty-five dollars, and told me that would be the last for a long, long time."

"Danny," Humphrey told Jenkins when it came time to replace Todd, "you've just lost a man and now you want to replace him. That's not progress."

When it came time to quit, as of course it would, Humphrey tried to get us to stay by telling each of us that we were being secretly groomed to replace Jack Gordon.

If you don't include its death — which came years after rigor mortis set in — the biggest thing that ever happened to the Fort Worth *Press* was shrinking from eight columns to a tabloid's usual five.

The *Press* went to its sensational tabloid form in the mid-fifties, not long after the death of Amon Carter, Sr., the iron-willed patriarch who ran the *Star-Telegram* and almost everything else in Fort Worth. In his lifetime, Carter could have killed the *Press* with a flick of his finger, but he allowed it to exist, possibly because it reminded him of something out of his childhood, a disfigured monk or maybe a mangy cat. In the weeks that followed, the *Press* circulation hit an all-time high, something over sixty thousand (it was forty-five thousand on Black Friday), but the novelty wore off and a deathwatch that would span two decades began.

Dick Growald celebrated the birth of the new tab-

loid with one of his ingenious cartoons. It showed a
bunch of midgets queuing up to the newsstand. C. L.
Douglas, the fat managing editor who wore a beret
and sat behind his desk eating green peas on a tooth-
pick out of a can, modeled the tabloid after the sexy
old New York *Graphic*, crimson headlines and all.
They loved to play weather headlines: GOLFBALL-SIZE
HAIL PUMMELS CITY. The city would turn out to be
Buffalo, New York. When it developed that the deer
hit by a police car and served up at the policemen's
picnic was someone's pet, Shrake scored with this
headline: POLICE EAT KID'S PET.

They tolerated and even appreciated ingenuity —
Mary Crutcher instructed her reporters in the art of
extracting murder confessions between editions.
Smart reporters learned the trick of removing photographs from the wallets of murder victims while
dumb reporters were across the room grilling some
idiot detective who just got there himself.

The specialty at the *Press*, however, was first-
person stories. Growald was mortified to pick up the
Press and see his by-line under this banner: I HELD THE
PLASMA BOTTLE THAT FED LIFE TO THE MAN CAUGHT IN
THE JAWS OF THE IRON MONSTER. The iron monster
was a machine that ground animal bones to fertilizer,
and Growald got an exclusive interview with the unfortunate operator by pretending to be part of the
emergency medical team. The *Press* printed Growald's picture with the story. In the best tradition of
the trade there was a cigarette hanging out of . . .
could it be? . . . yes, if you looked closely you could
see the cigarette was dangling from Growald's *nose*.

When they were constructing the Continental National Bank Building, Delbert Willis dispatched
Shrake and photographer Norm Masters up its fire
escape (the elevators weren't yet installed) to do a picture story on how you could see Dallas. Of course,

you couldn't see Dallas. Shrake was preparing to pose for a picture, lighting a cigarette and leaning against a railing, when the railing slipped off his elbow and dropped thirty stories.

"Damn you," Shrake screamed at Delbert. "I could have been killed!"

"Could you see Dallas?" Delbert asked.

"I couldn't even see Poly."

"Okay," Delbert said, waving his crutch at the rewrite desk, "give me about a thousand words."

No telephone tip was too trivial to ignore. One Saturday night a hysterical woman called the city desk and said she was about to kill herself. Mack Williams, who was assistant city editor then, yanked Shrake off the police beat and sent him out to reason with the wrought-up lady.

The address was a little shanty on a dirt road next to a garbage dump, way the hell and gone on the Northside. Shrake knocked on the door and a dog leaped out and tore his pants. Shrake kicked the dog through a hole in the screen, sent him howling and yelping clear into the kitchen, where he banged against the icebox. A man in overalls came out of the kitchen carrying a shotgun, and Shrake said, "Where's the lady who wants to kill herself?" The man pointed to a heaving, washed-out lump in a torn slip sleeping on a sofa, surrounded by empty gin bottles.

"I woke her up and asked if she really meant to kill herself," Shrake told me. "She said goddamn right she did, nobody cared about her anyway. I told her to go ahead, I wanted to watch. The man with the shotgun told me she threatened to kill herself every Saturday night and he sure wished she would hurry.

"Anyhow, I called Mack and told him what had happened. Then I went back to the police station, where all hell had broken loose while I was out. I worked my ass off the next few hours for two stories that barely got in the paper. Sunday morning I pick up the *Press* and there's my picture on page one. The headline said something like: I SAVED THE BEAUTIFUL BUT TROUBLED LADY FROM SUICIDE."

Covering the police beat, especially at the *Press*, was a great way for a young reporter to get off and grow up. We were right out of *The Front Page*. Growald ordered one of those stand-up telephones and charged it to the *Press*, which was a first and I'm sure a last for that worthy institution. Elston Brooks, who had once done the Teen Times page at the *Press* and was then covering police for the *Star-Telegram*, told all of us his professional secret: *Blend in*. Look like a detective. That meant you had to wear a gray hat, smoke Lucky Strikes out of the corner of your mouth, and call all women "sister." Growald listened to Elston's advice, then showed up in a straw sailor and checkered vest. This was Chicago, not Fort Worth. It was the twenties, not the fifties. Somebody had been putting Brooks on.

"The competition on the police beat was furious, especially if you covered it for the *Press*," Growald said. "Especially between me and Brooks. I tried to screw him any way I could, and I'm sure he did the same for me. I really got to him one time by plastering the police press room with Jesus Saves stickers. The whole room — the ceiling, the walls, the desks, the typewriters, even the chuggy old overhead fan — Jesus Saves stickers everywhere. This offended Brooks, because it offended the *Star-Telegram*. There *was* such a thing as image. Brooks got a tank of winos out to scrape them off, but they never could get the one off the fan. Brooks had to watch Jesus Saves in twenty rpm's."

One thing we learned at both Fort Worth newspapers was the meaning of *nigger deal*. We didn't write nigger deals. Or if we did, they didn't get in the paper. Once when I was still at the *Star-Telegram* I stumbled into a preacher story. There was an old black preacher who every day for forty years walked the short distance from his dirt-street hovel to the emergency room at City-County Hospital, there to pray for the sick and afflicted and pass the time with appreciative sisters of his flock. This was semiremarkable, since the old man was eighty-two years old and totally blind. Then they built the South Freeway, smack in the middle of his well-trod path. The inevitable happened: he was struck by a car and killed. And there he was when I first saw him, laid out among the weeping and wailing of that same emergency room.

I wrote it just like that and sent it by copyboy to the night city desk at the *Star-Telegram*, where a frightened and disturbed old editor, whose name I won't remember, read it and called me back. He complimented me on "a nice little yarn," then reminded me it was a nigger deal. But I *said* that—it ought to be in the first sentence of the second paragraph. But the old editor wasn't buying yarns; he was buying news.

"Just give us a couple of graphs to protect us," he told me in that whining voice that finally ran me off. "Say something in the lead about how many traffic deaths we've had in the city and county so far this year."

It wasn't any different at the *Press*, not where nigger deals were concerned. Growald told me: "I once turned in this sensational murder story to Mary, and when she finished yelling I understood that it was a nigger deal. She told me not to come back with any more nigger deals unless they were triple axe-murders. So the day before I left the *Press* to go into the Army, I got a triple axe-murder nigger deal. It got two paragraphs in the paper."

What you learned at the *Press*, and every other newspaper I ever heard of, is you can't tell the story. Not under those conditions. How could you describe detective Grady Haire flicking cigar ashes on his necktie and telling us, "Boys, that fellow's so crooked he can't carry shit to a dead bear!" Or Lieutenant Chick Matlock turning to the Houston detective with the opulent lifestyle, asking, "How long did you say you'd been on the vice squad?" There were gang wars in Fort Worth then, gamblers and hoods were getting blown away every week or so—frequently, it was said, by a professional badass named Gene Paul Norris. When Tarrant County and Fort Worth police, along with the Texas Rangers, riddled Norris with hundreds of rounds of live shells on a pleasant afternoon while Gene Paul was rehearsing to steal the Carswell Air Force Base payroll, the real story never came close to print. Gene Paul was grandly executed. They had been months setting him up for the Carswell job, and when they learned his plans also included kidnapping a woman bank employee and her young son, they decided to get it over with a day ahead of time. Get him on the run-through.

But none of it got written, except in one of Mary Crutcher's memos.

When I worked police for the *Star-Telegram*, Shrake was on the same beat for the *Press*. We trained a fourteen-year-old copyboy named Steve Perringer to cover for both of us. We practically gave him his own bureau. Steve was a bright, aggressive lad who learned quickly to check with the desk sergeant, get chummy with the dispatcher, butter up the nursing supervisor, check the hospital emergency calls against the desk sergeant's report, and never fall for any fire alarm before using the crisscross directory and calling a neighbor. We taught him about nigger deals, and how to be alert anytime two homicide detectives came racing up the steps or burned rubber down Tenth Street.

Once we got Steve working right, Shrake and I would retire to the Office Lounge, a dark little beer joint frequented by burglars and transvestites, and there we would while away pleasant hours talking about books we planned to write, if we could ever get around to it.

The great thing about Steve was he'd never bother us for anything trivial. Anytime he interrupted our drinking, there was a story there somewhere. No one was sober enough to recall all the insane details, but there was a murder one Saturday night, in one of the suburbs. Shrake and I and Harold Williams, another police reporter who worked for the *Press* then, were swilling free drinks at an osteopaths' convention when Steve raced in, his face red from running all the way from the police station. Heavily fortified with the osteopaths' liquor and ice and ice buckets, seven or eight of us crowded into Harold's old Plymouth with the police radio. I do remember we got stopped twice going down the wrong side of the Jacksboro Highway. We showed them our press cards.

When we reached the murder scene, everyone had gone. We backtracked to the district attorney's office, where the suspect had been taken for interrogation. The first person Harold spotted was a frail, frightened woman in a housecoat, sitting alone on a hard bench. I believe she was the victim's wife. Harold pushed his camera in the woman's face and quacked, "You sure don't look like a killer to me." That was enough. They threw Harold in the slammer, and threatened the rest of us, unless we got the hell out of there. Captain Jimmy Woods of the Fort Worth PD came to our rescue.

I don't know why I remember this, but one of the funniest lines I ever heard was delivered by Captain Jimmy Woods that night as he was driving us home.

Harold had said, "Jimmy, I think I'm gonna throw up in the backseat of your fine police car." And Jimmy answered, "Harold, if you do that, you'll kiss Alligator [the town drunk] good night tonight."

Ah, Alligator! Loved to cadge money from the press room. Shrake once got Alligator into a game of strip poker, apparently had him on the ropes, then gave up when Alligator offered to take off his pants.

And Steve Perringer, our little copyboy. God, he was eager. He loved the rush. He loved the action, the closer the better. He was blown up a few years ago when he got his TV camera too close to a flaming oil storage tank.

The *Press* was "that scandal sheet," which is a good tip-off of what constituted scandal in those days in Fort Worth. The *Press* took on the Ku Klux Klan and championed Alcoholics Anonymous and changed its mind according to its mystical reading of the public mood. Like underdogs everywhere, the *Press* talked a lot about "the people," but the word wore thin and the message long ago lost its punch. The biggest crusade I remember was Carl Freund's tireless (and endless) series exposing pinball machines.

From its beginning to its end, the *Press* was more style than substance. The principal reason that the *Press* was so interesting to read in the 1950's was its writers, particularly Shrake, who worked rewrite, along with six or seven other duties. There was a time when Shrake would write all the police stories, most of the city and country stories, handle club news, obits, stock markets, call-ins about five-legged dogs and eight-pound turnips. Then in the afternoon Delbert would let him write features.

"I'd do highly descriptive features about subjects I'd never met, except on the telephone," Shrake recalled. "Gene Gordon would go out and take some pictures,

The *Star-Telegram* might be a disgrace to journalism, but it was Amon Carter's paper. Whereas the *Press'* surrogate publisher, Walter Humphrey, went big for golden weddings, Santa Pals, enlarged turnips, spelling bees, teen news, and, if you can believe it, soil conservation (nobody ever discovered what Humphrey thought soil conservation was), Amon Carter, Sr., was partial to oilmen, ranchers, and government contracts.

Amon Sr.'s all-time hero was Will Rogers. He commissioned a statue of the old Oklahoma Cowboy and donated it to the city in November 1947. This was when Elston Brooks and the rest of us were in high school, but Elston remembers it well, since he was one of seven teenagers arrested for desecrating the statue, or rather the crate it was packed in.

The statue sat in front of the Will Rogers Coliseum for nearly a year, still crated in its shipping container. The reason was, old man Carter wouldn't allow anyone except Harry Truman to preside over the unveiling. Truman must have had other things on his mind that year. Anyway, it became a local pastime to go out at night and rip the boards away from the likeness of the old Oklahoma Cowboy. The last straw was when some of Carter's drunken friends at the Fort Worth Club decided to do it. Carter was outraged. The next edition of the *Star-Telegram* promised to bring future vandals to justice and offered a five-thousand-dollar reward.

It was the next night when Elston accidentally found himself swigged out in the backseat of a car parked in front of the crate, which six of his teenage friends were happily dismantling. The cops had them all by morning.

"I was just a teenager, but I was living alone in a flophouse at the time, paying nine dollars a month rent," Brooks recalled. "I had my own radio show and I'd do the captions. Then Delbert would put the features on his spike, where they'd stack up for weeks. At one time I had thirty-seven features on his spike waiting for space in the paper."

On an average day Shrake would write fifteen to twenty stories under other reporters' by-lines. He did a great Carl Freund, with a lot of references to "nickel-gulping monsters." He made Harold Williams' stories extra racy, using as many action verbs as he could, and making sly use of terms like "beautiful, scantily clad housewife." Under Shrake's keen eye all of John Ohlendalski's stories read like labels on detergent boxes.

There were other good writers on the paper, but almost all of them were in sports. Not that the *Press* sports page read like a sports page. Some of Jenkins' best columns had to do with how hard it was to open a package of crackers or buy gasoline. Todd was the only writer I ever knew who wrote his lead in advance of a game. Every *Press* sportswriter knew it was bad form to tell the score until at least the fifth paragraph. The first paragraph usually started out, "He was an old man who fished all alone."

Delbert Willis fancied himself a writer and longed to find the Jap who blew off his leg in World War II. This dream came true in 1966 when Delbert and his wife traveled to Japan for a reunion with twelve survivors of the Japanese battalion that had been blown apart at the battle of Morotai Island in 1945. Four of the Japanese soldiers who attended the reunion held out on the island until 1956. Delbert wrote a moving piece about the reunion, and about Morotai Island, "a little bit of real estate which no one really wanted."

The *Press* was "that rag" . . . "that other paper." What a beautiful disgrace. How pathetic. How like itself, and like the city it reflected. Lovely, crumbly, sad, misguided, vulnerable.

. . . *Ballads by Brooks* on KXOL . . . and I had produced a teenage musical called *Is Your Juvenile Delinquent?* . . . the answer, of course, was of course not. I mean we were sponsored by the Fair Department Store and all. Also, the *Press* was interested in hiring me to do the Teen Times page. Then suddenly I'm down at the police station, my whole career in ruins.

"They had all seven of us. The others brought along their parents and were taking it pretty well, but I didn't have any parents. Then Mr. Carter walked in in his camel's hair coat and Shady Oak hat. He walked with this aura of great power. Everyone except me and Blackie Sherrod, who was covering police then for the *Press*, stood up and came to attention.

"Carter was very kindly. He lectured us on what a great person Will Rogers was, then told us we wouldn't be formally charged. But he was going to do one thing, even though it violated his own long-standing rule. For the first time ever, the *Star-Telegram* was going to publish the names of juvenile offenders.

"Well, there was general *elation*. The other six went out and bought extra copies of the paper. But me . . . I mean, I was losing everything. Nobody was about to hire a teenage hoodlum."

The *Star-Telegram* eventually hired Brooks (he's now the amusements editor), but only after the *Press* broke him in on Teen Times. Brooks would have still been at the *Press* on Black Friday except he was fired by mistake by C. L. Douglas, who didn't understand that the reason Humphrey was taking Brooks off Teen Times was to have him become a full-time cityside reporter. The *Press* never learned to communicate too well at the top level, probably because no one up there ever understood for a minute what was happening or why or how.

The *Press* was a sanctuary for freaks, for idealists, for demonologists, for outcasts, for drunks, for honest young writers and reporters and curiosity seekers. I forget some of their names, but I remember them. The chap on the copy desk whose lunch always consisted of raw carrots, each bite of which he chewed exactly eighty-eight times. And Nat Lehmerman, who drove a cab, sold doughnuts, and wrote sports on the side. God, can I see that afternoon at Colonial! It's May and there is electricity in the air, the tortured figure of Ben Hogan is walking up to eighteen, leading the tournament by a stroke, the worshiping hometown crowd silent as a maiden's prayer. And right there with him, marching step for step in his tan cutoffs, waving his arms and talking a mile a minute, is Nat Lehmerman.

Nat is saying, "C'mon, Ben, baby, open up. What are you thinking right now?"

The *Press* brought out that side of you. If you didn't take yourself too seriously, how could you take Ben Hogan any other way?

Nobody will miss the *Press* except the people who used to work there, and maybe an occasional practitioner like one Fort Worth doctor's wife, who told me, "I liked it because it was little. I could take it with me in my sitz bath and fold it over when I got ready to turn a page."

A long, long time ago, a *Press* editor is supposed to have told a cub reporter, "The poor folks take us because we're the least expensive newspaper in town. The rich folks read us to find out what we're telling the poor folks."

A long, long time ago, that may have been true.

September 1975

Postscript

The Fort Worth *Press* is where I picked up my nickname Jap. Our heroes then were Hemingway, Faulkner (sort of), Lardner, and Runyon. We were straight out of *The Front Page;* snap-brims, trench coats, pocket flasks, the whole avenue. Sixth and Main was really Times Square, and the old fellow who sold papers outside the Hotel Texas was Nicely-Nicely. Everyone had a nickname. Sherrod was J. J. Hunsecker, after the brutally powerful columnist (Burt Lancaster) in *Sweet Smell of Success.* Shrake was Thor, and Todd was Rounder. Jenkins was both Perch and Pea-mouth. I think it was Puss Ervin (nobody tried to improve on his name) who first called me Jap. There had been a real Japanese intern at the *Press* the previous summer, and when my picture first appeared above my column (I had a tan, a burr haircut, and a face the shape of a volleyball), Puss observed: "Hell's bells, that damn Jap's back again!"

Puss is dead now, and so is Sick Charley. Blackie turned sixty a couple of years ago, and the rest of us are fifty, or pushing it. We're still friends. It was good times. Still is.

16

The Endless Odyssey of Patrick Henry Polk

Patrick Henry Polk III and his brood had been waiting for their welfare check. It was the worst winter anyone could remember. Henry Polk was forty-nine, destitute, and disabled by a bad heart. He was a rock mason and cedar chopper by trade, though Henry acknowledged that he hadn't "hit a lick at a snake" in months. Piece by piece, he had sold his chain saw, then his tools, and finally his furniture to feed his wife and seven children. They had stuck him in a hospital in Stephenville and scared the fool out of him with that talk about putting a plastic valve on his heart. And that's when Henry Polk did the only thing he could think to do: he put his wife, Cynthia, and the seven children, ages four to fifteen, in their '67 Chrysler station wagon and he *hooked 'em.* For most of September and October, they lived in their station wagon, cooking and camping on creek banks, accepting handouts from churches and charitable agencies, sometimes stopping to visit relatives as they zig-zagged through the cedar breaks of Chalk Mountain, Sipe Springs, Glen Rose, Valley Mills, Cranfills Gap, Lampasas, Marble Falls, and Liberty Hill, moving mostly south toward Austin, where Polk was born and lived most of his life.

By late October Henry was too sick to go on, and so was the baby, Kathy, who had a congenital heart condition. The transmission had fallen out of the station wagon, and they had traded it for a '67 Buick. By Thanksgiving Polk was in Brackenridge Hospital in Austin and Mrs. Polk had applied for welfare. Polk left the hospital a few days later, complaining that they wouldn't let him smoke. By now there was nothing left to sell, so Polk and two relatives went down to Onion Creek to look for some fern that they could decorate with holly and sell for Christmas wreaths. Sliding down the creek bank, he felt the familiar flash of pain in his chest and stomach. "The Claw," he called it: just like that wrestler on TV. A week before Christmas Polk was back in the hospital and they were talking again about surgery. By now the family had received $336 in emergency food stamps, and social workers had helped them locate a four-bedroom house in South Austin that would be covered by a federal housing program. But the welfare check for $225 still hadn't arrived.

Damned if Henry Polk was going to spend another Christmas in a hospital. He didn't trust hospitals, or doctors, or the city of Austin for that matter. "You know that song, 'My Kinda Woman'?" he said. "Well, that's Austin to me. I know ever' pig trail in it. You take a woman and seven kids and turn 'em loose in this town with no protection, you just as well tell 'em to go jump off a cliff. I told the doctor that, but he never savvied what I was saying. He just wasn't wearing the right pair of shoes. Long as I can move my hands and feet, there ain't no way I'm gonna let 'em cut me open."

Over his doctor's objections, Polk checked himself out of Brackenridge and went home for Christmas. It was a good Christmas. A Baptist church furnished dinner for the Polks, and a Catholic church brought toys, clothing, and certificates for some groceries and a tank of gasoline. One of Henry Polk's older sisters, who lived a few blocks away, and some other cousins, nephews, nieces, and in-laws found enough used furniture to make the house livable, and Henry borrowed a hammer, saw, and nails from a neighbor and built a kitchen table from an old door and scrap lumber.

"We was all together, that was the thing," said Cynthia Polk. "It was like a miracle." At thirty-two, having given birth to eight children and buried one, having survived two major operations of her own and enough trauma to fill a Russian novel, Cynthia Polk found miracles in the commonplace. She was a woman of faith, moxie, and country wit. When the kids bellyached about something they didn't have, the price of a movie for instance, she would turn it on them and say, "Gimme a dime's worth of dollars and you can keep the change." She was physically enormous—after the birth of her six-year-old, Jimmy Joe, or J.J., as he was called, her weight had soared and remained over 225 pounds—but she was amazingly pliable, good-humored, and, in a rough way, pretty. Cynthia had married Henry Polk nineteen years ago, when she was thirteen.

On Christmas, as any other day, the Polks clustered together like immigrants in steerage. When they ate, they ate together at the large homemade table. When Daddy and Mama sat in the living room, the kids congregated there. When the older kids played outside, they checked in every few minutes, reporting on the whereabouts of each member of the family. Four-year-old Kathy, who had epilepsy as well as a heart condition, was seldom out of her mother's sight: the family rule was that she would never be left alone, not for a minute. "If something was to happen to this baby," Cynthia said, "they'd have to put me in the grave with her."

Almost everyone in the family had medical problems. Lanette, the beautiful five-year-old with the blonde ponytail and imp's grin, had a blood disease one doctor had diagnosed as leukemia. Henry Polk's mother spent thirty-nine dollars on a long-distance telephone call to Oral Roberts, and within a week, through the miracle of faith in Jesus and AT&T, Lanette was pronounced cured. "The doctor couldn't believe it," Cynthia said. "He accused me of switching babies on him. No doctor cured that baby. It was the Lord." Colann, the thirteen-year-old, suffered from occasional convulsions; Cynthia Polk called it a form of epilepsy, though this had never been confirmed. Colann also had a hearing problem. Debby Sue, the brash, chubby eleven-year-old, needed glasses. Lanette needed dental work: her small teeth were already turning black. Billie Jean, the firstborn, who would soon be sixteen, had diabetes, as did her mother and grandmother. Billie Jean had also inherited her mother's addiction for sweets and propensity for gaining large amounts of weight.

The two boys, Patrick Henry, Jr. (Buddy Boy), nine, and J.J., six, had inherited their father's ruddy, flinty Anglo features and reddish-blond hair. If you had to guess their genealogy, you would guess Welsh. You could almost see the two boys following their old man down into the coal mines somewhere in South Wales, their fair skin already permanently stained. Though their true origins were long misplaced, Henry Polk and his fourteen brothers and sisters grew up in

South Central Texas, mainly in the Clarksville section of West Austin, a community of shacks, neighborhood stores, and churches founded more than a hundred years ago by newly freed slaves. His father was also named Patrick Henry Polk: the old man liked the name so much he named *two* of his sons Patrick Henry — II and III. Cynthia Polk, whose maiden name was Bates, grew up near Gatesville, the oldest girl in a family of eleven.

"We lived in a tent way back in the cedar breaks," she would tell her children, who never seemed to tire of the stories their parents told of hardships endured, of values learned and embraced, of other Christmas days sown along incomprehensible distances and yet ripening before their eyes: there was no tone of embarrassment, no sense of shame or regret or doubt that the ways of their people had happy endings. "Daddy would always run off, and pretty soon we'd be out of food. We'd look for armadillos or birds or wild onions, anything to eat. Mama was already sick with cancer and the sugar diabetes, and Granny was too old to be much help."

"Hey, Mama," Debby Sue would interrupt. "Tell us again about the man in the truck that broke down and your granny smelling bacon."

"Your granny always carried a broom," Colann prompted.

"Who's telling this story?" Cynthia Polk barked at her daughters. The other children laughed. They loved their mother's bark, which was considerably worse than her bite. "Oh, anyhow, we was out in the woods when all of a sudden Granny throwed down that old broomstick she always carried and yelled out, 'I smell bacon!' We walked down to the road, and sure 'nuff there was this feller with a pickup load of groceries broke down. Hundred-pound sacks of flour, sugar, beans, potatoes, bacon, everything you could think of. Mama said, 'Mister, if you'd like it, I'd be happy to fry you some of that bacon.' I guess he seen all us hungry kids, 'cause he said okay. So Mama built a campfire and started fixing the bacon while us kids sneaked back and took some of the provisions from the truck and hid 'em in the woods. He knowed we'd done it right off, and Mama said, 'Mister, I ain't gonna lie to you. My kids took them provisions 'cause they was hungry.' He let us keep what we already took, and the next day he come back with more groceries and mattresses and blankets and stuff we didn't even need."

Cynthia would remember the first time she ever saw Henry Polk, her future husband. Henry had been married and divorced twice by then—he has five grown children and numerous grandchildren from his earlier marriages. Henry had drifted up around Valley Mills where Cynthia Bates was living and it was love at first sight. "I was outdoors cutting wood," she recalled, "and I looked over and seen him lift this car motor up all by hisself. He was built like a bull back then, back before he took sick. I told my mama, who was on the porch shelling peas, 'I'm gonna marry that man there.' And sure 'nuff I did."

When Cynthia told her daddy she wanted to marry Henry Polk, he volunteered to drive them to the courthouse. "He said that would just be one less mouth to feed," Cynthia continued, not concealing her rancor. "After we was married, Henry tried to help out Mama and the kids. The last bottle of medicine my mama ever had, Henry bought it with his last ten dollars. When Mama finally died, all eat up with cancer and the sugar diabetes, Daddy took the nine kids who was still living at home and dropped 'em on the courthouse steps like you would a sack of puppies. We didn't know 'bout what he'd done for a few days. My Uncle Joe got there in time to 'dopt six of 'em. The other three we never saw again."

"Back then people wasn't so bad off as they are now," Henry Polk cut in, stubbing the butt of his Camel on the bare wood floor of the living room. There were not yet any ashtrays and hardly any dishes in the house in South Austin, though ashtrays were not a habit Henry cultivated. "Back then, we'd find us an abandoned filling station or somewhere and move in. I'd take that double-bit ax and cut me some cedar or post oak and sell 'em fifteen, twenty cents apiece. I was strong as a bull. I could cut wood all day long. When the weather was good, it weren't nothing to make twenty dollars a day."

Christmas passed, and so did New Year's, and as the Legislature convened to consider the problems of the state the Polks still had not received their first welfare check. They didn't know it, but the check was lost in the computer somewhere deep in the heart of the Department of Public Welfare (DPW) bureaucracy. This was partly the Polks' fault. From the time they first applied for welfare back in Stephenville, the family had left such a tangled trail that the DPW computer couldn't cope with their case.

The Dole

Patrick Henry Polk and his brood are not the typical Texas welfare family, but they are a fairly typical poor family. Only a small percentage of the poor in Texas actually receive welfare. There are approximately five hundred thousand poor families in the state — that's *families*, not people — and only about eighteen percent of them will get any government aid this year. Contrary to prevailing myths, most poor Texans are not black or Chicano: the largest group — almost half — are like the Polks: Anglo-Saxon Protestant, nearly illiterate, and totally puzzled by the complexities of life in the 1970's. Polk is not their real name. I changed names and a few other details because that was the only way the family would agree to a series of interviews that would cover two months. But the Polks are not a composite: details of their case, their medical and social histories, their habits and lifestyle are as accurate as I could report them.

Welfare is one of those five-alarm words, like *communist* or *rattlesnake*, and is customarily followed by descriptive nouns such as *chiseler* and *bum*. You have no doubt heard that welfare recipients drive Cadillacs. The hard fact is, most welfare recipients are barely surviving. Members of an Austin women's club were asked recently to guess how much cash a mother and one child would receive from welfare each month. Guesses ranged from $200 to $500. The actual figure is $86 — $24 for the child and $62 for the "caretaker." Only 325,000 Texans, seventy-five percent of them children, receive cash payments, or the *dole*, as it is sometimes cynically described. That's less than three percent of the state's population. The program that administers the dole is called Aid to Families with Dependent Children (AFDC). The key word here is *children*, though this seems to confuse a lot of us taxpayers. Under the rigid standards set by the Texas Legislature, the only persons who receive welfare are children (and one caretaker) who have lost one or both parents, or (as in the Polks' case) are deprived of basic necessities because the father is disabled. What makes the Polks so rare among welfare recipients is that both parents are living at home. The size of their family and the total amount of cash assistance ($225 a month) place the Polks in the upper one percent of the AFDC rolls.

The "average" AFDC family consists of a mother and two or three children. Daddy has either died, deserted, or been disabled. These children and their caretaker receive on average $32.06 a month (the national average is $72.35). That amounts to about $1 a day for shelter, clothing, laundry, utilities, and other necessities. Twenty to thirty percent of that $1 goes for the purchase of food stamps, which are not accepted for household items such as soap, detergents, and toilet paper—not to mention cigarettes, beer, or wine. Very few AFDC recipients live in public housing. All AFDC recipients automatically qualify for free medical care under Medicaid, which in terms of simple survival is far more important than actual cash. If the youngest child is older than five years, the mother is automatically enrolled in a work-training program and in most cases quickly returned to the labor force. The caretaker mother is allowed to deduct job-related expenses from her salary (usually about thirty percent), but if her bottom line exceeds $86 a month, the mother and child are dropped from AFDC and, after a grace period of ninety days, from Medicaid. The myth of the dole as a permanent gravy train finally collapses when you realize that the average income of a Texas family receiving both AFDC and food stamps is barely half the official poverty level of $5500 for a nonfarm family of four. Hardly your Cadillac crowd. Old Buicks and Oldsmobiles are more like it.

The actual payment to a specific family is calculated by an AFDC caseworker using a sliding scale based on 1969 cost-of-living figures. Because of inflation, the cost of living has increased fifty-six percent since 1969, but in the case of AFDC the Legislature has found it politically expedient to ignore this. *Except* for AFDC, none of the other twenty-eight programs administered by DPW has gone a single year without a cost-of-living increase. Once the caseworker has calculated the "needs" of the family, the next step is to cut that figure by twenty-five percent.

The philosophy here is that if the state pays a family less than it "needs," somebody in the family will have to go to work. Even though seventy-five percent of the AFDC recipients are *children*, the incentive theory is championed by demagogues and embraced by law-makers as an excuse to maintain AFDC payments below subsistence levels. "Incentive," says Bill Clayton, Speaker of the Texas House of Representatives, "is the only way we have to break the poverty cycle. Anytime you get support payments to a high level, you discourage incentive." The major flaw in this theory is that by no stretch of the imagination can $1 a day be considered *high level*. More than half the adults living in poverty in Texas are already working full time: they just don't earn enough (the Texas minimum wage is $1.40) to make ends meet. In fact, the incentive is to *stay* on the dole, if for no other reason than to qualify for Medicaid.

There is a technical but highly revealing factor in the Legislature's gut reaction to the Department of Public Welfare. It's not welfare that inspires the sanctimonious preachings in the statehouse, it's the dole. Welfare in fact embraces dozens of local, state, and federal programs that touch the daily lives of two million Texans (one in six) and cost $2 billion a year—but only $125 million ($92 million of it paid by the federal government) is mailed out each year to AFDC families. When you consider who controls all that money, and where it goes, the incentive theory takes on a new light.

Roughly one fourth of that $2 billion passes through the cash registers of the grocery stores, then filters down to distributors, processors, teamsters, farmers, and ranchers. "The food stamp program," says a DPW executive, "is heavily supported by the food industry. In fact, it's an industry *subsidy* program." Doctors, pharmacists, hospitals, and nursing homes pocket an enormous share of welfare money. "The strongest lobby in Texas, except maybe the highway lobby, is the nursing home lobby," an executive at DPW claims. "The last Legislature actually gave us *more* than we requested for nursing homes. The figure goes up every year—it'll reach about $436 million by 1978. This doesn't mean the patients are getting more benefits; it simply means the nursing homes are getting more money." Welfare, in fact, is a gigantic public industry controlled largely by special-interest groups.

"The reason AFDC is so unpopular," the DPW executive continued, "is that there isn't any interest group that can control it. It's cash, and it goes directly to the client. It's the only program where the client makes the decision what to do with it."

"I think one reason our welfare rolls are declining is it's easier to get a job in Texas than in most other states," says John Frannea, chief of management assistance at the Department of Public Welfare. "They don't pay very much, but you can get them. It's not the purpose of DPW to compete with the job market—nobody wants that—but we're not even close." Frannea points out that eighty percent of those being added to welfare rolls are coming on for the first time. On average, a welfare family drops from the rolls after eleven months. "There are few recidivists," Frannea adds. "What this means is that once you've had the experience [of welfare], you don't want it again. There's not much to come back to." Dr. Victor Bach, an expert on urban studies at UT-Austin's LBJ School of Public Affairs, is even more blunt: "The reason there is a low welfare fraud rate in Texas is because it doesn't pay even if you get away with it."

In light of the fifty-six percent inflation since 1969, the DPW recommended that the current Legislature increase daily AFDC payments from $1 to $1.23—or about $7 a month for each member of the family. The Legislative Budget Board, composed of the Speaker of the House, the Lieutenant Governor, and eight ranking members of the Legislature, rejected the request. With Dolph Briscoe also foursquare against it, there seems little chance the increase will be approved.

The Long Wait

It was the middle of January, and the Polks still hadn't received their welfare check. Henry was getting cabin fever. There was nothing to do with his hands and no way to explain, much less stop, the grinding of time. He had become a statistic. While the kids watched the fuzzy old black-and-white TV set rented from the 7-Eleven, and Mama worked the sewing machine, altering hand-me-down jeans and shirts, Henry cut little windows in a piece of cardboard and rolled it into a tube. "What's that, Daddy?" Debby Sue asked. "Nothing," he said forlornly, tossing it aside.

"The worst thing I ever did was sell that chain saw," he said.

"Now, Daddy, don't talk like that," Cynthia said. "We needed the money. 'Sides, that kinda work would kill you now."

"When you get sick," he said, "that's the end of the hump."

Henry remembered that his daddy used to make chairs of green willow and lariats of binder's twine. Henry was thinking of getting himself some binder's twine. Maybe he'd look around for some green willow, though he hadn't seen much willow since they cut the MoPac Expressway through Clarksville. Most of the cedar was gone, too. His daddy had a stationary buzz saw, powered by running a belt around the rear wheel of a '33 Ford, and Henry remembered how they used to pile overlapping layers of cedar posts in a mound, cover the mound with sod and cook it slowly until they had charcoal. They would use the sawdust for fertilizer, and the kids would sell the charcoal from door to door. They hunted coons and rabbits in what would later be called Tarrytown, now a quiet neighborhood of large homes and walled estates. There was always something to do, something to hope for. There were stories of Comanche gold hidden in caves along the Colorado River, and Henry's daddy claimed there were nine jackloads of Mexican silver buried near the Old Confederates Home, which stood on the southern edge of Clarksville.

Although Clarksville had started as a settlement for newly freed slaves, many poor white families had come later, and by the time Henry and his brothers, sisters, and cousins were growing up, the community was comfortably integrated, making it unique in Austin and probably anywhere else in Texas. "We played and fought with the niggers just like they was our own," Henry said. "There was two old ex-slave ladies, Aunt Eady and Aunt Jenny Moe, lived just down the street from our place. My daddy used to make us call all old folks uncle or aunt no matter what color they was. He said it didn't sound right to call 'em mister or missus. It was unrespectful." In the evenings they used to sit under the large live oak in front of Aunt Eady's frame shanty, which was about the same size and construction as their own place down the block. Aunt Eady would tell about the time of slavery, and about her white folks' pet parrot that would rat on her when she would sneak food from the kitchen or neglect her chores.

"When her white people would leave the house they'd let this parrot out of his cage so he could foller Aunt Eady around and tell on her, then when they come home they'd whup her. But one time they for-

got. They left the ol' parrot caged up where the nigger
could reach him. 'Nigger gonna get rid of ol' polly
parrot,' Aunt Eady said, and the parrot started crying, 'Oh, please, nigger, don't!' But Aunt Eady taken
the parrot and socked him in a pot of boiling water,
then put him back in the cage like nothing happened,
and she never got no more whuppings."

Obie Polk, Henry's older brother, would sometimes drop by the house in South Austin; and—when
he wasn't working—so would their cousin Jake Polk.
While Cynthia and the two oldest girls cooked, the
men would sit around the kitchen table playing forty-
two and talking and drinking strong black coffee. As
a young man, Henry had done his share of hooting
and drinking—the self-administered tattoo of a
spraddle-legged naked woman on his left biceps was
a living souvenir of one AWOL bender thirty years
ago—but now he was pretty much limited to coffee
and cigarettes. He wouldn't want this to get back to
his old lady, Henry said in a low voice across the
table, but having intercourse, or even urinating,
"hurts like somebody cut you between the legs with a
hot knife." Doctors at Audie Murphy Veterans Hospital in San Antonio had removed a malignancy from
his left testicle two years ago. "They said they cut out
the cancer," Henry said, "but I think they just spread
it around." Cynthia knew about The Claw, of course,
but the hot knife in his scrotum was a secret Henry intended to keep among the men. The men nodded.
They understood these things. It was like when Cynthia's younger sister's husband put a shotgun in his
mouth and pulled the trigger: the men swore it was an
accident, even though everyone knew he was dying
from cancer.

Jake Polk, who was in his late fifties, earned his living digging, hauling, and laying rocks. He was a rock
mason, as opposed to a rock cobbler. "The difference

is, a rock mason has to know what he's doing," Jake explained. Henry also took pride in the fact that he was a rock mason and regretted that he hadn't gone on to be a brick mason. For reasons that were not clear, Henry never mastered brick masonry. "But there's none better at rocks," he said. "All I gotta do is hang a string from each corner and get after it." Obie Polk, who was two years older than Henry, had never mastered rock or even learned to figure square feet and so was something of an outcast. Obie suffered from emphysema and chronic bronchitis and hadn't worked since he loaded watermelons in Weatherford last summer. Obie was a tall, very skinny scarecrow of a man who would have been in a veteran's hospital except for the misfortune of having deserted the Army in 1945. Since Obie had no children to qualify for welfare, he ate and slept wherever he could.

Of the three men at the kitchen table, only Jake Polk was physically able to hold a steady job and now that it was the dead of winter even Jake was idle. So they spent the long afternoons around Henry's kitchen table, talking about rock, about where to buy a rebuilt carburetor, about how what they hated most in the Army was saluting, and about mistakes in judgment that might explain their dilemma. Jake remembered the old black man who used to sit on the steps of the Sweet Home Baptist Church and ramble for hours about how someday there would be an expressway right through Clarksville. It would be years before they got around to building MoPac, but the old black man was right about it coming. In time the city would appraise the land in MoPac's projected path at two thousand dollars a lot, peanuts compared to its potential worth. Maybe if Henry's daddy had sold out in time. But he didn't. "The city come and took our homestead for six hundred and forty dollars' back taxes," Henry said. "Somebody got rich, but it sure wasn't us."

I had been around the Polks for more than a week now, and the hard-luck stories had become routine. It wasn't just Henry and his brood: there were brothers, sisters, cousins, in-laws so numerous I couldn't count, much less record them, and almost every one of them was a medical and social disaster. When they weren't talking about money they didn't have or hospitals that wouldn't have them, they talked about cancer and bleeding sores and broken hearts and faulty transmissions and relief checks that were nonexistent. When I first knew him, Henry Polk couldn't bring himself to say the word *welfare* — he called the DPW "those people down there" — but by now the family accepted my presence and even seemed to share a measure of relief that someone from the outside was there to listen. I gradually came to see them as a tribe, a clan of people who had never joined mainstream culture or had the least desire to. They were almost all cedar choppers and/or rock masons. They worked for cash or sometimes for the cedar itself, which they would sell after clearing land for some developer. They had never belonged to a union or paid Social Security or graduated from a school or had a title. They had never voted, and some of them had never thought of filing an income tax return.

Many of them were unemployed, but only a few qualified for unemployment since they had never worked for anyone except themselves. The ones who were old and disabled like Troy Tucker and his wife, Sara, lived on food stamps and Supplemental Security Income (SSI), a federal program for the needy who couldn't qualify for Social Security or state welfare. As in the case of unemployment insurance, only people who have paid into the program are eligible for Social Security. A few of them, such as Cynthia's sister (whose husband died from the shotgun blast), drew AFDC. Almost all of them were eligible for food stamps, but some hadn't got around to applying and others simply refused. Jake Polk never said it out loud, but you could tell that he'd rather die than accept welfare. At one time in his life, Henry Polk must have shared that aversion. Even now, when he heard someone bellyaching, Henry would say, "If you look around, you'll always see somebody worse off than you. God didn't make everybody to be rich. It would be a dull world if everybody was the same."

The house in South Austin, once so government-issue sterile, was gradually taking on a personality. Cynthia found some patches of cloth and sewed curtains. One of those velvet bullfighter paintings that you see in Mexican border towns appeared on the wall in the living room. Henry constructed a coffee table from some pieces of plate glass found in the city dump. They got an old king-size mattress and box springs from Goodwill. The two little girls, Kathy and Lanette, shared a cot at the foot of their parents' bed, the three older girls shared a second bedroom, and the two boys slept in the dining room (although the house was supposed to have four bedrooms, the two rooms at the back weren't heated). Apparently the Polks weren't familiar with thermostats, or maybe they were cold-natured—whatever the case, the house was always uncomfortably hot and smelled of used lard and burned sugar. Spectacular amounts of trash accumulated. Billie Jean and Colann swept the kitchen and living room two and sometimes three times a day, and still the floor was littered with crushed candy canes, spilled milk, partly eaten sandwiches, chicken bones, and cigarette butts.

Cynthia Polk had measured out the food stamps carefully, loading up initially on staples like sugar, flour, potatoes, and lard, then falling back on a lifetime habit of planning and shopping one day at a time. While the food stamps lasted, there was always meat or chicken, always fried. Every meal included potatoes, beans, and cake. (Henry's favorite meal was red beans and chocolate cake, mixed together.) Nobody in the family liked tomatoes or lettuce, and they weren't big on fruit either. In the afternoons when the kids came home from school, Cynthia would drive them to the bakery outlet and treat them to day-old fried pies, purchased ten for ninety-nine cents. There was one particular supermarket that the Polks visited daily, the chain that sponsored the TV sweepstakes show called *Let's Go to the Races.* Cynthia would select four or five items, then they would each head to a different checkout line, thereby multiplying their allotment of sweepstakes cards. On Friday nights, Cynthia and the kids would gather in front of the TV and cheer home their horses.

Henry thought this was foolish. Henry's motto was to "believe half of what you see and none of what you hear." It was like the stories about the Mexican silver and Comanche gold. He'd never seen any. He had crawled inside every cave along the west bank of the Colorado River and he had never seen any gold. He remembered one cave in particular. It was located straight across the river from the old Deep Eddy grocery near Clarksville. Henry, Obie, and Troy Tucker discovered it one day as they were hauling rocks across on a rubber raft. In his memory the cave was large as a house, and right in the center, partially covering a seemingly bottomless well lined with cedar posts, was an enormous boulder. The ceiling of the cave was black, suggesting ancient tribal campfires. He thought about this cave. He thought about it a lot.

"One of these days," he told his two boys, "we'll go look for it."

In the Trenches

Marie McAdoo was one of twenty-one AFDC case-workers assigned to DPW's Austin office. Each case-worker was responsible for ninety-five cases. Though she thought of herself as a social worker, her official title was Welfare Service Technician II, the bureaucratic way of saying that her monthly salary was fixed at $820. In a few months she was scheduled for promotion to Public Welfare Worker I, and though her duties would remain the same, her salary would increase to $876. That's tops for a full-time case-worker in this state. Considering their qualifications and work load, DPW's social and clerical workers are among the lowest-paid state employees. Many of them are teachers who couldn't find a teaching job. Few started out to be social workers. They majored in math, English, history, economics — in the subjects and skills that the market has little use for. The workers who deal in the food stamps and AFDC programs are the most overworked and the most criticized. "Nobody in those two programs has a good job," says a DPW executive. "Their work load is staggering. They come in daily contact with people who have very serious problems. Quality control is always looking over their shoulder, just like a factory. It's not surprising that they don't last too long." Marie was an exception. She had been with DPW for more than three years and she liked her job. Before joining DPW Marie taught grade school and worked with retarded teenagers. She's forty-eight, a grandmother, and a compulsive problem solver. Her husband makes a good income as manager of an insurance company, but Marie works because she enjoys it.

When Marie first learned of the Polks in early December, the family was camped on Slaughter Creek. She contacted them by telephoning one of

Polk's sisters, and an interview was arranged. "The immediate problem was to get them food," she recalled later. "They were down to one can of lard." Normally, emergency food stamps can be obtained in two or three days, but there was a technical problem. Rules set down by the federal Department of Agriculture, which funds the food stamp program (DPW only administers it), require that a family have cooking facilities, and a campfire along Slaughter Creek didn't qualify. Marie requisitioned groceries from the Travis County Department of Human Services, from a church, and from the goodwill of another social worker who was quitting and requested that her fellow workers donate food instead of throwing a going-away party.

Then she contacted David Keene, administrator of the HUD-funded Austin Housing Authority — known in the industry as Section 8. Section 8 is a federal program designed as an alternative to the dreary public housing projects that were in vogue during the Great Society of Lyndon Johnson. Poor people who qualify are allowed to find low-cost rent property in whatever section of town suits their needs. If the house satisfies government standards, payments are made directly to the landlord. The program is confidential. Since even a next-door neighbor would have no way of knowing that rent was subsidized by Section 8, there is no stigma. It is a very simple, direct program that helps both landlords and poor people and involves a minimum of red tape. The catch is there are never enough suitable houses to go around. In the case of the Polk family, a four- or five-bedroom house was required. But David Keene's office only had allocations for 31 four-bedroom homes and 5 five-bedroom homes. Maybe it *was* a miracle, as Mrs. Polk insisted: at any rate, the Polks located the frame house a few blocks from Polk's sister, and on December 13, after the landlord made some minor repairs, the family moved in.

Now that they had a roof over their heads and cooking facilities, the Polks immediately became eligible for emergency food stamps. Since their application for AFDC had yet to be approved, the food stamps they received were classified as Non-Public Assistance (NPA), which is not to be confused with Public Assistance (PA) food stamps, which go automatically to AFDC recipients. What it meant was that Mrs. Polk paid only $36 for $336 worth of stamps. Later, when their first AFDC check arrived, they would pay $108 for the same amount of stamps. If the Polks came across any additional income, they would pay more.

Meanwhile, Marie McAdoo was pursuing the Polks' case through reams of paperwork. Before their odyssey, the Polks had applied for welfare in Stephenville. For their new application to be accepted, the old one had to be denied in order to "clean the computer." The Stephenville office of DPW had forwarded the Polks' records, but the file was stacked up somewhere in the Christmas mail rush. Marie had verified from her interview that the Polks needed immediate help, but first she had to get Henry Polk's medical records from Brackenridge Hospital. That required a written release. On December 18, she carried a release form to the hospital, but Polk's doctor was out Christmas shopping. She telephoned again two days later, and nobody at the hospital could find the release form. She took a second release to Brackenridge. She called again on December 23. She was told that the release had been signed, but they couldn't find it. "I told them this was an emergency, so they looked again." Late that afternoon they finallly located the form — it had been sent by mistake to the children's section. By the time she got her hands on the release form all state offices had shut down until December 28. It was January 6 before all the records arrived.

By then, Marie had enrolled Colann, Debby Sue, Buddy Boy, and J.J. in school. Billie Jean, who was almost sixteen and had never lived in one place long enough to get past the ninth grade, couldn't be registered until March. Billie Jean wasn't really interested in going back to school. Marie suggested several alternate programs through which Billie Jean could learn a trade. Billie Jean had bad memories of her last encounter with education. When they were living in Lipan, a small community north of Stephenville, she enrolled in a vocational agriculture course and they wanted her to castrate a calf. If that was education, they could have it. Henry and Cynthia Polk didn't encourage Billie Jean. The parents shared an inborn distrust of education, maybe because they feared it would break up their tight family structure. To them children were assets, not too unlike horses and cows. This wasn't cynical or cruel, merely practical: when their own time came years ago both Henry and Cynthia had supported their dying parents; now the cycle was being repeated and it would be their children's turn. There were also moral implications. It was Henry's experience that "all schools are good for is sex and dope," and that wasn't what they wanted for their children. Although Billie Jean was already three years older than her mother had been when she married Henry, the girl had never been allowed to date or attend socials.

On January 6, Marie McAdoo filled out DPW Form 1-A, which in most cases goes straight to the computer keypunch operator. But in cases of "medical incapacity" the form must first be approved by the state office. Henry's medical report confirmed his chest pains as angina and myocardial infarction, and indicated it might be necessary to implant a valve to control the flow of blood through the heart. A week after Marie McAdoo completed DPW Form 1-A, the application was approved and sent to the computer where, for reasons no human could explain, it "bounced."

In mid-January, Marie McAdoo had been transferred from "financial needs" to "social services." "I guess you could say that what I'm doing now is dealing with physical instead of financial needs," she explained one afternoon when I dropped by the welfare office in South Austin. "Things like housing, health service — a lot of it is advice and counseling. A *lot* of it is just listening. The people I deal with have such tremendous problems they just need to talk to someone." There are two phones in Marie's tiny office, both ringing at once. Welfare workers joke that the only time the telephones are silent is when *As the World Turns* is on TV. There is a chaotic undercurrent in their work, a rumble like you feel in your legs when a subway train is approaching, an apprehension that an orderly world is only an illusion that protects our sanity. There is always a big rush on welfare after a holiday. One Social Security worker explained: "That's when old-timers sit around the stove and talk about their Social Security checks." It's the same when the weather is bad and arthritis acts up, or when there is an unexpected freeze and thousands of migrant citrus pickers are suddenly out of work. I noticed a mysterious sack of canned goods on the floor by Marie McAdoo's desk, but she didn't volunteer to explain it and I didn't ask.

Jean Bundrant, another social worker who had dropped by Marie's office to deposit two cans of turnip greens in the sack, told me: "Basically, people on welfare do not handle routine things the way you and I do. They don't think in terms of records or forms or programs. It doesn't occur to them to telephone and say they are moving. Right now I'm waiting to interview a mildly retarded woman with two kids. This is the seventh appointment I've set up for her and she's missed them all. Usually, after three times, the application is automatically denied."

"They need an advocate, someone to hear their problems and help solve them," Marie said. "If they can't find their way to Section 8, you take them. If they have problems with the landlord, you try to work it out for them. There are some doctors and pharmacists who won't accept Medicaid because of the red tape, so you help them find a doctor or pharmacist who will."

Sometimes the good intentions backfire. Welfare is so complex and so overweighted with conflicting rules and regulations that only a fool or a politician would pretend to understand it. Businessmen employ platoons of attorneys and accountants to deal with government red tape. Welfare recipients must face it essentially alone.

Jean Bundrant said that what really bothered her was people talking about welfare chiselers and Cadillacs and scrubby hippies on food stamps. Veda Douglas, a Medicaid worker who had come in to drop two cans of vegetable soup in the sack, offered a real case: "The husband had a job paying $600 a month. His wife had to go to a nursing home, which cost $650 a month. Welfare couldn't pay for the nursing home because the income limit in this case is $557.80. This means any kind of income—salary, retirement, Social Security, VA, trust funds."

"It gets very frustrating," Veda Douglas continued. "Every day we see people who need help and can't get it. If we're in the business of helping, we ought to help."

When I couldn't stand it any longer, I asked about

the sack of canned goods. Marie McAdoo handed me a clipping from a local newspaper. It told the saga of Slim and Pearl, an elderly couple existing on thirty-eight dollars a month from veteran's disability. Slim should have been eligible for Social Security, except his birth certificate was destroyed in a Colorado courthouse fire. Slim had mailed off eighteen dollars trying to get a duplicate, but for some reason it hadn't arrived. The shack where they lived had just been condemned. They were hungry. "If I just had four dollars," Slim said, "I could get me a fishing license and catch some fish." The sack of goods was for Slim and Pearl. Marie McAdoo intended to pay for the fishing license herself. In the two months that I spent hanging around welfare, this went on all the time. People so sensitive somehow coped with human misery in a system so insensitive. And yet almost every social worker I spoke with defended DPW as doing the best it could with what it had. I wondered many times what would happen if you brought the governor and every member of the Legislature down here to the trenches. But that would never happen: political slogans can't deal with specifics.

Manifest Destiny

It's hard to choose an exact date when Henry Polk became a social problem, but Henry would pick sometime about 1968, when he found the Lucifer bracelet. They were living out on Bluff Springs Road south of Austin, and things looked pretty good. They had collected two goats, three meat hogs, and 175 chickens, and there was plenty of work in the Hill Country cutting cedar or laying rocks. Cynthia, who was pregnant with Buddy Boy, still had an attractive figure. Life had hope and harmony.

Henry found the Lucifer bracelet while digging for worms in the backyard. As he recalls, the bracelet was a devil's head of pure silver with black ruby eyes. A small wooden cross was bound by twine across the devil's face. "I didn't know it at the time, but the Spanish lady next door had tooken it away from her boy and buried it. She had bounded up the devil with the cross. Anyhow, the bracelet was pretty, so I took to wearing it." Looking back on it now, Henry could see that God was punishing him for his backsliding ways. In those days, Jesus frequently spoke to Henry Polk. A few years earlier Henry had been "called" to preach in the Pentecostal church. When it came time to preach his first sermon, God told Henry to wing it. God's exact message, as Henry recalled, was "open your mouth and I will put in the words." As Henry approached the altar there was a great gust of wind from the north and the Bible pages blew open to Matthew 21:31. In a strange voice Henry read: "Jesus saith unto them, 'Verily I say unto you, That the publicans and the harlots go into the kingdom of God before you.'" What did that mean? Henry told his flock: "Harlots means whore, and publicans . . . that's like 'publicans and Democrats. Like senators and governors and hypocrites."

Later, Henry learned to speak in tongues. He took credit for a few modest miracles. The redemption of his nephew, for one. The boy was a disbeliever, so Henry asked the Lord to "not hurt him but scare him a little." That night as the nephew was sleeping on a mattress on the floor "a great ball of fire come rolling through the window" and there appeared Lucifer himself, fire in his eyes and carrying a pitchfork. The next day the boy joined the church. Not long after that, another nephew got in a bit of trouble—the police arrested him for robbing a grocery store and shooting the owner. "They was asking the death penalty," Cynthia Polk recalled, "but Henry and his sister got down on their knees and the Lord spared him." His nephew is now doing five to ninety-nine.

Anyway, at the time of the Lucifer bracelet, Henry hadn't exactly turned his back on the Lord, but he was standing sideways. Then bad things started happening. His dog jumped through a plate glass window. The son of the Spanish lady next door ran away, then her house burned down. There were weevils in the cornmeal. Henry got another cross and buried the bracelet where he found it, but the bad luck didn't stop. Henry wrecked his car and almost killed himself. One night the Polks came home and found seventeen chickens dead. "We thought the dogs done it," Cynthia said. "We put the dogs in a sack and took 'em out to the country and dumped 'em, and when we come back more chickens was kilt. We discovered it was a polecat done it. We shoulda knowed by the way the chickens was scalped."

Buddy Boy was born healthy, but in 1970 Cynthia gave birth to another boy who was named Oral Roberts Polk. The baby had a bad color and his head seemed too small for his body. He had trouble breathing. Cynthia recalled, "Henry told me right from the start, 'Don't get attached to that 'un, 'cause God never meant him to be raised.' I couldn't believe God just let me borrow him. But one morning when he was a few months old I woke up, saw blood coming from the baby's nose. When I felt him, he was cold as a bucket of ice. We was living then with Henry's cousin Jake and his wife, Dora, and I screamed, but it weren't no use. I knowed there was a Jonah where we was, and there wasn't nothing nobody could do."

Shortly after they buried the baby, the Polks got together with two of Henry's cousins and their families and reached a decision to move to California. Jake Polk, who was ten years older than Henry, had heard there were millions of acres of wood to be cut in the Sierra Madres west of Bakersfield. Jake and

Dora Polk had saved a little money. Their kids were all grown and Jake had bought an Army surplus truck large enough to carry their belongings. Henry bought a 1955 green-and-white Olds from a used-car lot on East Second. Cousin Woodrow Polk, along with his wife, Betty Frank, and their four kids, had an old Ford Ranch Wagon that the men put in shape. Everything they couldn't carry they sold.

In the spring of 1970, while the bodies of Vietnamese civilians were floating down the Mekong and Richard Nixon was pushing for the confirmation of G. Harrold Carswell to the Supreme Court, the Polk clan set out on a migration that could have happened during the Great Depression. U.S. troops would invade Cambodia and four students would be shot to death at Kent State, but the Polks didn't know it. H. Ross Perot, who had accumulated a fortune of $1.5 billion selling computer time, had chartered a 707 that would fly halfway around the world without reaching its destination in Hanoi, and Woodrow Polk, who had won a Purple Heart in Korea, would sell his broken-down Ford wagon for fifty dollars in Cordes, Arizona. Henry Polk's Olds used half a tank of gas getting up one side of Salt River Canyon, and on the down side the brakes failed. Henry saved the family by bumping against the rear of Jake's truck until they could grind down the canyon to safety. Dandelion soup and organic brown rice were big among movie stars and wealthy faddists in Southern California, and that wasn't too different from what the Polks ate.

Like thousands of migrants before them, the Polks soon experienced the nightmare of California. "You couldn't buy a job," Henry Polk recalled. "The unions had everything locked up." A procurer who worked for a collective of growers still holding out against César Chávez' United Farm Workers union found the

Polks destitute in Delano and gave them enough money to reach the fields. For the next three months the Polks picked tomatoes, strawberries, grapefruit, grapes, peaches. "It was like a concentration camp, only it wasn't," Henry recalled. "But you had to do what they said. We lived in little cabins right by the orchards. They'd shake us out at three-thirty in the morning so we could get in eight hours before noon when it got too hot to work." They were paid 22 cents a box for strawberries and 30 cents a box for peaches. The Polks had no way of knowing that César Chávez had just negotiated a contract that would pay farm workers $1.80 an hour, plus 20 cents a box, plus medical benefits.

"We'd take the kids out to the orchards with us," Cynthia recalled. "They'd play under the trees while we picked fruit. When it was dinner time we'd build a fire and cook what we had. The grape people was the best. They give us all the free grapes we wanted."

Henry said, "We had a hell of a time just keeping from starving that summer. Don't let nobody tell you that money grows on trees in California."

In the late fall of 1970, cold and broke and dispirited, the Polks headed home to Texas. Henry's Olds broke down and had to be abandoned near White Mountain, New Mexico. For the remainder of the trip all fourteen members of the Polk clan rode in Jake's truck. Colann and Debby Sue got whooping cough. When their food supply was down to a few overripe grapes and a little oatmeal, they sold their fishing poles and mattresses. "I happened to tell this woman in New Mexico about the baby dying and she give us a tank of gas and $135 in groceries," Cynthia remembered. "Otherwise, I don't know how we woulda made it home."

Over the next several years the Polks spent a good deal of time moving, looking for wood to cut or rocks to lay. J.J. was born, then Lanette, then Kathy. Lanette got lead poisoning from eating paint. Kathy was born with a heart murmur caused by a defective valve. Fluid had to be pumped from her chest every six months. Jesus still talked to Henry from time to time. "Sometimes He just told me to hook 'em," Henry said. It was Jesus who finally pointed the way to welfare.

Periodic entries in the Polks' thick dossier at the Department of Public Welfare describe what happened after that:

GRANBURY, May 1972 — This is the Polks' first encounter with welfare. A DPW caseworker writes: "Mrs. Polk says that she has been separated four months from her husband Henry. States she doesn't know where he lives. He comes around about once a month to see the seven children and leave $10." Mrs. Polk's application for AFDC in the amount of $146 is approved. She is also granted "commodities." Food stamps weren't available in Texas until the fall of 1973. When her case was next reexamined, additional AFDC payments were denied. The record does not reflect the reason for the denial.

GRANBURY, September 1973 — Henry has obviously returned to the fold because this time he is the one who has applied for AFDC, claiming disability because of a bad knee resulting from his car wreck in 1968. The doctor who examined Henry writes: "This patient's environmental background is poor and he has adapted inadequately to society and is very poorly motivated to improve." The doctor recommends X-rays to the right knee. The heart is listed as "normal." On September 9, the caseworker reports that "this applicant is healthy. He does not appear to meet the agency definition of AFDC incapacity." Application denied.

ROCKWALL, December 1973 — Cynthia Polk has

applied for welfare. Henry is hospitalized in Dallas with bleeding hemorrhoids. The hemorrhoid operation proves satisfactory, but doctors then discover "a mass in the left testicle." It is diagnosed as "a benign retention cyst." Polk also complains of chest pains. The report states that in the last five months Polk has earned only $278, and that his medical bills are enormous. (The law allows payment of medical bills back to ninety days from the date of the application.) AFDC payments of $245 and food stamps are approved, subject to reexamination on March 1. In another month the federal government will take over all cash-assistance programs except AFDC: the baby, Kathy, who is permanently disabled because of her heart condition, will be eligible for Supplementary Security Income (SSI) checks of $167.80 per month. The Polks don't yet know this, but little Kathy's SSI checks will keep the family going for the next three years.

GRANBURY, May 1974—Polk still complains of chest pains. An appointment is made with a Granbury doctor who will do "an EKG, chest X-ray, and upper G.I." The record shows that Polk never showed up for the appointment.

GRANBURY, July 1974—Cynthia Polk reports that her husband is working again and requests that they be dropped from AFDC rolls. Request approved.

SAN ANTONIO, May 1975—Polk is receiving outpatient care at the Audie Murphy Veterans Hospital. Cancer cells have been found in his testicles.

STEPHENVILLE, August 1976—Mrs. Polk has again applied for AFDC and food stamps. She complains that her husband has "heart trouble" and is hospitalized. The actual medical report is sketchy. A doctor writes: "Patient complains that he needs to go home to take care of his daughter, Kathy. He seems more concerned with his daughter than his own condition." The doctor suggests heart surgery may be required.

AUSTIN, December 1976—A medical report states: "Chest pains are not brought on by anything in particular but exertion definite problem." The diagnosis is "Angina and recent inferior M.I." Application approved.

Great Expectations

As January slogged on and the welfare check still hadn't arrived, Henry had a bad case of the *ol' hook 'em blues.* In his depression, he had almost forgotten The Claw. This was worse, much worse. The cash from Kathy's December SSI check had completely run out. So had the food stamps. "I can just feel it running all the way through me," he said. "I'm gonna have to make a move. I'm gonna have to do something." Cynthia was unequivocally in favor of hooking 'em back to Lipan, money or not. Kathy's condition appeared to be deteriorating: all day Kathy would sleep in her mother's lap, and all night she would cry. Cynthia had it in her mind that the girl would do better in the country. Cynthia purely hated Austin by now. "The only people I know here are Henry's relatives," she complained. "And the prices here—they'd stop anything. Eggs, ninety cents a dozen. Back home in Lipan you can go to Chicken City and buy a dozen cracked eggs for forty cents. You can get bacon on sale, fifteen pounds for eleven dollars and fifty cents." Cynthia had a hankering to see her sister, who was consoling the grief of her husband's death by dating a nineteen-year-old neighbor. She even missed her old daddy, who by now had married her mother's sister's oldest daughter.

There were several problems with hooking 'em, aside from the fact that they didn't have enough gas to get to Lipan. They worried they might never receive their welfare check if they moved again. But the main consideration was little Kathy. "If that's what's best for the baby," Henry swore, "that's what I'll do. They can keep their checks. They can keep their house. They can sue us. I never asked nobody when and where to go; I'm not gonna start now." To keep up their spirits — particularly Henry's — the nine Polks would lie for hours jammed together on the king-size bed, trading ideas about what might be done with the welfare money. Cynthia wanted a washing machine. The kids wanted a drive-in movie and a bucket of Kentucky Fried Chicken. Billie Jean wanted something special, but she wouldn't say what. Henry mentioned buying an old pickup truck to haul rocks, or maybe a chain saw, but you knew his heart wasn't in it. On second thought, Henry might buy an old school bus. "I'll fix her up and make us a home," he said. "We're gonna travel. If they got no rock to lay one place, we'll go where they is. If there's no wood to cut, we'll go find some. We'll see how it goes. Nobody's gonna live forever."

There was one day of total panic when Kathy's phenobarbital and Dilantin ran out. Without the medicine she would lapse into a coma. A refill cost twenty-seven dollars, and they didn't have anywhere near that amount. Besides, the prescription was written on a drugstore in Lipan. Late that afternoon, when the little girl could no longer keep her eyes open, they rushed her to Brackenridge emergency room where a social worker reminded them that Kathy already *had* a Medicaid card — it comes automatically with SSI, or "Sissy" as they say in the business. A doctor checked Kathy — she had "acute coryza," also known as a common cold — then he wrote a new prescription for her medicine, which Kathy's Medicaid card would pay for. "I had it right there in my purse and didn't know it was any good,"

Cynthia laughed as she carried her baby back to the car. She kissed Henry on the cheek and laughed again. "I told you it was still good only you wouldn't listen to me." Henry smiled, tugging on the beak of his grimy red BOWES SEAL FAST mechanic's cap.

On January 20, the day Jimmy Carter was inaugurated, Henry was in the front yard attempting to fix a broken water pump on his '67 Buick. His wife and all seven kids bustled around him, climbing on fenders to watch him work, asking endless questions about when they could go to the drive-in movie and have some fried chicken. Henry's only tools were a borrowed wrench and a piece of scrap metal that he used as a screwdriver, but the work itself was obviously a therapy and Henry seemed as calm and patient as a hound dog with ten pounds of kittens crawling over his back. In the living room a silent TV screen showed Jimmy Carter walking up Pennsylvania Avenue, waving, and promising, "No new dream . . . but rather . . . a fresh faith in the old dream." Suddenly, Debby Sue screamed: "It's the mailman, it's the mailman!" Henry kept on working and Cynthia placed his cup of fresh coffee on the fender, pushed through the yammering children, and threatened to "slap that silly off y'all's face if you don't behave." The letter looked official, though it didn't look like the welfare checks they had received in the past. It wasn't. It was a letter from the Texas Rehabilitation Commission (TRC) informing Henry that an appointment had been set for him at the regional headquarters for the following Monday. The letter said something about "evaluation, counseling and guidance, training, job training . . ." "What does it mean, Daddy?" Debby Sue asked. Henry just looked puzzled.

I timed it so that I would arrive at the Polks' home about an hour before Henry's Monday appointment with the TRC. The front door was open. The thermostat was turned to ninety degrees and it was hot enough to bake biscuits in the living room. Henry was lying on the couch with his head in his wife's lap. All the children were sitting around looking at him. "The Claw," he told me. "Tell him the truth," Cynthia said. "Over the weekend he climbed up to fix the carport roof and like a fool he jumped off and that's when it got him." After a while Henry said he was feeling better. Billie Jean brought us two cups of strong black coffee and Henry sat up, adjusting his cap. I noticed that the dogs were gone; Henry said he had taken them to the country and dumped them because his sister told him dogs weren't allowed in welfare houses. It turned out the sister was wrong: all he needed was a letter of permission from the landlord, which the landlord was willing to supply. Later that afternoon, when it was too late for the appointment, we all drove out to look for the dogs, but there was no trace of them.

That night I brought over some meat that was wasting in my own refrigerator and we watched the second episode of *Roots*. Cynthia said: "It makes you want to get mad at the white people." Henry retold the story of the old slave lady and the parrot, only this time there were tears in his eyes. I could tell something else was bothering him, and while Cynthia was putting the little girls to bed, Henry offered me some Bull Durham and said: "I'll tell you the truth about that appointment. I was just plain scared." Scared of what? "Superstition," he said. "I ain't even told my old lady this, but Sunday when we was out driving I saw a roadrunner. Ain't that foolish?" I told Henry I'd heard about black cats, but roadrunners being bad luck was news to me. "That's what I'm talking about. I was a fool. Roadrunners is bad luck for

some. I got to remembering later, after it was too late
to keep that appointment, that the last time I seen one
I got a check for eleven hundred dollars in back payments on Kathy's SSI. Don't that beat all?" I agreed
that it did. "But I'll do it yet," he promised. "I'll have
my old lady make me a new appointment. I don't
know from A to B what they're talking about, but if
they'll help me get some tools . . . or a job I can cope
with . . . they can keep their damn check."

But Henry Polk wasn't about to report to the TRC.
When a man is hanging by his fingernails, it takes a
mighty promise for him to lift a hand.

The Circle Is Unbroken

This may be difficult to believe, but Department of
Public Welfare Commissioner Raymond Vowell's
habitual tie clasp is a silver-and-turquoise *roadrunner.* Vowell is a sturdy, balding man with quick-study
eyes and the practiced poise of a man accustomed to
making large decisions. He might be a retired Air
Force colonel, or the president of a small college,
which he did once aspire to be. In fact, Vowell is a
professional administrator, the presiding officer of a
public-owned industry that employs fourteen thousand people and operates with a biennial budget of
$2.3 billion. If you thought of the DPW's budget as
"industrial sales" it would rank among the nation's
one hundred largest industrial corporations; it would
also rank among the top three hundred in employees.
Of all the state agencies, his is the least popular
and the first to feel the heat when something goes
wrong. It's also the first to duck when it is politically
expedient.

"The commissioner," as he is always called around
DPW, is admired among rank-and-file welfare workers, particularly those who worked for DPW before
his appointment in 1971. They feel that he has

streamlined procedures, improved welfare's public image, and reordered priorities where they rightly belong—in favor of the welfare recipient, or "client" as they say. "You feel that he really cares about the clients," says a social worker. The commissioner's passion for bettering the lot of his fellow man does not automatically extend to his own employees. "The commissioner will bust his ass for recipient benefits, but not for his own staff," says a DPW executive.

While administrating DPW is the chief purpose of Vowell's $42,000-a-year job, an equally important function is selling his department's biennial budget to the Legislature. Vowell enjoys pointing out that this year the department actually turned back to the state a $40.5 million *surplus* in its food stamp and AFDC programs. The reasons for the surplus were higher employment and a decline in AFDC families. Figures like this make good reading back in the legislators' home districts, but in fact this is an example of the way the lawmakers arbitrarily tangle the department in red tape. By budgeting each DPW program separately (which pleases the various lobbies), the Legislature also makes it unlawful for the DPW to transfer state funds where they are needed. Health service premiums paid to Blue Cross, for example, were projected and budgeted at $159.7 million, but the actual cost was $177.9 million. The department couldn't use the food stamp surplus to make up the difference but had to find surplus federal funds. Since individual members of the Legislature possess an abysmal understanding of the welfare system, Vowell must know at all times who to see and what to say.

Vowell's most popular decision was in the creation in 1974 of the department's investigation division, which claims to "uncover a half-million dollars a month" in welfare fraud. That is *uncover*, not *recover*. Last year $871,000 was recovered, or about

$72,600 a month. The cost of recovering this money is $1.7 million a year, almost double the reward, but of course there is a principle involved. Not all the criticism Vowell hears in his daily routine concerns welfare chiselers. At almost every subcommittee meeting some black legislator is certain to ask Vowell how many blacks DPW employs at the executive level. "None," Vowell says. Then he smiles and adds, "With the salaries we pay and the services we provide, qualified blacks won't take the job."

Pointing proudly to his charts and graphs, Vowell offers evidence that the state's welfare rolls are steadily declining: when Vowell became commissioner in July 1971, there were 384,682 persons on the Texas AFDC rolls. After peaking at 449,000 in the fall of 1972 (during the national recession), the rolls have dropped to under 325,000. This doesn't mean, though, that there are fewer impoverished Texans; strict enforcement of eligibility standards is cited as the main reason for this decline. Only 2.4 percent of the Texans on welfare shouldn't be there: no other state has such coldly impressive statistics. The national average is 7.5 percent. Increases in the state's per capita income levels mean that federal matching funds are decreasing proportionately. Seven years ago, for example, the federal share of medical assistance programs was almost 80 percent. That figure has dropped to 63.5 percent, and beginning next fiscal year it will drop again to 60.6. And yet, for all the billions spent, manhours utilized, charts and graphs and reports, Texas still has the highest number of illiterates and the highest number of poor people in the country. There is absolutely no evidence that the state's stopgap approach to welfare is doing anything to solve the real problem: what welfare experts call the poverty cycle.

"Before clients come into our system," Vowell told me, "something [bad] has already happened to them.

In most cases you can track it back to the time they dropped out of school. If we would go back to the roots of the problem and start doctoring it there, we could break or at least reduce the poverty cycle." Vowell cited a recent study claiming that of the students who entered the first grade last year in Texas, forty percent will never receive high school diplomas. Vowell suggested that I go to the DPW library and read the report of the White House Conference on Child Health and Protection, convened by President Herbert Hoover in 1930. "I think you'll see that we're dealing with the same problems today as we were then," the commissioner said. "The truth is, we haven't come very far."

The DPW librarian seemed surprised when I asked to see the 1930 White House report, which is about the size of a junior high school history book. "The commissioner is the only one who ever asks for that one," she said. The bulk of the report consists of flowery speeches and high-principled declarations from Hoover and lesser lights. The report claims that of forty-five million children, ten million were "other than normal" because they were improperly nourished. One million suffered from defective speech, and another one million had weak or damaged hearts. Lesser numbers had behavior problems, were mentally retarded, tubercular, deaf, crippled, blind, or delinquent. Hoover begins his speech extolling the virtues of motherhood (the Great Engineer added that he wasn't so sure about fatherhood), then there was a sentence underlined in red pencil, possibly by Commissioner Vowell himself: *"If we could have but one generation of properly born, trained, educated, and healthy children, a thousand other problems of government would vanish."*

And finally this warning, also underlined in red: *". . . if we do not perform our duty to the children, we leave them dependent, or we provide . . . the major recruiting ground for the army of ne'er-do-wells and criminals."*

Ray Lyman Wilbur, Hoover's Secretary of Interior and chairman of the conference, tacked on a final philosophical note, claiming that education, health, and welfare were jobs for "the local unit" of government. "We want a minimum of national legislation in this field," he said. "No one should get the idea that Uncle Sam is going to rock the baby to sleep."

You probably remember what happened next: the Great Depression. Then the New Deal. The New Frontier. The Great Society. Always, welfare was supposed to be a leg up. It never worked, possibly because politicians could never agree on whose leg needed the helping hand. Farmers, miners, small businessmen, even Lockheed got a nice share, but many of the states, Texas in particular, never got around to doing much about the crippled, the blind, the deaf, the disabled, the young, the old, or the plain old down-and-outer. There was hardly a trace of uniformity among the states, which of course precipitated migration, putting unbearable burdens on high-welfare states such as New York and California, and at the same time did little to alleviate poverty in tightfisted states like Texas. Uncle Sam's first all-out attempt at what welfare people call "whole income subsidy" was the food stamp program, which became mandatory for every state in 1973. On January 1, 1974, the federal government took over all cash-assistance programs except AFDC, which remained the province of each state. In other words, while the federal government set amounts for *adult* welfare, it remained for each state to determine cash payments for dependent children.

Like the commissioner says, we haven't come very far.

"The most difficult problem that we face is the attitude of the people," says Ed Horne, an attorney in charge of one of the DPW's regional Child Support Collection Units. "We have one of the most efficient welfare departments anywhere, but when people read wild stories about welfare fraud in New York they automatically assume that goes for Texas, too. We need to advertise, like the telephone company or Mobil. We're not going to change a lifetime of thinking overnight, but if people could at least understand welfare, society might be able to prevent the cycle sometimes in the future."

"The average legislator knows little or nothing about the welfare system," says Representative Mickey Leland of Houston, the only black on the powerful Legislative Budget Board (LBB), which routinely trims the DPW budget and sends it out to be rubber-stamped. "Fraud is used as an excuse to cut back or vote against welfare programs. The LBB doesn't have the resources to investigate the complexity of welfare, and what's more they don't want to investigate." I asked Leland how long it took the LBB to hear testimony and consider the DPW's two-thousand-page budget proposal. "There wasn't any testimony," he said. "I'd guess we spent about an hour on the total budget, maybe ten minutes of that hour discussing the constitutional limitations of AFDC." After sixty minutes of deliberation, the LBB voted to whack $231 million from the DPW request.

Representative Sarah Weddington of Austin told me, "When you reach the bottom line, welfare comes into collision with other programs — highways, prison systems, new parks. If you ask us to vote a five-dollar increase to an AFDC recipient or five dollars for a new park, we'll vote for the park. It's something lasting. The letters we receive say *don't raise taxes*, not *don't raise welfare*, but there is no effective lobby for poor people. The teachers are organized, the highway lobby is very organized, but when the poor try to organize they usually end up hurting their own cause. The poor are not people that a legislator feels comfortable with, nor are they influential in terms of votes." A member of the state Senate, who asked to remain anonymous, told me: "It's not that members of the Legislature are all that insensitive, it's just that it's politically expedient to vote against welfare. Poor people don't vote."

The mood of the current Legislature is to raise penalties for welfare fraud. Senator Bill Meier of Euless introduced legislation to make welfare fraud of more than $200 a felony (it is now a misdemeanor) punishable by up to ten years in prison. Meier's proposal originated at DPW, which claims that the bill is not designed to slap welfare mothers in jail but to prosecute major offenders, such as the Houston nursing home that collected $120,000 from phony billings, or the DPW worker in Dallas who made off with $14,000 in food stamps. Senator Carlos Truan of Corpus Christi views the bill as a method for legislators to score political points by punishing the poor. Says Truan, "This is a class of people that doesn't have an understanding of the law and its consequences. These are the most illiterate, most ill-educated, most ill-prepared people in our society. I'm sure that it is politically expedient to vote for this bill. Members of the Legislature are fearful that the folks back home wouldn't understand a vote against it. There is no concern for the effects of this legislation. The only concern is to demagogue."

Another "reform" bill that the demagogues can write home about is a piece of legislation that would prevent elderly persons from *giving away* property in order to get into a nursing home. An individual who owns at least $1500 in assets is not eligible for nursing home assistance. The maximum for a couple is $2250. Social workers cite numerous cases in which elderly couples have been forced to divorce in order for one of them to qualify for nursing home assistance.

Buried Treasure

Henry Polk and his brood were watching *As the World Turns* when the mailman finally arrived. They had returned the night before from a quick trip to Lipan with an old treadle sewing machine and a dog in the trunk of the Buick. Henry had insisted on doing the driving, and now The Claw had him again. His spirits were at rock bottom. "I'm just a backsliding Christian, banged up, beat up, wore out," he moaned to the children, who had stayed home from school out of sympathy for his condition. "Just a ol' holer roller. In my soul I don't believe I'm gonna prosper till I get down to the very bottom where I started."

But on January 26, the welfare checks arrived, two at once. The computer finally spit out both December and January. Combined with Kathy's $167 SSI check, the Polks suddenly found $617 in their pockets, though they had already spent about $50 of it on the trip to Lipan.

Thirty minutes after the checks arrived the entire family was at Payless Shoes, purchasing tiny cowboy boots (twelve dollars a pair) for the little girls, Kathy and Lanette. It had been almost two weeks since they had eaten meat, so the next stop was the supermarket, where they got five dollars' worth of round steak, some cigarettes and candy, and a stack of *Let's Go to the Races* cards. Debby Sue was still bellowing for some Kentucky Fried Chicken, so that was their next stop. Billie Jean now admitted a hankering for some peach-scented stationery at the drugstore. Henry gave her a dollar, then peeled off a dollar for each one of the kids. While Cynthia was purchasing some thread,

Henry and I admired what had to be the world's largest American flag across the street in front of the American Dream Mobile Home Center.

The following day the Polks bought a used washing machine ($35), a new water pump for the Buick ($27), and paid $92.82 to the gas company and $65.80 for water and electricity. They ordered a telephone, which cost $45 for deposit and installation, plus an extra $5 for the privilege of having their number unlisted. They spent $108 for a new supply of food stamps. Cable TV installation cost $4.95. They selected a used twenty-five-inch color TV in a dark oak Mediterranean-style cabinet, paying $55 down and signing a lease-purchase agreement to pay $59 a month for eighteen months (or a total of $1117). Then they bought another bucket of chicken, filled the Buick with gasoline, and went to see *The Town That Dreaded Sundown* at the drive-in. Two days after the arrival of the welfare checks, the $617 had been reduced to $60. It would be even tighter in future months when the combined AFDC and SSI checks would amount to only $392. Meeting payments on the car, TV, and utilities would eat up $300. There was definitely going to be a problem figuring out how to find $108 for the purchase of food stamps. When Cynthia mentioned this, Obie Polk, Henry's older brother, said: "Do what ol' Granny Tate used to do. She always carried a six-foot coil of barbwire in her apron. She be out gatherin' wild onions or poke salad, she'd come across a holler log and figure there's gotta be a rabbit in there. She'd just throw that barbwire in the holler and twist that little dickens out and have him for supper."

"Yeah," Henry said glumly. "Only I 'member one time it wasn't no rabbit, it was a ol' rooter polecat. She musta used a gallon of tomato juice and cedar oil getting that stink off her and the dogs."

"Some days it don't hardly pay to try," Obie admitted. Obie had more or less moved in with his brother's family. It had occurred to Cynthia that her brother-in-law's residency might qualify them for extra food stamps, but it had also occurred to her that an extra boarder might disqualify the family for the Section 8 rent program; she decided to let it go. It was never clear where Obie got his money, but he always had a few bucks in the pockets of the green twills that he always wore. One day in early February, Obie came home with something he called a "dowsing instrument." He had paid twenty-five dollars for it. It looked like a cheap, finger-size piece of hollow aluminum dangling from a cheap chain, but Obie believed it could be used to detect the presence of water, oil, and precious metals. He opened a badly soiled copy of a magazine called *Treasure Hunting Unlimited* and pointed to a diagram for aligning dowsing instruments with the shadows and the rays of the sun. "Exactly halfway between the marks is where the treasure is buried," Obie read.

"What treasure?" Henry asked.

"Them nine jackloads of Meskin silver buried by the Old Confederates Home," Obie told him. All the kids started yammering at once, but Henry told them to shut up. "Obie," he said, "you're touched is what you are." Obie looked hurt. He took his dowsing instrument to his cot in the dining room and stashed it under a pillow. "Don't pay no 'tention to Obie," Henry told me. "He's a little touched is all." Henry took his Bible from the top of the new color TV and walked to the bedroom.

One warm day in late February, Henry loaded his two boys in the Buick and we started out to visit his old friend, Troy Tucker. Troy, who is seventy-two and nearly blind, lives with his wife, Sara, in a picture-perfect one-bedroom fieldstone house they built themselves. The house sits on a ridge of cedars and boulders, hidden from the neighboring $100,000 homes and the highway that connects West Lake Hills with South Austin. Three dogs and about two dozen brightly plumed red-and-black chickens scrabble about the carcass of an ancient Dodge truck on blocks. Next to the house is the Tucker family cemetery, where four generations of Troy's people are buried. Years ago Grandma Tucker, who was born just below the ridge on Barton Creek, owned more than one thousand acres around here, but the family had sold it off a little at a time to stay alive and now all that remains is the cemetery and the three acres where Troy and Sara live. The most Grandma Tucker ever got for her land was $20 an acre; now it sells for up to $12,000 an acre. Troy had been one of the best rock masons around until failing eyesight and various other infirmities forced his retirement. "My wind's gone," he told Henry, who out of respect for the old man insisted on hunkering on the floor by Troy's rocking chair. "When your wind's gone, that's it." Troy had worked hard all his life. He remembered working a full year cutting wood along the Blanco River, and when the boss had subtracted his food and shelter only $394 remained. "That was for a full year's work, mind you," Sara said. Troy had never paid any Social Security. He had no savings, no retirement. He and Sara lived on two $125.90 SSI checks a month, plus $92 worth of food stamps, which cost them $62.

They talked about welfare, and about how bad it was to lose your health, and about the rock they had worked; then Henry got around to what was really on his mind. He asked Troy: "You 'member that big ol' cave we found that time when we was building that wellhouse across the river from Deep Eddy? *Big* sucker . . . with that big boulder in the middle of it mostly covering up that ol' Indian well?"

Troy said that he remembered it.

"You'd drop a rock down that well, you couldn't even hear it hit bottom it was so deep," Henry went on. "It was lined with cedar posts, like maybe it had been a ladder at one time?"

Troy said that was as he recalled.

"Well, me and the boys gonna go look for it," Henry said. "I been telling this man here about it, by golly I'm gonna find it for him."

"It's still there," Troy said. "I don't 'spect anybody come and moved it."

It was almost dark when we stopped searching for the cave. For the better part of three hours we had climbed steep bluffs and bellied along the edges of sheer limestone cliffs with nothing but air at our backs, through cactus and dense underbrush, climbing and dropping back and climbing again until we had covered every inch of the cliff as carefully as a hungry man might eat an ear of corn. We located several smaller caves with blackened ceilings and strange isinglass formations, and we happened across some rich man's trolley tracks used no doubt to transport family and guests from the hilltop mansion to the lake below, but we didn't find anything like the cave that Henry Polk had described. "Let's go back and look again," Buddy Boy suggested as we rested and picked stickers from our hands near the wellhouse that Henry and Troy Tucker had built years ago. Henry's face was beet-red and he was blowing hard. As a matter of fact, so was I. He swallowed some nitroglycerin tablets.

"It's gotta be there," he kept repeating. "They couldn't just come and move it. I know it's there. We'll come back some other day. We'll find her yet."

May 1977

Postscript

Most of the welfare programs described in this article have been canceled or greatly reduced, thanks to Reaganomics.

I sometimes wonder what ever happened to Henry and his family. I could make a guess, but I'd rather not. A few days after this story hit the stands in *Texas Monthly*, Mrs. Polk called me, crying and telling me I'd ruined their lives. Say *what*? "All that stuff about spilled chocolate and chicken bones on the floor!" she told me. "What are my neighbors gonna say?" I reminded her I had made up names for the entire family: how could anyone *possibly* know? Well, she told me, she'd told a *few* people herself, and word had kind of got around they were "about to be wrote up in *Texas Monthly*."

A welfare worker called me a few days later and said the Polks had decided to hook 'em. My story had shamed them out of town. They didn't leave a forwarding address.

As Herbert Hoover's Secretary of the Interior so aptly phrased it: "No one should get the idea that Uncle Sam is going to rock the baby to sleep."

If there is a lesson here, it's that some of the highest officials of our government, past and present, are uncaring. More's the pity.